AMERICAN EDUCATION

Its Men,

Ideas,

and

Institutions

Advisory Editor

Lawrence A. Cremin
Frederick A. P. Barnard Professor of Education
Teachers College, Columbia University

AMERICAN EDUCATION: *Its Men, Ideas, and Institutions* presents selected works of thought and scholarship that have long been out of print or otherwise unavailable. Inevitably, such works will include particular ideas and doctrines that have been outmoded or superseded by more recent research. Nevertheless, all retain their place in the literature, having influenced educational thought and practice in their own time and having provided the basis for subsequent scholarship.

FOUNDATIONS OF METHOD

Informal Talks on Teaching

BY

WILLIAM HEARD KILPATRICK

ARNO PRESS & THE NEW YORK TIMES

*New York * 1971*

Reprint edition 1971 by Arno Press Inc.

Reprinted from a copy in
The Newark Public Library

American Education:
  Its Men, Ideas, and Institutions - Series II
ISBN for complete set: 0-405-03600-0
See last pages of this volume for titles.

Manufactured in the United States of America

Library of Congress Cataloging in Publication Data

Kilpatrick, William Heard, 1871-1965.
    Foundations of method.
    (Brief course series in education) (American
education: its men, ideas, and institutions.
Series II)
    Bibliography: p.
    1. Education--Aims and objectives.
2. Educational psychology. I. Title.
II. Series: American education: its men,
ideas, and institutions. Series II.
LB1025.2.K5 1971   370.15   74-165721
ISBN 0-405-03710-4

Brief Course Series in Education

EDITED BY

PAUL MONROE

FOUNDATIONS OF METHOD
INFORMAL TALKS ON TEACHING

FOUNDATIONS OF METHOD

Informal Talks on Teaching

BY

WILLIAM HEARD KILPATRICK

PROFESSOR OF EDUCATION, TEACHERS COLLEGE
COLUMBIA UNIVERSITY

New York
THE MACMILLAN COMPANY
1926

PRINTED IN THE UNITED STATES OF AMERICA
L. H. JENKINS, INC.
RICHMOND, VIRGINIA

PREFACE

This book is based on a course which I have been giving for a number of years under the name of "Foundations of Method." Its aim is, accordingly, not to present details of specific method procedures, but rather to discuss the principles on which method in general may be founded.

Among the conceptions that determine the trend of the discussion, two stand out prominently: first, that the individual of whatever age, being complex, responds in many varied ways as he reacts to a stimulating situation and that education must care for all these responses; second, that there must be considered the dominating part played by the individual's mind-set or attitude in determining what varied responses he shall make and which of these are to be fixed as habit in his character. Method, in consequence, becomes then much more than a question of how a child best learns any one thing, as spelling or silent reading. Such inquiries are good and proper but they do not suffice. Method must look further. In particular the broader outlook upon method asks how the parent or teacher shall so manage the total situation confronting the living child as to call out the most and best of all his inner resources and how then to guide the ensuing experience so that the aggregate learning results of knowledge, attitudes, habits, and skills shall be best. Among these learning results, attitudes and habits here receive emphatic attention, because they have heretofore been too much overlooked.

For the solution of this broader problem of method the

element of purpose is herein presented as a factor having peculiar value, promising as it does at one and the same time to call out the child's available resources, to direct and organize his varied responses, and, by the resulting satisfactions and annoyances from success and failure, to fix in his character the learning results properly accruing.

How method thus conceived becomes probably the greatest essential factor in moral character building need not here be elaborated, nor its consequent significance in the very insistent problem of adjusting our total educational scheme more effectually to the demands of democracy and of a changing world. However, it may not be out of place to say that the conception of method here presented finds its proper position in an educational philosophy which consciously intends to look these demands of modern life squarely in the face. It may be added that, in such a philosophy, method and curriculum will be found more inherently related than is usually conceived.

No particular age of learner is here contemplated. The considerations urged are believed to apply to all ages — to all who can learn. Nor is the work directed solely to teachers, actual or prospective. It should appeal as truly to parents and to any who lead others. To some teachers it may seem unfortunate that the discussions are not more explicitly directed to ordinary school work. A partial rejoinder is that the contentions here made would, if admitted, demand a different type of school.

It would be ungrateful not to mention my indebtedness to those whose teachings have most helped to make the ideas here presented — Spencer, James, Dewey, Thorndike, and Woodworth. Their ideas, particularly those of Dewey and Thorndike, permeate these pages. What I have to offer is built largely on their foundations, though of course I alone am responsible for what here appears. Some of the chapters have already appeared in the *Journal of Educational Method*, and for the use of these my thanks are hereby tendered.

As regards the unusual style of composition, it may be said that this was chanced upon in an effort to lighten a presentation that otherwise threatened to become too involved and heavy. Being tried, it has been retained, partly for the reason named, partly to encourage more independent thinking on the part of those readers who come as learners to the book. Other readers may possibly feel regret at my choice in the matter. In keeping with the conversational style, the organization of the several topics is somewhat less systematic than is usual. Students of the book are accordingly urged to use the index in connection with any topic studied in order to consider at one time all the references to that topic. This use has been kept in view as the index has been made.

For reading the manuscript and making valuable suggestions, hearty acknowledgments are due to the Rev. Dr. Thomas S. Cline of the General Theological Seminary and to my colleague, Professor Fannie W. Dunn. For valued help in the preparation of the manuscript and in seeing the book through the press my best thanks are due to my assistant, Miss Marion Y. Ostrander.

W. H. K.

MAY, 1925.

TABLE OF CONTENTS

FOUNDATIONS OF METHOD

CHAPTER I

THE WIDER vs. THE NARROW PROBLEM OF METHOD

" 'Method,' 'problem of method,' 'wider problem of method,' — what do you mean? What is it all about? What is the 'wider problem of method'? I have never heard of that. And is there a 'narrow' problem? I didn't hear the address — I've just come. Was method discussed?"

A group of teachers are talking

"That's just the point. The speaker gave us a new discussion of the problem of method. He did not, as is so commonly done, talk about the newer ways of selecting subject-matter or the scientifically devised special methods of teaching spelling, handwriting, and the like. He talked instead about the part which he said method, broadly interpreted, can and should play in education."

The problem of method

"Was there any discussion at the close?"

"Yes, rather an animated discussion. Many asked him further about the broader problem of method; but as most had never before heard of it they couldn't make out what he meant."

"You object to his position then?"

"No indeed. I cordially approve so far as I can understand it. It seems to me almost, if not quite, the most important problem in the whole field of education."

"Well, I should like to know more about this most important problem in education. I have heard more or less

1

of this position but I have never fully understood it. Is this what the speaker called 'the broad problem of method'? How did he discuss it?"

"Let's take it up and go to the bottom of it. I mean let's go into the ins and outs of this matter of method. We can all ask questions, whoever knows or thinks he knows can answer, and we can all judge. Let's do it."

"I for one should be glad to discuss it, for my own ideas need clarifying. Where shall we begin?"

"Let me begin with my earliest recollection. I can't help so much on the recent developments, but I well remember the first time I ever heard method discussed. I was a child of about ten — more years ago than I care to tell. I recall to this day what a furor there was in our backwoods community when a new teacher said that she didn't teach the alphabet first, she taught the words first, and letters and spelling later. She called it the 'word method.' My head went round. It sounded like building a chimney from the top down. My uncle said it was foolishness, that it couldn't possibly work, that the school board ought to turn off such a teacher. He certainly was surprised, however, to find his little Tommy actually reading in less than half the time his older children had taken."

"Yes, and then we had the sentence method, which some claimed was better than the word method; and later ~Various~ we had all kinds of method: the phonic method, "methods" the phonetic method, and I don't know how are recalled many others. The Grube method in arithmetic came and went; and then we had the Speer method, I believe. In those days our institute lecturers had a great deal to say about methods. They spoke bravely about the 'new methods' as something great; but I think of late years I have noticed a superior sort of smile sometimes as 'methods and devices' are mentioned. Am I right?"

"You are right, I am sure; but there is still another way of looking at method. Last summer at the university I took a course in educational psychology. Our professor said that some day we'd have a science of method, or rather that the scientific psychologist would tell us which of two ways of learning anything is more economical and would give us definite rules. He talked a great deal about the laws of learning, about set, readiness, exercise, and satisfaction. It was awfully hard at first, because I had never heard of such things; but after a while I got into it, and now I believe he is right. I have been watching myself and how I learn, and watching my class, too. Those laws of learning certainly work — it's all a matter of exercise with satisfaction or annoyance."

The psychological study of methods is mentioned

"Well, suppose your psychologist is right as you think. I don't see much difference between method when we talk about the 'word method' of reading and the study of method by your psychologist. It seems to me that the psychologist is just doing more carefully what we all did when we decided that children learned quicker and better by the word method than they did by the old alphabetic method. I was at summer school myself last year, and in one course it was brought out that science and common sense don't differ much except in degree; science is more exact. Whether you proceed by common sense or by science, method seems to me to be a matter of the most economical way of teaching or of learning anything."

The old and new are compared

A definition of method is proposed

"The speaker to-day referred to that, but he objected to restricting method to this scientific procedure."

"And that's where he is exactly right. There are more reasons than one why I should prefer the 'word method' or the 'sentence method' or any of the modern combinations of these to the old 'alphabet method.' It is not simply because the child sooner learns to read. That's good, but there's more to it than that. That old dry humdrum alphabet and spelling method made the children hate the school and hate the teacher. The newer methods of teaching reading somehow encourage the children. They seem more alive. If I wanted to make the children just docile, like the old serfs, you know, and always 'keep them under' and 'break their spirit,' and if I wished to run the world on the principle that 'children should be seen and not heard,' then I'd favor such spirit-killing methods as the old alphabet method or even some of the drill methods now used. But if I believed in all that old slavish docility, I'd be consistent and give up democracy and accept Prussianism outright."

A wider notion of method is suggested

"Yes, I know; I have heard you on this before. I am not going to dispute now whether your way of treating children is better or not. I know you'd begin by telling me that children are less refractory in school than they used to be; I remember what you said before about child suicides in Germany caused by the harsh school treatment. But I am interested in your idea of method. You mean, if I understand you, that the problem of method includes more than the best way of learning the lesson immediately at hand, that method is more than a matter of the most economical way of teaching a child how to read or how to learn a long poem. This sounds reasonable, but I don't quite understand. I wish you'd discuss it more fully."

"Well, it is just this. There is, as I see it, a narrow way of looking at method and a broader way of looking at it. It might be better to employ different words for the two uses, but so far no one has proposed the different terms. The narrow way is all right as far as it goes. It asks what is the best way of

The two views of method are contrasted

learning to read, what is the best way of learning a French vocabulary, and so on. This is what the older generation had in mind when they made so much of 'methods.' Only they had little or no scientific procedure for testing whether one method was better than another. If the difference between two rival methods was great, the better would probably win out in the end. In this way the old alphabet method, as was said before, has gone entirely. Scientific psychology and the tests and measurement movement will undoubtedly place method, considered narrowly, on an increasingly scientific basis. This will prove of great advantage to all concerned if only we know how to make it all work together for the best education of children. But right there comes the rub. I have seen children, after they had passed a history examination, slam their books down and say, 'Never again! I hope I may never look into another history book as long as I live!' Now it seems to me that our pupils ought to learn not only what is in the history course, but also to love history. I have seen older children study civics and government and come out not caring a rap whether their city was well governed or not. There is something to learn besides what is written in the books, and a child may learn the one without learning the other. Then I know too that some of the pupils who make the highest marks — at any rate under some teachers — are afraid to call their souls their own. They can't think independently; they don't know how. They are afraid to trust their own judgment — they hardly have any judgment. If it is in the book, or if the teacher says it, then it's true and that ends it. But surely that isn't the kind of citizens we need in a democratic country." Is it method

"Do you mean that whether pupils come to or subject-like history or to wish good government or be matter? able to think independently is a matter of method? It

seems to me that each of these is something to learn just
as truly as is the subject-matter of history or government.
How about it?"

"It is something to learn. You are exactly right. Learning the subject-matter of history is one thing. Learning
to love history is another thing, related but different.
Learning how to reach independent but dependable judgments in history is still another thing. Each learning is
valuable and needs consideration. We should not trust to
luck in the last two any more than in the first."

"But you have not answered my question. You admit
that all these things are something to learn, but you say
nothing of the method. A few minutes ago you were
making big claims about method; you said you were widen-
ing the reach of method. In the end it seems that everything is something to learn, everything merely some kind
of subject-matter — different kinds of subject-matter to be
sure, but all subject-matter. Why not agree with those
who say that after all curriculum is the one question?
For curriculum seems to me to be nothing but a selection
of desirable subject-matter, of desirable things to be learned.
How do you answer that?"

"In one way it is all a question of things to be learned.
But the problem of method comes in. It won't be kept
A second defi- out. It cannot be kept out. To each thing to
nition of   be learned belongs its own way of being learned.
method   To learn anything we must somehow practice
that thing. To learn how to form judgments we must
practice forming judgments — under conditions that tell
success from failure and give satisfaction to success and
annoyance to failure. To learn to think independently we
must practice thinking independently. Now the problem of
method is exactly the problem of providing such conditions
for learning as give the right kind of practice for learning —

a practice that will tell success from failure and attach
satisfaction to success and annoyance to failure. To each
thing you call 'subject-matter' (the term is a slippery one)
belongs its own style of method. Self-respect is a thing
needful to be learned — you wish it called 'subject-matter.'
At any rate, to the learning of self-respect belongs its own
style of method, namely discriminative practice in exercising
self-respect. Now, isn't it true: to each learning, its own
method? Do we see how method attaches to learning
history, to learning to love history, to learning to think
trustworthily in history, to acquiring self-respect in such
matters?"

"Yes, I must admit it. I had not before seen how inti-
mately subject-matter and method are related to each
other. They seem strict correlations of each Is it not one
other. To each thing to be learned belongs its typeofmethod,
own appropriate method. Perhaps I'll wish to after all?
ask you more about that later. But I have now another
question. You spoke, earlier, of a wider sense of method
and a narrower sense of method. I don't yet see any two
senses of method. You have pointed out perhaps unusual
fields in which to seek and find method, but all the instances
you have given — once they are found — belong to the
same kind. All reduce themselves to one formula: the
most economical way of learning the thing at hand. There
may be more things at hand, more things to be learned at
one time and together than I had thought; but the same
notion of method — your narrower sense of method — fits
them all. What then becomes of your broader sense of
method? I believe you have forgotten it or rather have
been confused in your thinking."

"Don't be too hasty. Perhaps we shall yet locate the
broader kind of method. You spoke a moment ago of
several things at hand to be learned, many things to be

learned at one and the same time. Can a child learn several things at a time or must he learn in fact but one at a time?"

"I don't understand. I have always heard that we can do only one thing at a time, or at any rate can pay attention to only one thing. How then can we learn more than one thing at a time?"

"I'll tell you how several things may be learned at one time. Suppose a shy little girl enters the kindergarten. **Many learn-** She shrinks at first from the other children, she **ings go on at** is unwilling to engage in any of their activities, **once** but at length she is coaxed into trying the 'slider.' (You know our kindergarten has in it a children's toboggan slide.) This little girl learns how to mount the stairs, how to get herself ready, how to let go and slide down. She forgets her shyness and enjoys sliding tremendously. The next day she comes to school a different child. Why different? I'll tell you why. She has learned some things. What has she learned? Wherein is she different? She already has decided that she likes the kindergarten assistant who helped her yesterday. She likes Mary and Tommy who helped her on the slide. She likes the slide. She knows how to use it, how to take her turn. She is less shy. She told her mother, when she reached home that night, that she liked the kindergarten. Each of these things represents a something learned. Each represents an exercise with satisfaction. Did she learn these several things, one at a time, in a set order? Clearly not. Nor did she learn them all exactly simultaneously or in one moment. But they are inextricably interwoven. Learning each was in some measure bound up with learning the others. It would have been impossible for her to practice with the slide without at the same time acquiring some sort of attitude toward the other children using it, some sort of attitude toward the kindergarten assistant who supervised, some sort of attitude toward herself in the total situation, some sort of attitude toward the kindergarten as a whole. And note how large a part method played. Suppose the assistant were an impossible sort of kindergartner who had greeted the shy stranger sternly and had gruffly ordered her at once to mount the slider stairs. Would the child's learning have been the same in any way? On the contrary, wouldn't it all have been different?"

"Of course it would have been different. Anyone can see that. The teacher's way of handling the situation must have its effect."

"Then we have two factors that together make up the wider problem of method. First is the fact that while the child is responding in significant fashion for any length of time to any situation, he responds not singly but variously, variously to the many different parts and aspects of the situation. What he learns by these varied responses I am calling 'simultaneous learnings.' The second is the fact that the teacher's way of handling any pupil-learning situation affects for good or ill the aggregate of these simultaneous learnings. They are all tied together; they must be considered together. These two facts or factors present for us the wider problem of method: How shall the teacher so act as to make finest and best this aggregate of 'simultaneous learnings'?"

"You seem to imply that what you call 'simultaneous learnings' are inevitable. Is that true? I can see that it's true in child life and with such childlike experiences as that with the 'slider,' but how is it with our school subjects — with grammar, for instance? Does a boy learning a grammar lesson inevitably have these simultaneous learnings?"

"Indeed, yes. Simultaneous learnings are inevitable. In the half hour when a boy is facing his grammar lesson, An illustration he is not only learning or failing to learn that from specific lesson, but he is also fixing or unfixing grammar an attitude toward the subject of grammar, another attitude toward his teacher, another toward schools, another toward himself with reference to grammar and school and his ability and disposition generally. He may be getting interesting suggestions for further study into language when a favorable moment shall present itself, or he may be hardening his heart on the whole matter. He may be saying, 'It's no use. I can't learn anything.' He may be deciding that school and parents and the whole tribe of governors are unfeeling tyrants, that wrong to them is right to him, that right to him is success in 'getting by' with his unbridled impulses. These are some of the heads under which this boy has been learning during his half hour of grammar study. Does this make it clearer?"

"That point is clear — the simultaneous learnings are there; but I don't see where method comes in. We were discussing the 'wider' problem of method. Have you forgotten that?"

"Method was there all the time, whether I mentioned it or not. Does the teacher have any part in influencing The wider which learning under all these different heads sense of a boy will make? Is it not true that what method the boy thinks or does not think, what he feels or does not feel, what, in short, he brings with him out of the total situation depends in large measure upon the teacher, upon his way of handling the boys in and about the school? The narrow sense of method singles out for consideration one specific thing to be learned and for the time being pays exclusive attention to that as if it were the *only* thing going on at that time. The wider sense of method knows that in actual life one thing never goes on by itself. This wider method demands that we consider the actual facts, the real world. The narrow sense of method faces always an abstraction, an unreality — a part of a total situation, a part that can no more exist by itself than could a man's head continue to live apart from his body. We have to make such abstractions for the sake of economy in studying; but we should know what we are doing — we must never make the mistake of supposing the abstracted element is real life. The problem of method in the wider sense is thus very general: How shall we treat children, since whether we like it or no they are going to learn well or ill not only the thing we choose to set them at, but also at the same time a great many other things perhaps of far greater importance?"

"That is just what the speaker said to-day. Method in the wide sense must be studied. Too much is involved. Without this method the study of education walks on one leg instead of two. Curriculum alone does not suffice."

"But this problem of method puts a great responsibility upon the teacher. I am almost sorry I see it. Why, I cannot teach 'Stocks and Bonds' next week without wondering whether I am doing more harm than good! I cannot shut my eyes any longer to what you call the wider problem of method. But what shall we do about it? How can we study it, and how is it related to the narrower problem of method?"

"We do thus have these two problems of method, one narrow, the other wide: one has to do with learning the details, as such, that go to make up education; the other concerns education as a whole, education considered as the correlative of the whole of life. We can and must study both. The psychologist and experimental educator will help most

Method in the wider sense is the problem of life

on the first problem, the problem of method in its narrow
sense. The second problem is in a way the problem of life
itself. The answer to the second problem, the wider problem of method, will depend on the answer we give to the
problem of life. That is why the old Prussian type of
method doesn't suit us in America. Military Prussia wanted
some of her children to fill this station in life; others, that;
but all to be docile and obedient. She wanted some to be
tradesmen and shopworkers, others of the upper classes to
be officers in the army and government officials, but all to
accept the rule of the Kaiser without question. So her
school officials hunted out a way of treating children that
made them able each to do his own work, but did not make
them independent in judgment. I once heard Dean Russell
of Teachers College discuss this. He said the method was
the same for all the Prussian children whether they went,
as the common people, to the *Volksschule* or whether they
went, as the upper classes, to the *Gymnasium.* The
curriculums of the two schools were different, to fit
each group for its place in the scheme; but the method
was the same, to mold them all into the Prussian type
of character."

"That's exceedingly interesting and very important for
us. I begin to wonder if we don't have some Prussians
in this country, I mean people who are anxious to fit our
immigrants into some sort of lower working class. I have
heard certain persons talking a great deal about 'instinctive obedience,' as if they wanted some of our people to
grow up especially strong in obedience while others perhaps
should grow up especially strong in commanding those
more obedient ones. It doesn't sound like democracy to
me."

"Yes, it is a very important problem, and it is equally
important that it should be recognized. If we are going to

make a success of our democratic experiment begun (formally) about 1776, we must have a type of education that fits democracy. A democratic society should have a democratic school system, and in this system a democratic method will play a most important part."

A democratic society should have a democratic method

"I have just come in and I don't know about the two problems of method that I am told you have been discussing. If the others don't mind, I wish you would summarize what you have been saying, so that I may take part with you."

Another teacher joins the group

"With pleasure. Our first conclusion was that just as we need to study the curriculum to find out *what* to teach, so we need to study method to find out *how* to teach. When we came more closely to the question of method we found there were two problems of method: one, long recognized, the problem of how best to *learn* — and consequently how best to *teach* — any one thing, as spelling; the other, less often consciously studied, the problem of how to treat the learning child, seeing that he is willy-nilly learning not one but many things all at once, and that we teachers are in great measure responsible for the aggregate of what he learns. The first of these problems we called the narrow view of method; the second, the wider view of method."

"I begin to see what you mean. But why do you say 'narrow' and 'wider'? Do you mean to disparage the one and exalt the other?"

"By no means. The one is narrow because it considers only one thing at a time, the other is broader because it takes into account the many learnings all going on at once. But there is no wish or willingness to disparage the narrow view. Some of us think the psychology of learning which undertakes to answer the first problem is the most notable single contribution that psychology has thus far to offer.'

"Won't you say a further word about the wider view of method? I don't get exactly what you mean. The idea is so new that I don't fully grasp it."

"Well, if the others don't mind hearing it again, I'll gladly explain how we saw it. As it seemed to us, any child during an educative experience learns not merely the one thing he is supposed to be engaged in, say a grammar lesson, but is also at the same time learning well or ill a multitude of other things. Some of them may be: how he shall study, whether with diligence or the reverse; how he shall regard grammar, whether as an interesting study or no; how he shall feel toward his teacher, whether as friend and helper or as a mere taskmaster; how he shall regard himself, whether as capable or not; whether or not he shall believe that it pays to try (in such matters as grammar); whether to form opinions for himself and to weigh arguments in connection; how he shall regard government, of all kinds, whether as alien to him and opposed to his best interests, a mere matter of opposed superior force, or as just and right, inherently demanded, and friendly to his true and proper interests. This by no means exhausts the list, but it will give you some idea of what we mean by 'simultaneous learnings,' some idea of what we had in mind in saying that many things are being learned at once. You will also see how important some of these attendant learnings are, and I believe you will agree with us that whether they are well learned depends in great measure on how the teacher treats the children."

The wider view of method is summarized

"Please don't think me stupid. I have been here from the first, but I still don't see the difference. I don't see the two problems. I see that grammar is one thing and that a liking for grammar is another, and I can well believe that each has to be learned in its own way; but I should

say that each presents essentially the same problems of
method, how to use the laws of learning so as to get that
thing best learned. Where are the two different problems?"

"Perhaps an illustration will help. Imagine an athletic
coach so anxious for his team to win that he preaches
'Anything to win.' What do you think of the   The athletic
probable effect on the morals of his boys?"   coach: "Any-
"I fear they'll do 'anything to win.' I should   thing to win"
expect a bad moral effect. But I don't see that this illustration is any clearer than the other. We have here two
things to be learned, the game and the morals involved.
But doesn't each follow the same laws of learning? I see
two instances of one problem, both instances of what you
called the narrow problem of method. I do not see two
problems. I see only one. I see no 'broad problem.' "

"You stopped me too soon. I agree with most of what
you say. The problem of how best to learn the game is
one instance of the 'narrow problem.' The problem of
how best to build morals through the game is, as you say,
but a second instance of the same 'narrow problem.' But
I maintain there is yet a second problem — one you have
not named."

"I don't see it."

"Let me then ask a further question or two. Suppose
you are coaching a team and know the best way to teach
the game as a mere game, and you also know
how best to teach morals through games; will   The problem
you teach the two separately or together?"   of teaching
"I don't know. I hadn't thought about it.   two things
                                                 at once
I suppose I should teach them separately on the principle
of 'divide and conquer.' What do you say?"

"Suppose the two things were so tied together that you
couldn't separate them but had to teach both at the same
time, what then?"

"That's not so easy to say. I can see how attention to either one might distract attention at a critical time from the other, and that this might interfere with doing either well. I believe I should take them separately."

"Suppose we had not simply two things to consider but many. What then?"

"The more reason for separating them and taking each in turn."

"But suppose for some sufficient reason you had to teach all together?"

"Then I should have the problem on my hands of how to manage all, and I don't now see how I could do it. I suppose I should have to compromise somehow, slighting some things and stressing others."

"And that problem would be another and a different problem from the problem of how to teach each alone provided you could separate them all out from each other?"

"Indeed, yes. I begin now to see."

"I am glad you do, but there is yet more."

"More yet?"

"Yes. Suppose you faced a group of children and knew that they were certainly learning many things simulta-

The problem of what is being learned

neously, but you didn't know just what these many things were. What then would you do?"

"I suppose my first step would be to find out what were the different things they were learning."

"And after you had found out, you would still have to ask how to manage the situation so that the total outcome would be best?"

"Yes."

"And these two problems would still be different from the problem of teaching each thing separately, would they not?"

"Yes, I see that."

"And finally is it not true that any class is inevitably learning many things simultaneously?"

"Yes, I must admit it. We have sufficiently discussed that before."

"And we cannot, even if we would, separate them so that only one is learned at once?"

"Yes, that too is true."

"Then every time I as teacher face a class I must consider (*a*) what things they are simultaneously learning, and (*b*) how I can manage so that this aggregate as a whole may be the best?"

"I see no way out of it."

"And these together constitute a different problem from the problem of how to teach each if I could, by a miracle, have it all by itself?"

"Yes, I now see your two problems: one is a problem of seeing and adjusting many things together, the other is a problem of how I would manage each by itself if I could so isolate it. I see now." Two distinct problems of method

"How many things are being learned at once? Do you think of them as few, many, or very many?"

"Possibly in strictness there is no limit to the number. Practically the most significant ones are seldom more than a dozen, I reckon. What do you say?"

"I agree with you."

"Am I right in thinking of the narrow problem as primarily psychological?"

"Yes, that's how I see it."

"And the broad problem is rather moral and ethical, or perhaps better still philosophical?" One is psychological; the other is philosophical

"Yes, I think so. When we face life and have several demands simultaneously on us and they get somewhat in each other's way so that some must be made to yield in a measure to others, then we have a moral or philosophical problem. It is a conflict of values, you see, and that's always philosophical."

"And each learning situation inevitably presents the broad problem of method?"

"Yes, and we must face it. Duty demands it. In so far as we can help matters, we are morally responsible for what happens."

"And, besides this, each learning situation may well present to us one or more fruitful problems of method narrowly considered?"

"Quite true. The alert teacher will always see them."

"Then, if I understand it, the problem of method properly considered looks to psychology to tell us how to make learning go well in each of all its several details?"

"Yes, but a full consideration of method makes us ask at each time and all the time what kind of character is being built through all the learnings simultaneously going on, and how we can with it all help a finer character to grow."

"Then if we are to do our full duty as teachers we should make a serious study of method in both these aspects."

"Yes, and for us psychology is probably the next step."

REFERENCES FOR FURTHER READING [1]

KILPATRICK — "Method and Curriculum," *Journal of Educational Method*, 1: 312–318, 367–374 (April and May, 1922).
KILPATRICK — "Dangers and Difficulties of the Project Method," *Teachers College Record*, 22: 311–314 (September, 1921).
KILPATRICK — *Source Book in the Philosophy of Education*, No. 480. (This item repeats part of the preceding reference.)
DEWEY — *Interest and Effort in Education*, pp. 8–11.

[1] It is advised that the student use the references in the order given.

CHAPTER II

What Learning Is and How It Takes Place

"I wish I understood the 'laws of learning.' Wherever I go, some one refers to them. They sound very imposing — and mysterious — but do they really amount to anything? How did the world manage to get on so long without them?"

Another meeting of teachers

"Well, you may be interested in the laws of learning, but I'm not. I don't see the use of teachers' worrying their heads about psychology. Teaching has to do with children, real live children; but psychology is as dead as other things that live only in books. Teaching is hard enough and dry enough without having to learn psychology besides. If I went to summer school, which I don't intend to do, I'd study photography or something else interesting, but you'd never catch me in a class in educational psychology. Besides, when I go off in the summer I don't want to be always reminded of my work. September to June is enough for me."

Do teachers need psychology?

"Yes; we all know how you feel on such matters; but I believe one reason why you find teaching dry and hard is exactly because you don't study it. At summer school last year I found out so many new things about children and how they learn, and heard so much of the plans and experiments of the other students, that I could hardly wait for school to begin again, I was so eager to see those things in my pupils and to try some experiments of my own. You will perhaps say that I have always liked teaching. So I

The study of education makes teaching more interesting

19

have, in a way, but teaching the same way year in and year out was getting to be pretty monotonous. Now it's a different thing. I have more interesting things to watch than you can imagine. But I must admit that I don't seem to see all my psychology as clearly now as when we were discussing it in the class. More difficulties have arisen than I had ever dreamed of. For one thing the psychology seems more complicated, not only when I watch my pupils in relation to it, but also when I try to straighten it all out in my mind. There's nothing I'd like better than to talk it over, but I warn you I'll raise many questions; for I want to know."

"If psychology or anything else will make teaching my brats anything but humdrum, I'll say, 'Yes, let's study it.'
Does psy- I am willing to listen awhile and see how your
chology fit all discussion starts off, but I tell you beforehand
children? I'm skeptical of it all. You don't know my pupils. Psychology may help your nice well-dressed children who come from good homes, but it takes something stronger for mine. My first step with each new class is to put the fear of God into their souls. After that I can sometimes do something with them. Perhaps I might use even psychology then, if I knew enough about it."

"Where shall we begin? Some one suggested the laws of learning."

"That's my first question: Why do you say 'law'? I know you don't mean that we have to obey Thorndike or whoever first made those laws; so why say 'law'?"

"A law of learning is like any law of nature. Newton didn't *make* the law of gravitation; he *discovered* it. As I
The meaning understand it, a law of nature is nothing but
of the term a statement of an observed regularity. Galileo
"law" discovered certain laws of falling bodies, but bodies fell afterwards just exactly as they had fallen before.

They didn't pay any attention to Galileo. He only told
what they do, regularly do, always do, so far as he could
tell. The laws are merely exact statements of how bodies
fall."

"Well, if that's all, I don't see the use of laws. Why
bother with them?"

"The use is this: If we know what to expect of falling
bodies, we then know how to act where falling bodies are
concerned."

"That's nothing but common sense, isn't it? Where does
the science come in?"

"Science is itself nothing but common sense, common
sense more careful of its steps. Science is based on experience just as common sense is, but it has more exact ways
of measuring and of telling. In particular it tries to include
many experiences under one statement. A law of nature
is merely a very inclusive, very careful, and very reliable
statement of what to expect."

"That sounds reasonable, but apply it to our topic.
What is a law of learning?"

"A law of learning would be nothing but a very carefully
made and very inclusive statement of how learning takes
place."

"Give us one of the laws of learning. I'd like to know
how learning takes place. Perhaps I'd know better how to
make my pupils learn."

"I'll give you the Law of Readiness: When a bond is
ready to act, to act gives satisfaction and not to act —"

"Now there you go with your outlandish jargon. Why
don't you use everyday English. Bond! What is a
bond?"

"That is the trouble about trying to be exact. As a
matter of fact, I fear I have over-simplified it now. I
think, though, we'll have to begin further back. We'll

have to get some preliminary terms or give up the effort to use understandingly the laws of learning."

"Go on. Only don't give us too many."

"Let's begin with this symbol, S → R, and build up from there. S stands for stimulus, or perhaps, more exactly, for situation acting as stimulus; and R stands for response. Any act of conduct is a response (R) to some sort of situation (S). I hear a child crying (S); I stop and listen (R). I meet a friend on the street (S); I say 'good morning' (R). My friend sees me and hears me speak (S); he responds in like fashion (R). He notices that I stop walking (S); he stops (R). I see that he is within close hearing distance and attentive (S); I speak commending his address of last evening (R). He hears me speak (S); the meanings of my words arise in his mind (R). He understands my meaning (S); his face flushes and he feels gratification (R)."

The symbol S → R

"You haven't said a word about bond or connection. Please explain that. I told you I'd raise many questions."

"Notice the next to the last instance given: 'He hears me speak (S); the meanings of my words arise in his mind (R).' If he had not in the past *learned* the meanings of these words, my voice would have struck in vain upon his ears. The meanings could arise in his mind only because in the past he had learned to associate thenceforth these meanings with these sounds. That is, his past experience had built up somewhere in him — in his nervous system, in fact — such connections or bonds that when a particular sound is heard (e.g., my spoken words 'magnificent address'), its appropriate meaning arises as a thought in his mind. Each such language connection or bond has to be learned — that is, built up — by and in experience."

The term "bond"

"But not all bonds are built up or learned, are they?"

"No, that is what I was about to say.   My friend flushed with pleasure (R), when I commended his address (S). His being pleased at commendation and his Innate *vs.* flushing in connection were not learned; these acquired responses are innately joined.   Each one of us bonds is born with many such responses already joined by strong bonds to their appropriate situations."

"What is the arrow in S → R? Is that the bond connecting S and R?"

"Yes. It is usually better to think of the situation (S) as being sized up or received by one nerve structure (or mechanism), the response (R) as made by a second, and the arrow as a third nerve structure that carries the stimulation from the receiving structure (or mechanism) (S) to the responding structure (or mechanism) (R). There are some difficulties in so simple a statement, but we shall not go far wrong so to take it."

"Do you mean that this S → R holds true of everything we do?   Everything?"

"That is exactly what I mean.   All conduct of whatever kind is so described.   Of course some situations are very simple, while others are very complex.   And All conduct similarly with responses, some are simple, can be described in others exceedingly complex.   The bonds also terms of vary.   Some are so simple, definite, and 'strong' S → R that as soon as the stimulus comes the response follows with almost mechanical promptness and certainty.   You know how it is if one is struck sharply just below the knee cap, the knee flexes in spite of anything we can do to prevent it. Other connections or bonds are so weak, so little formed, that the least interference will prevent the response.   If I ask a third grade pupil what is 2 x 2, he will say '4' at once. If I ask 7 x 6, he may tell me '42,' but he is likely not to feel very sure of it.   If I ask 8 x 13, he is almost sure not to know. Now it isn't a question of knowing 42 as a number in and of itself, it is precisely a question of having or not having built a bond that joins 42 to 7 x 6, so that the thought of 7 x 6 (S) is followed by 42 (R). The arithmetic connections or bonds have to be built in order to be available for use. I wonder if the word 'learn' doesn't begin to take on a more definite meaning?"

"I see that S → R does join up with arithmetic and language; but does it fit all learning — geography, for example, or composition?"

"Most certainly. If one should ask about the capital of North Dakota, some will answer at once; others will hesitate, making perhaps several guesses; some won't know at all. The presence or absence of the bond and its strength, if present, tells the tale. So with composition work. One child will leave a straight margin at the left of the page, another will write as if there were no such thing. The difference is the presence or absence of the appropriate bond. One child will join with *and's* many short sentences. Another will consciously avoid it. So with morals: One boy in a tight place (S) will lie out of it (R). Another in the same tight place (S) will tell the exact truth unflinchingly (R). Everywhere it is a question of what bonds have or have not been built."

"Now tell us about readiness and satisfaction and annoyance. They are fairly clear to me, but there are still some difficulties."

"And others of us know nothing about them as yet."

"Readiness is easier to see than to tell. I like to think of it as connected with the degree of stimulation needed at any given time to bring about a given response, the greater the readiness, the less stimulation Readiness discussed is needed. Imagine a small boy and a heartless experimenter. One hot day the boy begs for ice cream, boasting recklessly that he can eat six helpings. The experimenter dares him to do it, saying that he will furnish the ice cream. The contest is on. Situation: a plate of ice cream before a small boy on a hot day. Response: the boy falls with alacrity upon the cream. Readiness is high. The second helping finds, if possible, even greater readiness. But toward the end of the third plate readiness sharply declines. The fourth sees readiness reduced to the zero point and even below. Readiness is thus a condition of the neurone measuring the degree of its craving for activity."

"That is clear so far, but are there not other causes of readiness or unreadiness?"

"Indeed, yes. Fatigue, due to extended exercise, is a common cause of unreadiness. (The case above was different. It was not so much exercise of jaw or palate nerves as it was fullness of stomach that reduced below zero the readiness for ice cream.) Preoccupation with something else of an opposing kind may also bring unreadiness, as when fear or sorrow cause unreadiness for mirth. A most important source of readiness is *set*, one's mental attitude at the time." *Conditions making for readiness or unreadiness*

"I wish you would tell us about set. I have heard so much about set and purpose that I just must straighten them out. What is the connection between set and purpose? But first, what is the difference between set and readiness? They seem much alike to me."

"They are much alike and sometimes confused, but I believe we can make a clear distinction between the two. Set is broader than readiness. Readiness is best thought of as belonging to one response bond (possibly a compound response bond), while set refers to the mind acting more or less *"Set" and "readiness" discriminated and related* as a whole (or for our purposes, set more precisely belongs to an aggregate of bonds that for the time being have practical charge of the person or organism).[1] The term 'mind-set-to-an-end' brings out perhaps more clearly what I mean. The emphasis here is on one controlling end which seems to possess the mind. The organism is bent or set upon attaining this end (typically an external end). The practical relations between set and readiness are here most interesting. A boy gifted in baseball is anxious that his team shall win in the match next Saturday. We may say that he is 'set' on winning the match. This set reaches out to many allied and auxiliary response bonds and makes them *ready* for the part they may possibly play in attaining the end in view. The boy's ear will be 'wide open' to hear any useful 'dope' on the game. His eye will be 'peeled' to see the curves of the opposing pitcher. This effect is general, the mind-set-to-an-end in fact makes more ready all one's inner resources (response bonds) that by previous inner connection seem pertinent to the activity at hand. Nor is this all. Simultaneously with passing on readiness to pertinent bonds, this set also makes unready all those response bonds whose action might interfere with attaining the end in view. The same thing that made our baseball boy ready for the necessary practice during the preceding week made him correspondingly unready for anything that might interfere with that practice. Every teacher knows that little study is given to books just in advance of any engrossing contest. Some college teachers say no serious study is possible till after the Thanksgiving games."

"You have struck something live now. But you seem almost to make a thinking being out of mind-set. It entertains ends. It seems to know what will help and what will hinder action to these ends. I don't see what becomes of the person — his self, I mean."

---

[1] There is still a slightly different sense in which the mind-set makes one see everything as "roseate" or makes one "blue."

"Your inquiry raises a real difficulty, but it is a difficulty rather of language than of fact, I believe. Imagine a little girl walking by a toy shop. Her shoes have been hurting her feet. All at once her eyes fall *The action of the mind-set* on a fairy vision of a doll. Her 'heart' (aggregate of S → R bonds capable of forming a mind-set) responds at once. She wants the doll. A set for possessing the doll is in possession of the girl. Shoes are forgotten, by-standers vanish. She and the doll for one brief moment make up the whole world, but in another moment the mother is included: 'O Mother! I want her so much. Please get her for me.' Then that world enlarges to include in succession shopkeeper, price, money, possible sources of money, Father, Uncle George.

"A formal analysis will perhaps make clear the life history and action of this psychological set: (*a*) there must be available for stimulation certain end-setting-up S → R bonds (here the doll-appropriating response and, likely enough, bonds for doll-carriages, ice cream, etc., as well); (*b*) something (here the chance sight of the doll) stimulates one such available S → R bond (more strictly an aggregate of bonds); (*c*) a response follows, wherein an end is set up (here the strong wish for the doll); (*d*) from this set there spreads readiness through previously made connections to allied and auxiliary S → R bonds (here become 'ready' the bonds for asking Father or Uncle George); (*e*) a similar and simultaneous spread of unreadiness to such other S → R response bonds as might thwart or unnecessarily postpone the doll-appropriating activities (the pains from the shoes are forgotten); (*f*) then follows the auxiliary action of the most ready of the allied S → R bonds ('O Mother, please get her for me'). Thus instead of using the mysteries of self and thinking to explain what has here gone on, we must, I think, ultimately explain from the inside and along these lines what a self is and how thinking proceeds. But that's another story."

"Well, we have to admit that psychology is not as dead or dry as I said. But how are you going to use all this? What bearing has it on your laws of learning that you began to talk about?"

"Possibly when we take them up our digression will be justified. Suppose we begin now? Thorndike gives three **The three** major laws, those of Readiness, of Use and **Laws of** Disuse (or Exercise), and of Satisfaction and **Learning** Annoyance (or Effect). The Law of Readiness follows well what we have been discussing: *When a bond is ready to act, to act gives satisfaction and not to* **The Law of** *act gives annoyance. When a bond is not ready* **Readiness** *to act, to be forced to act gives annoyance.* Think what we have been saying about readiness, and see if this law does not sound reasonable."

"Why, yes indeed. That boy and the ice cream — as long as the ice-cream-eating bonds were ready to act, he got satisfaction from his eating; and the less ready he became, the less satisfaction he got from his eating. I suppose if he had been compelled to eat all six plates, it would have proved very annoying. Yes, this law is clear, but I have been wondering if it isn't a kind of definition of what is meant by satisfaction and annoyance. What do you say?"

"The question is a very interesting one. I am inclined to agree with you. But probably we had better not go into that discussion just now. Fix attention on readiness as a state of the neurone (or nerve structure) which disposes it to action; then this law throws its light on the meaning of satisfaction and annoyance. Probably our general experience has something else to add in any particular case. I am inclined to say that this law partly defines and partly

joins things of which we have otherwise independent
knowledge.   Let us now go to the Law of Satisfaction and
Annoyance."

"You skipped the Law of Use and Disuse.   Do you
wish to keep the order you first gave?"

"So we did skip it, and I believe it is best to take the
other first.   Before taking it up, consider what we are
about.   Some S → R bonds we bring into the world with
us; others — the great majority — we acquire after we get
here.   Of the innate bonds some fit our civilization and need
to be maintained; others don't fit so well, and
need to be changed or killed off.   Acquiring Learning defined
new bonds or changing old ones is what we
mean by learning.   Perhaps our commonest work is strengthening or weakening bonds."

"What do you mean by strengthening a bond?   When is
a bond strong and when weak?"

"We strengthen a bond when we change the connection
between any S and its R so that the response (R) will more
likely follow the stimulation (S) or will follow
more promptly or more definitely.   Weakening Strengthen-ing bonds
is merely doing the contrary;   though often
people speak of weakening a bond when they really mean
strengthening a substitute bond.   Of course, pedagogically,
this is usually the best way of weakening an undesirable
bond."

"Can all bonds be changed?   Or are there some beyond
our influence?"

"There are some bonds practically beyond the power of
education to modify.   These we call reflexes.   They belong
especially to certain more mechanical actions of the body.
Education too has limits fixed for it by nature.   Of course
then when we are speaking of learning we restrict ourselves
to modifiable bonds."

"We are ready now to state the Law of Satisfaction and Annoyance (or Law of Effect): *A modifiable bond is strength-*

The Law of Satisfaction and Annoy-ance *ened or weakened according as satisfaction or annoyance attends its exercise.*"

"When we studied this last summer our in-structor led us to repeat many times: 'Satisfaction strengthens; annoyance weakens.' And then he would have us repeat the whole law. As a result, in the end we fixed it strongly in mind. It is certainly a great law. I never dreamed when I first heard it how much help it can give a teacher. But the more I watch my children learning, the more I believe that this law is the very bottom on which our learning rests and upon which we must base our school procedure."

"Let's go on and see how this law tells us what to expect in our teaching."

"I believe I see already how it is all going to work out. Mind-set-to-an-end is purpose. If the child has a strong purpose, this as mind-set pushes him on to attain his end. This mind-set makes ready his inner resources for attaining the end. When he succeeds, these ready neurones and the success both mean satisfaction; and satisfaction means strengthening the bonds used. He learns by doing. His purpose helps him learn. It must be so. Mind-set, readiness, success, satisfaction, learning — they follow just this way. Am I not right?"

"You have certainly caught the clue."

"Does this explain the value of interest in learning? I have always believed that interest helped learning, but now I seem to see more in it than ever before."

Interest and learning "Exactly so; to take interest in doing any-thing is to have a mind-set towards it. That means, as we saw, an inner urge to engage in that thing and readiness in sense and thought for whatever helps it along."

"Why say 'readiness in sense'? Do you mean that my eye actually sees things I am interested in better than it sees others? I thought the eye was like a mirror or camera and saw everything in front of it."

"The *eye* does see everything in focus before it, and, as a mere mirror, sees them indifferently; but *you* don't see them that way. *You* pick out from all the things in front of your eye certain ones to pay attention to. When I say 'You pick out,' it would be more exact to say that your mind-set at the time, your various readinesses, pick out the things significant to these readinesses. Don't you know that a girl on her way to buy a hat will see the shop windows of the milliners more certainly, more readily in fact, than the windows of the hardware stores? Her eyes, as bare optical instruments, may see the hardware windows, but that seeing meets no response within. Actual and effective seeing is selective according to the mind's set at the time. So with hearing and all the rest."

"Then the working of interest is a scientific fact, and not mere sentimentality. I had got the idea that really hard-headed thinking ignores interest. Haven't we been told that?"

"Possibly you have heard something like that, and some sentimentalists have brought just reproach on a good cause. But it is true beyond a doubt that interest is a significant factor in mental life and a positive help to learning."

"It seems, too, that you don't oppose interest to effort. I thought some people held that you have to choose between interest and effort, that you can't have both."

"You are certainly right that I don't oppose Interest and effort interest to valuable effort. Exactly the contrary. Interest is the natural, indeed the only, basis of effort; the stronger the interest, the stronger, if need be, will be the effort."

"You gave the Law of Effect as if it were scientifically established. Is it not true that some psychologists reject it?

Satisfaction and learning

It seems to me I've heard about some rats learning a path quicker when they were punished for going wrong than when they were rewarded for going right. What does this say about the effect of satisfaction?"

"There are two replies to be made to that. First, the Law of Effect includes, as its statement shows, both satisfaction and annoyance. Whether the rats learned faster by punishment or by reward matters not to this law; either learning was by effect. The fastest learning, other things equal, is where both are used, satisfaction when they go right, annoyance if they go wrong. The other reply is that among psychologists Watson alone, so far as I have heard, denies the law, and he gets little if any backing in his contention. It is true that some very good psychologists have questioned whether the law as stated is ultimate. They do not deny the law as a fact, they merely propose to explain it by appealing if possible to more fundamental considerations."

"Suppose any one denied the law, could he consistently use punishment?"

"If this law is not true, punishment has no place in the learning process strictly considered. To be consistent, one who denies this law would have to deny that the pain attached to going wrong helped the rats to learn more quickly the way out."

"I wonder if everyone understands the word 'satisfaction' in the same sense. Do you mean by satisfaction pleasure and by annoyance pain?"

"No. I do not mean to make satisfaction the same thing as pleasure. Sometimes they may be the same thing, more often not. If I had to choose single words as synonyms I'd use success and failure. Indeed Woodworth uses these words instead of satisfaction and annoyance.''

"Well, won't you please leave off this hair-splitting and arguing! If the laws you talk so much about are of any service, please go on and explain how we can use them.''

"Very well. Take the very specific case of John who has not learned well his number combinations. Suppose he is called on in class for 7 x 9. He hesitates; it **How the Law** might be 72, or 56, or 63. Which is it? He **of Effect** tries them in this order. When he says 72, the **works** teacher looks unimpressed, certain pupils quickly raise their hands, one or two actually snicker, the teacher says 'No.' Now this response of 72 did not bring satisfaction because it did not succeed. He saw by the words and manners of teacher and fellows that 72 was the wrong response. The failure brought annoyance, and the snickers served to increase it. When he ventures 56, he is by reason of the previous attendant annoyances the more anxious to find it right. This very anxiety increases the annoyance of failure. When finally he says 63 and it succeeds, his satisfaction is all the greater by reason of his previous failures and their attendant annoyances. Now the Law of Effect says that the next time he will be less likely than he was this time to say 72 or 56 and more likely to say 63. If this happens often and consistently enough, he will eventually say 63 at once without fail.''

"When you say 'often enough' you are using the Law of Use, are you not?''

"Exactly so. Any teacher knows that joining 42 correctly to 7 x 6 just once is not sufficient. More is needed to fix the learning. As we have always known, repetition is necessary. The Law of Use (or Exercise) **Law of Use** tells us that within limits the more often a response is made to a situation the closer becomes the bond connecting the two; that is, the more surely and smoothly is the response made when the situation presents itself."

"I am interested to ask how the two laws of Effect and Use work together. So far as I can see the Law of Use or Repetition merely says that the Law of Effect holds for the second instance and for the third and so on. Am I right or wrong? If the effect is satisfactory once and again and again, we build a habit of acting that way. If the effect is annoying once and again and again, we build a habit of not acting that way, even of aversion to acting that way. Is it not so?"

"You are right as far as we have gone; at least that is what I think. But there are some instances where Use or Exercise seems to be independent of satisfaction or annoyance. Suppose while we were here talking we heard a tremendous noise, the most deafening we had ever heard, do you think we should remember it?"

"We certainly should and for a very long time."

"Do you think the satisfaction or annoyance it gave us to hear it would make us remember it? Or would its intensity be the main thing?"

"If the noise were intense enough to be the loudest we had ever heard, it would hurt our ears and be rather annoying than satisfying. Still we should surely remember it, and the more, I believe, because it hurt. Don't you think so? But this seems a denial and reversal of the Law of Effect. I am puzzled. What do you say?"

"I think we had better say that the intensity of the hearing exercise is the main thing."

"We seem then to have two parts or aspects of the Law of Exercise, the *number* of repetitions and the *intensity* of the exercise."

"Yes, and there is a third, often called *recency*. Of two experiences otherwise equal we are more likely to recall the more recent one."

"Isn't that merely the Law of Disuse stated Recency and disuse the other way about?"

"Yes; if John goes many months without having 63 follow 7 x 9, the connection weakens and he is less sure to think 63 when 7 x 9 confronts him. All learning tends thus to weaken and drop away."

"Do you mean that eventually we shall forget everything?"

"Oh no, not that. I said *tends* to weaken and drop away, and this is true. But if it is once very well learned it may stay 'on tap,' as it were, a very long time, and in any event is more easily re-learned. Besides every time we do use any such connection (with satisfaction), we give it new life. You hear people say they remember things that happened when they were three or four years old. They may be correct, but most of such memories have been kept alive by telling them every few years or at any rate by thinking them over."

"Haven't I heard that people remember the pleasant things of life longer than the ordinary or the unpleasant things?"

"There is some reason for thinking so. Al- Remembering pleasant things most all grown-ups look back on childhood as a period of almost unalloyed bliss, but most children do not think so at the time. This stronger hold of the pleasant may be due to the 'effect' of the original pleasure, but it may in greater part be due to the fact that we tend by the Law of Effect to think over the things that it gives us satisfaction to dwell upon in our minds, and similarly to turn away from recalling the unpleasant things. So the pleasant memories get more exercise than the unpleasant."

"If I understand you, we might sum it up as follows: Whether I am more or less inclined to repeat a response depends then on the number of times it is used with satisfaction or annoyance, as the case may be. Each instance of satisfaction inclines me more to repeat it; each instance of annoyance disinclines me to repeat it or, if you prefer, inclines me against doing it?"

"Yes, the laws of Effect and Exercise work together that way."

"And if I go a long time without using a response, I lose in some measure the power and tendency to use that response?"

"Yes, that is the factor of Disuse."

"But whether I shall *remember* an event depends largely on the intensity of the experience, independently of whether it was pleasant or unpleasant?"

"Yes, with the understanding that on the whole we tend besides to dwell on and so to think over pleasing things more than unpleasant ones, and in this further way the memories of the pleasing tend to outlast the memories of the unpleasing."

Brooding over slights "But some people seem to take pleasure in brooding over unpleasant things, such as slights and rebuffs."

"Quite right; and since they get satisfaction from such brooding they remember these things longer. Many of the slights and rebuffs were only imaginary in the first place, but brooding over them fixes them in memory as truly as if they were real."

"Does all this mean that the way we think about our experiences may determine their subsequent influence in our lives?"

How thinking guides "effect" "It certainly does, as moralists have always known. Thinking may make all the difference. Suppose that I get angry with a man and while angry tell

him what I think of him and of his conduct, does it give
me satisfaction or annoyance?"

"If you are really angry, you'll enjoy telling him, especially
if you see that it hurts. But later when you think it over,
you may regret it. You will most likely regret it if you made
a spectacle of yourself and if there were other undesirable
consequences. The man may have been an old friend.
The annoying circumstance may have been totally misunderstood. In such circumstances, your initial satisfaction may
turn to very great regret and annoyance."

"What is the 'effect' then? Am I more or less inclined
next time to give way to angry words?"

"If the annoyance of regret outweighs all the satisfactions
involved, you are next time less inclined."

"But doesn't it make a difference what I regret? I may
regret losing control over myself; or as a small man I may
regret having tackled unsuccessfully too big a man; or I
may regret the injustice I was guilty of while still approving
the use of angry words in resentment. Doesn't the 'effect'
depend on what I regret?"

"You are quite right. If I regret losing my temper (no
matter whether the other man was right or wrong, or large
or small), then next time I shall more likely keep my temper.
And if I do hold my temper next time successfully against
provocation (and the greater the provocation the better for
my subsequent self-control, if only I succeed) and if later
consideration approves, then I have taken a step toward
holding my temper as an abiding characteristic. I am becoming a man of self-control.

"But if I only regret having picked too big a man, then
next time, I'll pick my man with more discretion, and I am
on the road to making a pugnacious fellow of myself, perhaps a prudent one, perhaps even a bully; but still I am
more likely thereafter to give vent to anger if only I think I
can succeed in the controversy."

"Much depends then on thinking — much more, I see, than I had believed before."

"Isn't there a lesson here for all teachers, that we should get our pupils to think carefully over what they do, so as to see wherein they have been right and wherein they have been wrong?"

"Yes, and it holds of all they do — writing a letter, baking a cake, making a box, playing a game, settling a quarrel."

"I don't agree with you here. You may laud thinking all you want to. My opinion is that thinking without doing is worthless, even worse than worthless. People that are always thinking about their sins never have anything but sins to think about. They don't help the world along. I had rather have one sturdy sinner that works than a dozen snarling hypocrites. Young hypocrites grow into old hypocrites. Your plan gives them a bad start while they are young. You are wrong with your mere thinking. It's action we want."

"Not quite so fast. Who said we believed in thinking only and not in doing? Didn't you notice a moment ago we said: 'And if I do hold my temper next time?'

Action ought to follow thinking

Do you think that actually holding your temper under provocation is not *doing* something? No, you have spoken too hastily. You are right in saying that thinking without doing is worthless, but you are wrong in intimating that we do not mean to stress doing."

"Haven't we forgot that we were to discuss the laws of learning? It seems to me we've got off the track. This is all very interesting and I think valuable, but are there not some other laws? Last summer I heard a good deal about 'Association' or was it 'Associative Shift?' My

Associative Shift

roommate talked about them a good deal, but I was not in the course with her. What do these things mean?"

"Let me give an illustration I found. I think it makes this 'association' clear. A man put some savory meat in a dog's mouth and at the same time rang a bell. Because of the meat the dog's mouth watered; Pawlow's dog that is, saliva began to flow. This was done frequently for many days. In the end, if only the bell were rung the saliva would still flow."

"Yes, that is a well known instance of Association or of Associative Shift or, as many prefer, of Conditioned Reflex. Can you tell us more about how it happened?"

"I think so. At the beginning, of course, it was the meat only that made the saliva flow. The bell could have no such effect. But the bell being for many days rung in *association* with the presence of the meat and so in *association* with the actual flow of saliva, it finally came about that the bell's ringing alone would suffice to start the saliva flow. This might seem mysterious if there were not so many other instances of the same thing in man and brute."

"This story sounds very curious to me. You say it really happened? I don't know whether I believe it or not."

"Oh yes, it is a well authenticated experiment, in substance often repeated. Haven't we all seen dogs taught to stand at the word of command? That's the same thing. You show the dog something he wishes and you hold the object so that he must stand up to get it. At the same time you say 'stand up.' You repeat this till the 'association' is made. It's all the same."

"Yes, I see that it is. Have you any more illustrations?"

"Yes; a little child was shown a rabbit. She put out her hand to play with it. Just then a harsh noise was made close by. The child, being frightened by the noise, drew back her hand from the rabbit. The next Origin of fears day the same rabbit was shown and the same frightening noise made; the child shrunk away and showed other signs of fear. This was kept up for several days until the sight of the rabbit without the noise would frighten the child. This is a very interesting case. At first the child had two natural (innate) responses: one, on seeing the rabbit (S), to wish to play with it (R); the other, on hearing the loud noise (S'), to draw back in fright (R'). In the end the response (R), playing with the rabbit, had yielded entirely to the response (R') of fright. The sight of the rabbit (S) now made the child draw back in fright (R')."

"Don't you think children learn many things in this way? I mean things like being afraid of the dark or of frogs or of gruff Uncle Henry, as the case may be?"

"It often so happens. I think too that with young children punishment often acts by association in much the same way. After punishment the word of command may, by reason of its association, suffice."

"Why do you say with young children? Is it different with older children?"

"It may work differently with older children. Go back to the child and the rabbit. Suppose the child has seen how the noise was made. She might then not have associated the noise with the rabbit but with the experimenter instead. If so, the child would not have come to fear the rabbit. The older the child the more likely she is to separate in thought the noise from the rabbit, and accordingly the less likely she is to fear the rabbit. So with punishment — it does not as a rule work so well with older children. This is partly the reason."

"Do you mean then that punishment succeeds better with children too young to think much?"

"Yes, this artificial kind of punishment does on the whole succeed better with young children. They are, you might say, more easily fooled. The association seems closer to them. With older people, other things being equal, the more arbitrary the punishment the less likely will the desired association be set up; while the more inherent the punishment the quicker and and better is the lesson learned. From the artificial kind of punishment they may even learn wrong things, such as resentment, for instance, or cunning." Punishment and association

"Isn't part of this the same question we had before about regret? We learn according to where we place the satisfaction or annoyance?"

"Yes, the older child makes distinctions that may break up the wished-for association and he naturally places his annoyance according to his analysis of the situation. When people whip children, or punish them in any way, they ought to be careful how the child thinks and feels about it. If he regrets his wrong-doing, he is less likely to repeat the evil act next time. If, however, he merely regrets being caught, he is less likely to be caught the next time. Possibly some husky boy might afterwards regret that he stayed to take his punishment instead of running away. If this is how he feels, he will the next time be less likely to stay. He may run away."

"This is all very interesting. You know I never dreamed that psychology could tell us so much that we as teachers have needed to know. Of all this discussion about the laws of learning, what one thing do you think we need most to keep in mind?"

"If I had to choose one thing, I should say the Law of Satisfaction and Annoyance. It has more new things to tell us than all the others. It is strategic."

"What do you mean?" Strategic value of the Law of Effect

"I mean that our schools do not as a rule pay as much attention to this law as they might. They fail to arouse readiness. They fail to see that the child gets satisfaction from desirable things. They often seem to think that exercise alone suffices. They forget that exercise with annoyance may tear down. If our teachers thought more about these things, they would succeed better."

REFERENCES FOR FURTHER READING

See references at the end of Chapter III (page 51).

CHAPTER III

ANOTHER VIEW OF LEARNING

"When we were talking last time, nothing much was said about the nervous system. I didn't know that any one could talk about learning without discussing The neural neurones and synapses. We did last time ex- basis of actly what I had thought could not be done and thinking we managed pretty well, but I still think it helps to know about synapses."

"Well, I don't know anything about synapses or those other things you mentioned, and I don't want to. You people seem to revel in long words. I am dead against all such long-winded terminology. I have heard about a 'terminological complex,' and I believe some of you have it. Why isn't common sense good enough?"

"All I can say is that this additional way of looking at it helps many people, including me. Perhaps if you studied it you'd like it. Any word that we don't know seems strange. Surely you are not going to balk at words of no more than two or three syllables."

"Do I understand that there is another way of studying about learning? I thought we had found a pretty good way last week. Does the new way add anything to that way? Do the two ways fit together or does one contradict the other?"

"There is another way, but the two ways do not contradict each other. Suppose we look at the other way. I think it helps greatly. You remember we said that all

43

conduct could be described by telling first the situation which calls for the conduct, and then by telling the response called forth. We call this the stimulus-response formula and we write it, as you know, $S \rightarrow R$. Suppose some one tells you of a particularly spoiled boy and you ask for details. You may hear something like this: If you ask him a question (S), he just sticks out his tongue at you (R); if his mother tells him to be quiet (S), he goes right on hammering or shouting (R). Our question now is, What is there in this boy that makes him respond in such ugly ways when his sister is so different? If you ask the little girl a question (S), she answers very prettily (R); if her mother tells her to be quiet (S), she not only stops at once but says she is sorry she has disturbed (R). The outward situations are the same for both children, but the responses we get are quite different. What makes the difference? Is it that the little girl cannot stick out her tongue or that the boy cannot answer our questions? No, either child could, in point of ability, do what the other one does. What then is the difference?"

"The boy is just bad and the girl is just good, that's all there is to that. What more can you say?"

"Wouldn't you rather say that the boy has formed bad habits, while the girl has formed good habits?"

"To locate the goodness or the badness in habits is much better, I should say, than merely saying 'good' or 'bad'; but even these answers don't carry us as far as we should like to go, or can go. We can study the nervous system as the carrier or immediate cause of behavior. Suppose we take a very simple case of conduct, one so simple as to be 'automatic,' the knee jerk, for example. A man sits with one knee crossed over the other; the experimenter taps on the tendon just below the knee, and the man's foot shoots forward with a jerk. This knee jerk is very quick. The time has been measured and found to be about three-hundredths of a second. But short as this time is, the movement is not so simple as might be thought."

"I think I have heard that in all such cases a nerve or set of nerves carries the stimulation in to the brain or backbone and another set brings out the motor response. But can this be true of so simple a case as the knee jerk response? Three-hundredths of a second seems too short a time."

Sensory and motor neurones

"It is not too short a time. What you had heard is correct. There is always one set of neurones that carry in the stimulation and always another set that bring out motor response. Generally, if not always, there are 'central' neurones connecting these two."

"A moment ago you said 'nerve' and now you say 'neurone.' What is the difference?"

"A nerve is made up of many neurones, somewhat as a telephone cable is made up of many telephone wires. It is easier for us to think in terms of neurones."

"Do I understand that the neurone is the unit element in a connected system of communication?"

"Yes, that's about right."

"And what is the synapse that was mentioned along with neurones earlier to-day?"

"A synapse is a junction point for two neurones, through which, or over which, a stimulation leaps. A neurone has always a receiving end branching out like a tree (called in fact a *dendrite*); it has a long central cord (sometimes called *axon*); it has finally a discharging end branching out like a brush. A synapse is a contact point where the branching receiving end of a second neurone is close enough to the branching discharging end of a first neurone to allow the current to jump across."

A synapse defined

"If I could see a diagram I think it would help. What I can't see, I can't grasp."

"Here is one which may be taken to illustrate the knee jerk reflex. This system consists of two neurones, ABC called the 'sensory' neurone, and DEF the 'motor' neurone. You can see how the stimulation follows the arrows. The experimenter tapped at A. The stimulation, A simple being received by the many sensory branches, reflex arc then ran along the neurone ABC to a connection ('center') in the spinal cord (the cord is not given in the figure). There it started a motor response stimulation

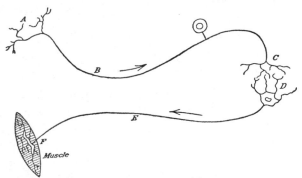

FIG. 1. Two neurones with synapse.

which, running along the neurone DEF to F and spreading out there through the discharging endings, caused the appropriate muscles to act. This made the jerk."

"Do you mean then that in the knee jerk the stimulation ran along a neurone to the spinal cord before the jerking response could be started?"

"That is just what I mean. But generally, if not always, the connection is more complicated. There "Central" might be a 'central' neurone running along the neurones spinal cord joining the sensory neurone with the motor neurone. And of course the reflex is the

simplest kind of behavior. Voluntary acts are more complicated still. Many other neurones involving the brain are
then to be found."

"You said this knee jerk is one of the simplest systems
of neurones, requiring only three-hundredths of a second
to take place. Do more complicated instances of conduct
take longer?"

"Yes, and the more complicated the instance is, the
longer the time required. To respond by pressing with
one hand on an electric button as soon as the other hand is
touched takes about fifteen-hundredths of a second. To
respond similarly to sight takes about eighteen-hundredths
of a second. When one must choose between two stimulations, responding to one and not the other, it takes longer.
In general, the more thinking required, the longer it takes
to respond."

"Do you mean that in these longer time intervals there
are more neurone connections involved?"

"Yes; that is, in general, true. Of course some people are
quicker than others, but that is a different matter."

"Do you not think that so simple a diagram does more
harm than good?"

"I had thought it does more good, but what have you in
mind?"

"Just this. I once heard a very competent student and
lecturer say that novices in this field are so likely to be
misled by over-simplified diagrams that he for his part
refused to use them."

"You think that the one we have just seen may be so
simple as to mislead?"

"I don't know. I am asking for information."

"I look at the matter this way. There is danger that
such simple diagrams may lead the novice to think the
nerve structures back of behavior more simple than in

fact they are; but, on the other hand, there is good reason to believe that simplified diagrams help much in understanding how learning takes place."

"As between the probable good and the possible danger you think the good outweighs?"

"Yes, provided we are careful to put the learner on his guard."

"This all sounds very pretty, but what's the use? How much more do we now know about learning and teaching?"

"Yes, tell us about learning."

"One other thing is necessary. In life nothing is more common than to keep trying further responses if the first one doesn't work. We spoke last week about
Repeated trials a boy's trying to recite his multiplication table and not knowing 7 x 9. We imagined him trying first 72, then 56, and finally 63. This kind of conduct means the branching of neurones. A very simple case might be like this.

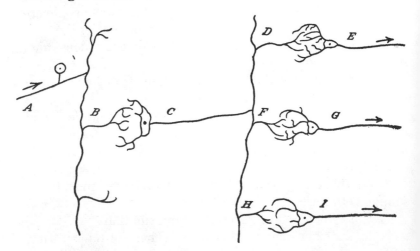

FIG. 2. Multiple response by the branching of a central neurone. (Adapted by permission from Woodworth, *Psychology*, Holt, New York, 1921, p. 39.)

"Before the teacher speaks the boy is ready (though he may not yet know it and he may of course change at any friendly suggestion) to offer answers in the order suggested, 72, 56, and 63. This means that path (synapse) DE (the path to 72) is in better working order than either of the other two, the connection (synapse) being closer; and that path (synapse) FG (the path to 56) is in turn more closely connected than HI (the path to 63).

"The teacher says '7 x 9?' John answers, '72.' It doesn't succeed and some degree of annoyance ensues. The teacher repeats, '7 x 9?' John then tries '56.' Again failure and annoyance follow. The teacher again asks, '7 x 9?' John hazards his third try, '63.' This time success and satisfaction result.

"Suppose the teacher at once asks again, '7 x 9?' What will happen?"

"If the teacher asks at once and John is even normally bright, he will answer '63' immediately."

"Suppose she waits ten minutes and then asks John?"

"He may say '63' or he may not, depending."

"Depending on what?"

"On whether he remembers."

"Could we say it in terms of the diagram? Perhaps we can find out something about remembering. At the beginning, path (synapse) DE was most closely connected, and path (synapse) HI was of these three least closely connected. If we ask at once after his success with 63, what then?"

What learning means

"Why, I suppose HI would then be most closely connected, and the other two less closely connected. But I don't know. I have never thought about it this way before. Do you mean that something happens to the paths? Something physical, I mean? Do these little branches change or get closer together or wider apart, as the case may be?"

"That is exactly what happens.   Or at least that is the best opinion we have.   Woodworth thus pictures four stages of a synapse as it is more and more **Learning re-** closely connected through successful exercise, **sults pictured** and a fifth where the connection has through disuse grown less strong.   Of course, according to our preceding discussion, failure and annoyance would also weaken a connection as truly as does disuse."

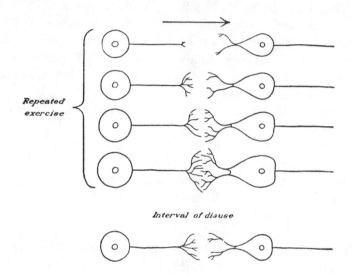

Fig. 3.   The Law of Exercise in terms of synapses.   The diagram shows four stages of a synapse as it is more and more closely connected through successful exercise and a fifth where the connection has, through disuse, grown less strong.   (Adapted from Woodworth, *Psychology*, Holt, New York, 1921, p. 415.)

"Then learning means such a change in a synapse as makes closer that connection, thus rendering it more likely that the stimulation will take that path in preference to others?"

"Exactly so; that is what learning means, if we understand that the connection is made by use (and not, as we may suppose sometimes happens, by mere bodily growth — the maturing of the child)."

"Then that's what learning means. I now see why you were so particular about that S → R. Learning means changing the path among the neurones so as to join a new R to an old S. Yes, I see it now. This does add to our other discussion. I see better now what we then discussed."

"And those laws of learning all have reference to carrying stimulations along new paths so as to bring new responses?"

"Yes. Success and satisfaction bring a closer connection. Failure and annoyance or disuse weaken the connection. I like to see it in terms of those little fibre endings reaching out toward each other or shrinking away — shrivelling up. It helps me a great deal."

"I have a rather ridiculous thought in this connection. Have you ever seen a snail put out his horns, his feelers? If all goes well, they stick far out; but if trouble comes, the horns come in. Perhaps you'll laugh at me. But I think something like this of those little branching fibres. Success and satisfaction make them reach out. Failure and annoyance bring them back. Of course there is the difference that in permanent learning the fibres become (relatively) fixed. There the illustration breaks down."

"What does 'readiness' mean according to this idea?"

"It means a temporary livening up of connections. Imagine a man who speaks well in two languages. If one addresses him in French, all the French word connections liven up, as it were, and the English connections go to sleep. When he sees a horse he thinks and says *cheval*." **Readiness and set**

"Wouldn't you call this 'set' rather than 'readiness'? It seems to me too inclusive, too widespread, to be called 'readiness.'"

"If you think of the whole thing as one big inclusive

change, I should say 'set.' If you think of the particular connections, I should say 'readiness.' 'Set' applies to the aggregate, 'readiness' to the individual neurone."

"I think we can see this better than before. Each readiness comes because the appropriate neurone is joined up effectively with the others of the set."

"How do purpose and will enter in this physiological discussion?"

"We have practically answered that already. Remember that purpose is much the same as mind-set-to-an-end. If we speak of holding an end in view and of striving to attain it, we are but describing in other terms how set and readiness work. You will recall, in this connection, the little girl and her wish to get the doll. The set is a persisting tendency of organized neurones to respond in a certain fashion. The 'effort to attain the end' is the name we give this tendency. When this response is balked by any hindrance, the tendency may be strong enough to find a path for itself through related neurones. These neurones then become ready; and if they act, the resulting acts constitute what we call the 'step' or the 'means' to attain the end in view. If they succeed in attaining the end, they give satisfaction and learning ensues."

Purpose and will

"This reminds me of a passage from Thorndike:

"'Purposive behavior is the most important case of the influence of the attitude or set or adjustment of an organism in determining (1) what bonds shall act, and (2) which results shall satisfy.'[1]"

"Yes, that's a good statement of the facts in the case."

"But where does will enter?"

"Opinions differ. But mine is that will is merely another name for the action of a mind-set, especially where

[1] *Educational Psychology*, Vol. II, p. 51.

there have been conflicting tendencies and one tendency finally wins out."

"Then you locate the will in the action of neurones?"

"Yes."

"And learning results from the action of set and readiness?"

"Yes, and habit and learning are respectively result and process. Learning has its results in habit, that is, in an abiding synaptic connection."

"Yes, I see it all better now. It is clearer. The S → R is now richer in meaning. The S makes me think of the branching sensory receiving end, and the R the final branching discharging end that makes the response. The → is the whole path in between. Learning means such a change in those little synaptic fibres as makes the stimulation take a new path. This means of course that a new → now joins a new R to an old S."

"Then neurones and synapses do help us to understand better what learning is and how it takes place?"

"They help me."

REFERENCES FOR FURTHER READING [1]

THORNDIKE — *Education*, pp. 53–67, 95 ff.

GATES — *Psychology for Students of Education*, pp. 23–27, 31–33, 45–62, 222–236.

WOODWORTH — *Psychology*, Ch. 2, 13, 16.

THORNDIKE — *Educational Psychology*, Vol. II, 1–16 (*Brief Course*, pp. 125–137).

[1] In this instance the readings are so arranged as to indicate the thoroughness of treatment, the most exhaustive last.

CHAPTER IV

SIMPLER INSTANCES OF LEARNING

"What I should like to see is how this psychology will work in school. I don't care much for theory till I see it at

Psychology to be put to work

work. Some people seem to be satisfied with the beauty of mere theory, but I don't feel that way. I want it put to work."

"That pleases me, and I wish we could begin with my class. Ever since we have changed the schedule and my pupils have had so much marching through the halls they drive me crazy. March! They don't march; they run. Unless I am there and watch them with an eagle eye I can't get decent behavior. My principal is not overly exacting, but I have had several strong hints that my class needs toning up, or 'toning down,' if you prefer."

"In answer, let's see what one teacher did in like circumstances. She said one day to her class: 'Your going through

An instance from marching

the halls is not so orderly as it might be; you know it and others have been speaking of it. Today I am going to ask you to notice yourselves as you go, and when you come back I shall ask each

Each pupil was to report his own disorder

one who thinks he did not walk exactly as he should to raise his hand. I tell you in advance I shall not punish you. I shall do nothing about it beyond the show of hands, but I do wish you to notice and tell me.'"

"Much good that would do my pupils. For many it would only add lying to noise. If I didn't punish, or at least threaten it, they'd raise the roof."

"Wait till we have finished, and then see. These children
at first seemed to take the matter much as you say yours
would. They made at least as much disorder
as usual; and when the hands were called for, Not all
reported
not very many were raised."

"Just what I told you. Children are naturally born that
way. They won't keep quiet and they will lie. At least
some of them will. You have to punish. I admit I mainly
threaten, and that doesn't do much good. But what did
the teacher do? She'd give up her sweet and gentle ways if
she listened to me. But go on; I want to hear."

"The teacher stood and looked at the class, a bit discouraged. Then one boy, ignoring her, spoke up, pointing
his finger straight at another boy near by: 'You One boy re-
ought to raise your hand. You made just as buked another
much noise as the rest of us and you know you for not
did.' At this Boy Number 2 looked sheepish reporting
and squirmed a little. Some others didn't seem very happy.
The teacher let it 'soak in' a while, then said: 'To-morrow
we'll try it again; and we wish then to see *all* the hands that
ought to go up.'

"The next day she reminded them seriously, but not
naggingly, that they were to walk quietly and that all hands
were to come up where there had been disorder. Next time:
This time there was less noise, but more hands; less noise,
and what was equally significant, there was an more hands
air of conscious success about the class, not of smug satisfaction nor of having got ahead of anyone, but almost as if a
victory had been won. The teacher, sensitive
to such matters, could feel the difference. Class feels
the victory
Moreover, although more pupils had confessed
to disorder there was little or no sense of opposition between
pupils and teacher. They seemed somehow to feel themselves on her side. I need not prolong the story. They did

the same thing each day for a goodly number of days. The hands grew fewer and the order grew better. In the end the class could control itself reasonably in walking through the halls without teacher or monitor, and would, so far as the teacher could judge, tell the exact truth.[1]"

"A good story of a good teacher, but I don't see where the laws of learning came in. It was personality that did it. The class was good material to begin with. The teacher's personality supplied the rest. I have always said that personality is the main factor in successful teaching. I knew a ——"

"But the laws of learning did enter. The teacher's skill is evident, I grant you, and doubtless her personality was a **How the laws** factor, but the laws of learning were skilfully **of learning** and tactfully used. The teacher may not have **were utilized** thought about it in just that way, but the laws entered just the same, and we can see where and how."

"Recently I saw two maxims that pretty well sum up our laws of learning: 'Practice with satisfaction,' and 'Let annoyance attend the wrong.' Let's try these in this form and see how they work. I believe the short form maxims will help."

"Very well, if you wish, we'll use those. Let's ask first, what did the teacher wish these children to practice?"

"Walking quietly through the halls."
What was "Was that all?"
practiced "Telling the truth."

"Yes, she wanted them to practice these two things — walking quietly and telling the truth. Did they practice these two and with satisfaction?"

"At first, no. Well, I am not sure."

"What happened? Did the children walk quietly the first day?"

---

[1] The incident is substantially true though details have been changed. W. H. K.

"Some probably did. Many didn't."

"Did they 'practice with satisfaction' or did 'annoyance attend the wrong'?"

"Not much of either on the first day so far as I can see."

"Did they practice telling the truth?"

"Some did. Some didn't."

"Did annoyance attend the wrong?"

"Not at first, but after that boy spoke I think it did. I think all who had untruthfully not held up their hands were ashamed. That was annoyance. And all who had held them up were then glad they had told the truth. That was satisfaction. And those who had walked quietly were more pleased than before that they had walked quietly. That was satisfaction. I think that boy made them all think, and thinking directed satisfaction or annoyance to the right place." Annoyance after the boy spoke

and satisfaction too

"How was it the second day?"

"More practiced walking quietly, and they got satisfaction from it both then and later when the time came to make a show of hands. Apparently all practiced telling the truth, and I am sure they got satisfaction from that. I don't know what the teacher would have done if it hadn't been for the first boy; but taking both together it worked finely. I can see how much more ready the children were after the first day both to watch their walking and to tell the truth afterwards." Practice with satisfaction

"Your word 'ready' is very apt, though perhaps you used it independently of our discussion of 'readiness.' They were 'readier' to notice their walking and they were 'readier' to tell the truth. You recall our law, 'When bonds are ready to act, to act gives satisfaction.' Did these children get satisfaction because of their readiness?" How readiness entered

"I think they did. Satisfaction if they walked better.
Satisfaction if they told the truth."

"It was a master stroke for the teacher to say she wouldn't
punish. They could tell the truth more easily, and they
had no incentive to try to get ahead of her. It
changed the whole situation. If the pupils controlled themselves in walking, their thought in
so doing was directed to the real thing and not to fear of
punishment or other artificial elements."

How it
helped not
to punish

"One of the best things in the situation was that pupils
and teacher could get together in the matter. I think
children often look at teachers as in some sense their ene-
mies."

"For those who walked in a disorderly manner, did annoyance attend the wrong? Were they not so pleased at telling
the truth that they forgot about the wrong of disorder?
And if they did forget wasn't this 'practice with satisfaction' in wrongdoing?"

"For the first few times there might be something in what
you say but, as between the two, truthtelling is more important. We could wait to get the other. However, telling
the truth (as regards this particular thing) would easily be
learned and then would come the wish not to have to hold
up their hands."

"Are we agreed then that this teacher did use the laws
of learning?"

"There is no way out of it. She did use them and use
them wisely."

"And do we see how much better it is to see what the
teacher *did* and how the laws were used than to fall back
on a blanket term like 'personality'?"

"Personality"
a poor
explanation

I wonder if we don't mean by personality
the power and disposition to use (consciously
or unconsciously) these laws skilfully and tactfully?"

"Perhaps so, if we add to it a nice consideration for others."

"Do I understand from this illustration that we should try to arouse a 'readiness' for practicing the right (whether of conduct or of lessons) and then be sure that satisfaction attends the right and annoyance the wrong?   Is that all?"

"That's the most of it.   Readiness, exercise, and effect, these three sum up the conditions of learning."

"I wonder if public opinion didn't play a part in this case, and if so what the laws of learning had to do with it."

"Almost surely public opinion entered, at any rate after the first.   When that first boy spoke, all who had told the truth felt that the others had acted unfairly. How public This boy's words directed and voiced the dis- opinion approval.   This public opinion was keenly alert entered the next day and afterwards to see that the truth was told."

"That's all right, but I don't see any laws of learning."

"Why, this public approval or disapproval would increase the satisfaction or annoyance as the case might be of all who acted with or acted against the public opinion.   It increased the *readiness* to prac- How public tice the right.   This brought more surely the utilized the *exercise* of the right, and then gave greater laws of learning *effect* to the satisfaction or annoyance according as right or wrong had been done.   Certainly the laws of learning entered."

"From this discussion one would infer that the laws of learning enter always and everywhere.   Is that true?"

"Certainly it is true.   The laws of learning are always present in conduct just as the laws of chemistry are always present in chemical phenomena." Laws of

"If that is true, why bother about them? learning al-If they are bound to be present, they will take ways present care of themselves.   Why all this fuss?"

"They are always present, but they need not work for us. They may work against us. In the chemistry labora-

We must see that they work for us tory, explosions sometimes do great damage. The laws of chemistry work in such explosions as truly as when things go the way we wish them. It is our business to know how things will work so that we may make them work for good rather than for evil.",

"Do you mean that when a mother 'spoils' a baby she is following the laws of learning?"

"Certainly she is following the laws of learning, and this whether she ever heard of them or not. Let's follow up

"Spoiling" and the laws of learning the illustration. What do we mean by a 'spoiled' child?"

"If he wishes anything, nothing else must get in the way. If you won't give it to him, he'll make himself disagreeable till you do."

"A child who acts as if nothing but his wishes count. If he can't have what he wants, he'll make himself disagreeable till he gets it."

"Very good. Now these characteristics are habits of conduct, habits of thought and behavior. How did it come about that this child thinks that nothing but his wishes should be considered? Did he not learn it?"

"If it is a habit, he must have learned it."

"And if he learned it, he must have practiced it. I suspect that he 'practiced this with satisfaction.' What say you?"

"I suppose you are right. His mother or nurse or grandfather — somebody — let him 'practice with satisfaction' this wrong idea."

"And when he learned it he was following the laws of learning?"

"Yes, I see that he was. It can't be otherwise. He got what he wanted by being disagreeable; that is, he practiced being disagreeable and satisfaction was allowed to attend.

I see it.   The laws hold all the time.   It is our business to
see that they work for the good and not for the wrong."

"Why can't we have an illustration from arithmetic or
geography or English composition.   If the laws of learning
are useful, why shouldn't we teachers put them to work
for us?"

"There is no reason why we shouldn't, and every reason
why we should.   Only it is not always easy."

"Why isn't it easy?"

"Because for one thing we don't always adapt school
work to child nature.   If we don't — and in the degree that
we don't — we shall find it difficult to get readiness for our
lessons, or to get in any high degree satisfaction from learning them.   We are in danger of getting mostly annoyance."

"You are right there I suppose, though I don't just
know what you would do.   But can't we find some illustrations that fit ordinary school work?"

"Certainly we can.   Have you ever seen children interested in writing a letter?"

"Yes, I remember when my fourth grade was going to
invite the fifth grade to see their play, they planned to
write a letter inviting them to come and ex- Letter writing
plaining why the play was given.   They were and the laws
much interested." of learning

"Did the questions of spelling or of capitalization or of
margins come up?"

"They did, and the children took more pains to get that
letter right than any other they wrote for me."

"Was there readiness for learning the right forms?"

"Indeed there was readiness.   That is what interest
means, doesn't it?   They applied what they found to be
the best practice, and they showed great satisfaction when
at last they had a letter no one of them could find fault
with."

"Did they learn anything?"

"Surely they learned. After that we had almost no trouble with the right form of letter arrangement. I think I never saw a class learn it more quickly. They got some new rules about capitals that stayed with them too. There were still other things they learned — how to entertain guests, for one thing. They had a committee to meet the incoming class, show them seats, give them programs, and after the play was over to serve them refreshments. They were as pleased as Punch over it all. Two years later the sixth grade teacher told me that some of the girls with her had used this experience as a kind of model for an entertainment that class was giving."

"Did the laws of learning enter?"

"Yes, indeed; there was readiness, exercise, and satisfaction all along the line. There was annoyance too over some mistakes made. They talked it all over afterwards to see what was right and what was wrong. In this I think satisfaction and annoyance were well directed to successes and failures."

"But we still don't have illustrations of everyday lessons. You all get eloquent over exceptional instances. I want something to help the daily grind. Do you give it up?"

"By no means. Take the dryest lesson of them all. Maybe it ought not to be dry, maybe it ought not to be taught where it is, or perhaps not taught at all. But supposing it is going to be taught, we can still help. Perhaps the best place of all for helping is to work for success, for nothing succeeds like success, and nothing fails like failure."

How success utilized the laws of learning

"What do you mean by 'work for success'?"

"I mean, plan your work so that each child can feel that he succeeds. If he succeeds to-day, he will be readier to attack to-morrow. This new readiness not only makes success likelier but adds to it increased satisfaction. And satisfaction means learning. I have seen bad boys almost made over when they at last got hold of some work they could really do."

"Would you then make the work easy so that they would surely succeed? Or is there danger from this?"

"There is great danger of having work too easy. In fact success is hardly sweet unless it follows effort. Difficulties that challenge are best. To succeed Neither too after putting forth all short of the last ounce of easy nor energy is of all successes the most satisfying. too hard We wish then activities difficult enough to challenge us, to put success really in jeopardy, but not so difficult that success does not come at last."

"If I understand you, success in the face of such difficulties brings greater satisfaction and so increases the learning. Is this true of all the details of the activity?"

"The question is a good one. It is true of all the details in so far as greater difficulty gives increased consideration. Much beyond that I should not care to go. It is further true, moreover, that one's interest along such lines is likely to grow, and favorable attitudes toward teacher and school are likely to be built as well as toward the subject and toward one's fellow-workers who share the difficulties and the successes."

"You speak of attitudes. Are they acquired in accordance with the same laws of learning?" Attitudes and

"Exactly the same. It is 'practice with the laws of satisfaction' that builds an attitude, just as learning truly as it builds good handwriting or truthtelling or anything else."

"Haven't I heard that good teachers are using problems more frequently in geography and history than formerly?"

"Yes, and these illustrate well our laws of learning. A problem, felt as such, challenges thought. This guides the search for an answer, and gives satisfaction when pertinent material is found. Having a problem, we have something to tell us when we have found the solution, and finding the solution is satisfying in the degree that we were anxious to find it and had to work for it. This satisfaction makes an earned solution stick in mind in a way that need not be expected of the merely 'handed out' solution."

How a problem utilizes the laws of learning

"What do you mean, 'earned' solution, 'handed out' solution?"

"Did you ever work an original problem in geometry? If so, you will remember how much easier it was to remember your demonstration than even a shorter demonstration given in the book. You had earned it. The other was 'handed out.' The same holds in geography or history or physics or economics, everywhere that man is man. An earned solution sticks."

"An earned solution gives self-reliance too."

"Indeed it does. Success after a challenge adds to one's confidence in such matters. It is an awful pity that teachers do not play more consistently for such successes among their pupils."

"Then you believe in the modern tendency toward the use of problems?"

Modern tendency to use problems

"Indeed I do. I hope we may discuss the matter later in much greater detail."

"Isn't this problem attitude really an instance of mind-set with all the attendant readinesses?"

"It is exactly that and that is the very subject we ought to consider next — mind-set and learning. Meanwhile, before we separate, let us see where we stand. What have we discussed to-day? How shall we say it?"

"The laws of learning hold all the time. They may work against us. We must make them work for us."

" 'Practice with satisfaction' and 'Let annoyance attend the wrong.' These together made an alternative statement of the law of effect. I like these short forms myself."

" 'We cannot learn what we do not practice' has been implied at several points, though I believe it was not so worded."

"Readiness, exercise, and effect — these three include practically all."

CHAPTER V

MIND-SET AND LEARNING

"Shall we begin where we left off last time, with mind-set and learning?"

"Yes, do. I think I see how it goes but I want to hear the discussion. Mind-set brings readiness; and readiness and successful effort both mean satisfaction; and **Mind-set and learning** satisfaction means learning. Couldn't we have a practical illustration? They always help me."

"By all means if you like. Suppose a girl has asked her mother's permission to make a dress 'all by herself' and her mother has at last consented. What do you say? Is there any mind-set?"

"I should say so; there is a very definite mind-set. I remember something like this when I was young, and I was nearly wild with enthusiasm and determination. I was bent on showing all the family that I could make a dress. I chose a party dress, because I had been invited to go to a more important party than usual and I thought I had no suitable dress. Yes, there is a definite mind-set."

"And what about an inner urge?"

"What do you mean by 'inner urge'? Is there also an outer urge? And are the two different?"

"Let me answer that. I know the difference. Sometimes I find a boy determined to do something, say make an airplane. The urge is inside the boy. I may try to discourage him, others may laugh at him, he may find difficulties; but as long as he feels that way inside he will persist in spite of all outside interferences. That's an inner urge. But suppose the boy's father tells him to mow the lawn, and the boy does it only because his father makes him; the urge here is outside. With an outer urge, one will give up at the first opportunity. If any interference comes along, he will try to take it as an excuse to stop. This girl had a strong inner urge to make the dress. A strong mind-set to accomplish an end means exactly a strong inner urge. Am I not right?"

"Exactly right. But now tell us what else this girl's strong mind-set means besides an inner urge?"

"You called it further back a 'mind-set-to-an-end.' I should say it means a clear and definite end in view, a strong purpose with a clearly defined end. Here the end was to make a dress that would fit and be becoming, and call forth favorable comments from all who saw it and arouse their wonder that so young a girl should make so pretty a dress. The strong mind-set meant setting up this sort of end."

"And what about readiness or unreadiness?"

"I know; it was just what we had before. The mind-set makes this girl ready to see and examine dresses and styles and patterns and fabrics, and to hear people talk about such matters, and to read *Vogue* and the *Delineator*." Set and readiness

"Yes, it will make ready for action all the mechanisms in the girl's mental make-up that might have to do with making the dress. But what about unreadiness?"

"We had that too. It makes the girl unready to do anything else. I dare say she is more or less of a nuisance about the house till the dress is finished, for she won't want to be called on to care for the baby or to set the table or even to be told that it's bed time. Yes, all the mechanisms whose action might interfere will be distinctly unready to act."

"What does all this mean for thinking? Does this girl think?"

"Certainly she thinks. She has to choose the style in which she will make the dress. That takes thinking and a great deal of it. I fancy she'll have everybody in the house nearly crazy looking and passing judgment, unless she is the kind of girl who somehow already knows her own mind. Of course she has to choose the material, and watch the price so as not to exceed her supply of money. After that there will be the pattern and how to lay it on, how to cut out the material, etc., etc. Yes, she has to think.

Thinking

"An important matter is this — What guides her thinking? What tells her what to think? It is the end in view that guides. Here it is exactly the kind of dress she wants to make that guides her thinking. In this case it is a party dress. Her purpose to make this dress guides her thoughts, at least in a large way, all the time. Some smaller purposes, specific subordinate ends I suppose you would call them, guide at other times; but all have to fit together."

"You say all have to fit together. Is this what some call 'organization'?"

"Exactly, this is what is meant by organization. Everything she does — buying, planning, cutting, sewing — all have to work consistently together or she will not have the kind of dress she wants. I should say there is opportunity here for the best kind of organization. How to organize her efforts is part of what she had to learn, and an important part."

"But are you not leaving out the most important thing? I mean the learning. I can see how the girl's purpose means a definite end in view and an inner urge to attain that end. I can see too how these things mean an efficient organization of effort — in fact the whole thing seems to be working for efficiency of

Purpose and learning

action. But I don't yet see where learning comes in. Can
you explain more clearly?"

"All we need is to apply the results of our previous discussion. Learning mainly comes by the Law of Effect. Any
movement of mind or body that succeeds (or brings satisfaction) has for that reason a better chance of being used
again. Similarly any movement that fails has a smaller
chance. This better (or lesser) chance of being used again
we call 'learning.' The greater the feeling of success or
failure (satisfaction or annoyance) the more definite the
learning.[1] Now if the girl has a strong interest in making the
dress, what she does by way of successful planning or execution brings great satisfaction. Wherein she fails, she feels
annoyance. This success (satisfaction) fixes in her nervous
system the success-bringing movements. The annoyance
in like manner tends to cut out for the future the failure-
bringing movements. When the girl has finished her dress,
each step that helped make it a success is more firmly fixed
in her (as a habit or skill or memory), and each step that hurt
will less likely be used again. And not only are the separate
steps thus fixed (or dropped out, as the case may be), but so
likewise are the connections of one step with another. The
organization as an effective whole is fixed in the girl's mental
make-up. The stronger the purpose and the more definite
the success (or failure) the stronger and more definite the
learning."

"You have said nothing about the factor of readiness
here. Does that play any part?"

"Yes, indeed. The readiness we discussed as growing
out of the mind-set not only prepares each pertinent mechanism for use but accords satisfaction when used. We then
have, as it were, satisfaction coming possibly from two

[1] Except in some extreme cases where such factors as consternation or
paralysis of action interfere with the learning process.

sources: first, from the readiness of the mechanisms used, and second, from the resulting success. This fact means the possibility of better learning."

"How does consciousness help? Does it have any part in the learning process as here described? I have heard some say that this too is an important factor."

Consciousness and learning "Indeed it is an important factor in learning. Its function here is at least three-fold: first, to connect more surely and definitely the various responses with their several appropriate stimuli that they may be properly and strongly joined together for learning; second, to attach satisfactions or annoyances more precisely where they severally belong and so bring about the right learning; and third, by emphatic attention to heighten the satisfaction or annoyance felt and so increase the learning. It is for these reasons, among others, that we are most anxious that pupils think while they act and consciously intend the several steps they take."

"You do not mean then that in purposeful activity all the success-bringing movements or steps are equally well learned or remembered?"

"Indeed, no. At one time the girl who made the dress needed to pick up her scissors from the floor. She probably did so as a matter of course and will never think of it again; but she will think of the store in which she bought the goods for her dress. One movement has significance; she thinks about it, and she will remember it. The other has such slight significance to her that she doesn't think about it at the time and so will not remember it in the future."

"But you don't mean to say that remembering is all there is to learning?"

"Most certainly, no. As thinking is not all of life, so remembering is not all of learning. Remembering, that is, recalling to mind, is a very important kind or instance of learning; but the skill to use a tool or the tendency to repeat an act are instances of learning that are not well described as remembering."

Remembering not the only kind of learning

"Didn't the older education mainly think of learning as remembering?"

"Yes, I think it did; and it was, as we say, too exclusively bookish. We are now stressing habits, attitudes, and appreciations, which our schools formerly too much overlooked."

"And you think that purposeful activity, under a strong mind-set, helps in all kinds of learning, habits, skills, attitudes and appreciations as well as in things properly to be remembered?"

"Yes, that's what I think."

"What about the presence of a difficulty? Does it help or hurt?"

"If not too great, it may help appreciably. Success after overcoming a difficulty yields greater satisfaction."

"Once before we spoke of the effect of a difficulty to spur to action. Ought we not say something about that here?"

"You are quite right. It is recognized by competent psychologists that when one is pursuing an end any obstacle (not too great) serves to spur to greater energy and effort. Not only then are more of one's inner resources thus called into play, but success attained under such circumstances is sweeter when it comes. The increase of attention occasioned by the obstacle and the greater satisfaction from success both increase the learning. You are right; reasonable difficulties enhance the probable educative effect of the enterprise."

How an obstacle spurs to effort

"Does this mean that we are to put hindrances and difficulties in the way of students? Is there not danger that they will resent this?"

"There would be great danger of resentment. No, I

should not place artificial difficulties in the way. Rather should the teacher know these psychological facts and encourage the students to undertake enterprises neither so easy as to fail to challenge their powers nor so difficult as to discourage. Between these limits lie the best educational results."

"Won't you please sum this up for us? I think I have the main points, but I should like to have it in more systematic form."

"That it may be clear that the same analysis holds true of academic activities as in the case of the girl with her dress, suppose we make a tabular statement showing how a strong mind-set acts in both kinds of activities. Imagine now that Summary of a boy who likes mathematics is brought face to mind-set and face with a certain difficult problem. The learning teacher says that this is an unusually hard problem, that he doesn't know whether any member of the class can solve it or not, though they have now had enough mathematics to enable them to solve it. He'd like them to try, but he is not very hopeful. The boy feels in this a definite challenge. He proposes to solve that problem and to solve it all by himself. He attacks it, but it doesn't yield at once. He redoubles his efforts. We have then a clear case of study and, let us suppose, of eventual success under the influence of a very strong mind-set-to-an-end. We find accordingly for this boy (and for the girl making her dress):

"1. *A definite end in view.* The boy is definitely determined to solve the problem all by himself. (The girl is definitely determined to make an excellent dress.)

"2. *An inner urge to attain this end.* The teacher has not required the problem, but the boy is strongly urged on by himself from within to solve it. (So with the girl, making the dress is her own enterprise. She acts from her own inner urge.)

"3. *Readiness in all the boy's pertinent inner resources.* All his knowledge and skill, all his available ideas, are in a state of readiness. They rise up, as it were, earnestly desiring to be used. (It is the same with the girl.)

"4. *An unreadiness for thwarting activities.* He has real difficulty for the time being to enter wholesouledly into his other lessons. He can hardly cease thinking about the problem. (The same is true of the girl.)

"5. *The inherent difficulties spurring to greater efforts.* The difficulties met, being not insuperable, do not discourage but call forth more conscious attention and stimulate to even greater efforts. (True of boy and girl alike.)

"6. *The end defines success for him.* He won't count it success unless he solves the problem beyond a question and by his own unaided efforts. (Success with the girl means a dress that she and others will approve, made all by herself.)

"7. *Success attained brings satisfaction.* The stronger the mind-set and the greater the difficulties successfully overcome, the greater will be the satisfaction of success. (True of both alike.)

"8. *Satisfaction means fixing the responses that brought success.* When he finally sees the solution, the way out of the difficulty, the satisfaction attending will by the Law of Effect fix in him the success-bringing steps. (The satisfaction will fix in the girl's nervous system each success-bringing step, whether of knowledge or of skill, and the organization of all into one whole.)"

"Do you mean by 'fixing the success-bringing steps' that the boy will remember the solution?"

"Yes, I mean that and more. Solving the problem means seeing the elements of the problem in a certain appropriate relationship. Now the satisfaction of success will fix in him this relationship. It will *How success acts* be almost impossible for him to forget it. Moreover, his mind will in sheer pleasure at hard-earned success play back and forth over the main success-bringing steps, so that exercise with renewed effect will fix this yet more strongly in his mind. Each time he shows his solution to an appreciative listener, this fixing process will again be repeated. And there is yet more. This present success will make him more inclined to attack the next challenging problem he meets; and he will for the same reason find it easier the next time to get into the spirit of seeking; the mind-set to study having this time brought success will the next time more readily call into play the boy's available mathematical resources for solving such a problem."

"And are the like things true of the girl?"

"Indeed, yes. The results to her are in effect the same. Her success fixes it all in her mind. She too will delight to think it over and talk it over. She too will be encouraged by this success to attempt more difficult feats of sewing. Another time it will be easier for her to get into the mind-set necessary for successful dressmaking. The next time her experiences will be better available when needed."

"Is this why purposeful learning is so much advocated now?"

"Yes, only there are still other reasons for wishing to utilize the child's purpose. There is in the first place more likelihood of success. The strong inner urge will mean stronger efforts. Then there is greater probability of a good organization's resulting. The definite end makes it easier to form an effective organization, because there is something to guide the steps. This is more evident where the effort to attain the end involves the assembling and uniting into one whole of many obviously different steps. The third reason for wishing the strong purpose is the one above described, that the learning takes place better. The learning not only comes more quickly, but it is more abiding when it does

The function of purpose

thus come. The satisfaction following success brings about this result by the Law of Effect."

"You have not said anything about annoyance. Does that not enter into the situation?"

"Yes, but negatively. The steps that lead nowhere bring annoyance, and for that reason they tend to drop out, not to be repeated the next time. This is the other half of the Law of Effect." How failure and annoyance act

"Doesn't the satisfaction of such success affect also the associate suggestions and the concomitant learning that we discussed in Chapter I?"

"Indeed it does; but we must leave that until we have taken up the subject of coercion."

"It is good to talk about such things. Already teaching means more to me. Heretofore I have been an artisan in the work. Now I see that we may become artists at teaching." Artistic teaching

"And the art is based on science."

"Yes."

REFERENCES FOR FURTHER READING

KILPATRICK — *The Project Method*, pp. 8–11.

THORNDIKE — *Educational Psychology*, Vol. II, 213–234 (*Brief Course*, 208–224).

WOODWORTH — *Psychology*, pp. 69 ff., 74 ff., 542.

KILPATRICK — *Source Book in the Philosophy of Education*, No. 501, 512, 513.

CHAPTER VI

COERCION AND LEARNING

"I understand we are to discuss coercion and learning. I hope we may take a clear case of coercion and carry through the whole process. I want to see each step, for I find it a difficult subject."

"Before you do that, I have a preliminary question. What does coercion mean? Must there always be another person to do the coercing or might impersonal circumstances coerce? Might one even coerce himself? I wish you'd make this clear."

"To say what meaning a word shall have is not easy. Different people see things differently, and differing situations sometimes require differing senses of meaning; but if there is possible doubt we must say what meaning we propose to use. Let's begin with the clearest case of coercion, which is certainly where one person forces another into doing something he wouldn't otherwise do. Suppose a boy has planned to go swimming with the other boys and his mother in spite of his tearful pleading forbids, and 'forces' him, as we say, 'against his will' to stay at home and 'mind the baby.' Suppose further that before he will yield she has to threaten punishment, and even after the other boys have gone she has to speak sharply to 'make' him treat the baby decently and care for her properly. What, now, are the characteristic elements in this instance of undoubted coercion? As it is an extreme case, we may expect the elements to stand out in unusual relief. First, in point of

76

time we find a mind-set already occupying the stage of action. This mind-set would, unless thwarted, result in a certain line of conduct; namely, in his going swimming with the boys. Second, there arises some interposition, felt by the one coerced to come more or less from the *outside*, which sets up the essential coercion; namely, a state of affairs that thwarts the activity already under way and *against the will* of the coerced directs experience along another and, under the circumstances, *undesirable* line. Third, the one coerced *accepts, but against his will,* the new line of conduct because he fears a threatened and still more unacceptable alternative.

"This is of course an analysis and description, not a logical definition. The emphasized words must have been experienced in order to be understood; but, having been experienced, their meaning is fairly definite. With these understood, the essential elements of coerced activity stand out."

"It seems to me, then, that whether you call any such experience a case of coercion depends upon the attitude of the one concerned, whether there arises in him Coercion is a a contrary set which inwardly rejects while matter of there is outward yielding." attitude

"Yes, I think you are right, and the more definite the inner rejection, the clearer is it a case of coercion."

"Might it not happen that what began as a clear case of coercion would cease to be such because the coerced person changed his mind, the inner attitude shifting from rejection to acceptance?"

"You are quite right, and the possibility of this is a matter of great practical importance for the educator."

"Would you not also need in this discussion to say whether you were thinking of the one who did the coercing or the one who felt coerced?"

"Perhaps so, and the instance given above was in terms of the attitude of the one coerced. Whether he learns or not is our concern; so we have given our analysis and discussion in terms of his attitude. We have in our past discussions seen clearly that the attitude of the learner affects his learning. That's why it is emphasized in our present discussion."

"Have we sufficiently answered the question as to whether coercion must come from another person or might proceed from circumstances?"

"I think so. The question is one of fact. This inner attitude of rejection is most easily and most typically aroused by persons, possibly because their motives are both complex and hid and are accordingly the more easily mistaken, and resentment is thus more readily stirred. Resentment, I may add, seems a typical accompaniment of coercion. The young and hotheaded may entertain feelings of resentful and rebellious rejection against mere impersonal circumstances, where older and calmer persons would accept such thwarting as inevitable. To the one group this kind of thwarting would be coercion, to the other it would not. But the two undoubtedly merge into each other in intermediate cases."

"Can, then, a person coerce himself?"

"After the discussion given, the question is, as stated, for us now one of fact. Do we see anyone rejecting with inward rebellion what he imposes on himself? If we do, then one may coerce himself. The cases that seem most like this may, however, upon reflection, turn out to be examples of the coercion of circumstances rather than of one's self. The question thus becomes rather academic than useful."

"Well, may we not go on to something interesting? When you people begin splitting hairs, you never know when to stop. It gets very tiresome to the rest of us. Are we never to take up the effect of coercion on learning?"

"It is too bad to spend so much time on what may seem unnecessary. We are, however, now ready to go on with our topic. Shall we take an illustration and follow it through with the same steps we used at the outset?"

"By all means. An illustration always helps."

"Suppose, then—John has lately been so much interested in football that he has slighted his lessons. At length the teacher in desperation tells him that he must stay away from practice that afternoon and An instance
of coercion work on some problems he has repeatedly missed. As soon as he can do the work, he may go. To make a clear case, suppose John feels rebellious the whole time, but doesn't dare actually to rebel. Our problem, then, is to find out what kind of learning will go on, and how it will take place."

"Shall we take into account only the learning of the problems, or shall we consider all the learning that takes place? I mean, shall we ask about all the simultaneous attendant learnings that we discussed before [Chapter I]?"

"Eventually we must take account of all, because they are all taking place, but for our immediate purposes let's begin with the problem solving."

"Well, if the boy is going to be rebellious the whole time, he won't learn much. Anybody knows that. I don't need to study psychology or pedagogy or pedaguese or anything else to tell me that. Why don't you ask something that people want to know?"

"Yes, we went over the same point earlier in connection with learning through interest. The main results in the clear cases may already be known, but if we can find out *how* the rebellious attitude works to prevent the learning, we have learned something new. Perhaps then we'll know better how to manage rebellious cases. Shall we go on?"

"Yes, for gracious' sake, do."

"Well, consider John. He stays because he's afraid not to stay, and he studies at least after a fashion. Is there any mind-set?"

"Certainly, he is dead set against the whole performance and, as you said, this contrary set continues throughout."

Opposed mind-sets

"Is that all? Is there any other mind-set? Remember, he can get out with the other boys only if he will convince the teacher that he can work the problems. Does this mean anything?"

"Yes, it probably means that he will try to convince the teacher, and so will study the problems."

"Then he will have a mind-set for the problems?"

"To a degree, yes; but he may try to convince the teacher by some kind of bluff or, it may be, even by cheating. But whatever the means he adopts for convincing the teacher, he will have at least some temporary mind-set for that."

"Why do you say that his mind-set for the study or for the cheating, as the case may be, will be temporary?"

"Because he is really intent on getting to the football practice. That's the end for him. The study and fooling the teacher are only means. For the football he has what we called an *inner* urge. For what he does to convince the teacher there is only an *outer* urge."

"What is the effect of the rebelliousness?"

"It acts, as it were, on the side of the football urge. The two work together. They are almost parts of the same thing."

"Yes, I see that, but what is the effect of the rebellious spirit on these temporary sets? Doesn't the feeling of opposition keep him from trying to persuade the teacher?"

"I don't think so. I was wondering if this rebellious feeling of opposition doesn't work against the boy's studying, but in favor of his fooling the teacher."

"I believe you are right. The teacher undertakes to force the boy to study. To get ahead of the teacher and so get out of study would afford an outlet for the boy's spirit of opposition. Yes, the rebelliousness works against study and for getting ahead of the teacher."

"But suppose the boy is in the end forced to study. Is there or is there not any set for the problem solving?"

"Let's see. Suppose one of the problems involves a long subtraction. Will the boy remember throughout that he is subtracting, or will he forget and either begin adding or have to go back and ascertain anew what he is trying to do?"

"I see what you mean. Certainly, if he is to solve the problem he must in some measure have a mind-set that puts his mind on it. In such case he probably would go ahead consistently in his subtraction."

"But the contrary mind-set roused by the coercion would interfere with this mind-set, wouldn't it?"

"Yes, as a rule the contrary set would interfere to some extent with his attention to the arithmetic, at times so much so as to prevent anything but a very mechanical How the contrary mind-set acts sort of attention. In other cases there would be less interference. In still others, he might really give pretty good attention to the arithmetic."

"Would it not depend on the strength of the contrary set and on the degree of rebelliousness, as to how much interference there would be?"

"Exactly so."

"This discussion sounds very reasonable, but I thought we were to hear about the psychology of learning under coercion. You seem to have overlooked that."

"Suppose we take the eight definite steps in purposeful learning under a strong favorable mind-set as given before [pages 70-71], and discuss the effect of coercion under those heads."

"Very well. In that case we had a strong mind-set-to-an-end that favored, as you say, the learning. How is it here?"

"We have here also a strong mind-set, but it is opposed to his staying in or to studying. We find also a certain temporary and relatively weak mind-set for the problems. The stronger the rebelliousness that attends the opposed mind-set, the weaker this mind-set for arithmetic is likely to be."

"What about (1) the 'definite end in view'? "

"There is one main end, to get to the football practice. There may be a kind of subordinate end, to solve the problems; but there may be in place of this a plan of deceiving the teacher."

In coercion there are opposed ends

"What about (2) the 'inner urge'? "

"The inner urge is to get to the football practice. There may be a derived and temporary inner urge to deceive or otherwise cheat the teacher, but any urge for the problems would in this case be typically outer. It will let up as soon as the external pressure is removed."

"What about (3–4) 'readinesses and unreadinesses'? "

"Each mind-set will have its own system of readinesses and unreadinesses; and these will greatly interfere with each other. So long as the contrary mind-set is acting — especially so long as the rebellious feeling is present — it will be psychologically impossible for the best arithmetical thinking to go on. The thoughts just won't come with fullness and freedom. Under such circumstances it would be only relatively mechanical work that could result."

Resulting unreadiness

"Won't there be actual readiness for thwarting activities?

Don't pupils under such conditions actually take to a kind of sabotage, as they call it in labor discussions?"

"There certainly is likely to arise readiness for thwarting activities, and sabotage is not an inapt term to describe many of them; but often an older and uglier word is even more apt."

"You mean cheating, I suppose, and you are certainly right. Many children under unwise management readily feel great 'readiness for thwarting activities.' In answer to such readiness, children hitherto and otherwise good may find a natural if unholy satis- Tendency to deception faction in 'beating' the teacher?"

"Yes, here as elsewhere the Law of Readiness holds: 'Where a bond is ready to act, to act gives satisfaction.'"

"And does this satisfaction fix the cheating habit in these children?"

"Yes, unless there is some counteracting annoyance. Only we mustn't say they will surely cheat under all other conditions. The rule of no general automatic transfer holds here as well as elsewhere."

"And what about (5) 'hindrances spurring to greater efforts'?"

"So far as studying the arithmetic is concerned, exactly the opposite will hold. As with all 'outer urges' each new difficulty is a new suggestion to stop, to cease efforts. No, where one works under coercion a difficulty encountered in a problem will not as a rule spur to greater efforts at problem solving. Just the contrary will generally happen."

"And (6) what is success for this boy?"

"It all depends on the ends set up. The Ambiguous success main success, if success there be, will be getting out with the other boys. There may be the subsidiary success in his efforts at cheating, or the milder success at the problem solving."

"And what about (7) the satisfaction that attends success?"

"Each success carries its own satisfaction, the amount of which depends on the strength of the corresponding mind-set. If the boy can beat the teacher, considerable satisfaction ensues; he has escaped and he did it by his own contrivance. If he solves the problems and so gets out, the main satisfaction may still be in getting out. The satisfaction in the problem solving as such is lessened in the degree that he has felt resentfully that his work has been under compulsion."

"What, then, shall we conclude about (8) the learning that results from coercion?"

"First, in so far as the opposed mind-set begets unreadiness for the problem solving, in that degree the necessary **Coercion gives** thoughts are unlikely to arise. There is then **less promise** danger that psychologically he will be unable **of success** to do a good job of thinking. In other words, his chances of successful solution (as the teacher counts success) are lessened in the degree that the boy feels opposition and rebellion.

"Second, the satisfaction that results from successful problem solving (supposing he does succeed) is probably the **Less satis-** smaller, both on account of the lack of readiness **faction** for the necessary effort because of his opposition to the coercion, and also by reason of the overshadowing feeling of satisfaction that he has at length escaped coercion.

"Third, since the satisfaction is small there is small learning. The Law of Effect must play its part. There **Less learning** may even have been built up a growing distaste for the whole subject of mathematics. If so, this is merely the negative side of the same law."

"Do you mean that the annoyance of the whole proceeding may disgust him with mathematics? It isn't the mathematics that is at fault, it is his own previous idleness or lack of attention to duty. Won't the annoyance thus serve to keep him from being idle again? Why Aversion
may result do you pick out the mathematics to suffer?"

"It all depends upon the boy's own reaction. If he lays the blame on his idleness, he will less likely be idle the next time. If he blames the teacher and the dryness of mathematics, then he may build an aversion to both. Which he will probably blame, you know as well as I; but the Law of Effect will work in any case."

"Do you conclude that coercion has no place in school?"

"No, I wouldn't say that. I think it has a place. But I would say that if my coercion of children is of such kind as to arouse a strong feeling of active resentment, then I need not expect much useful learning to The place
of coercion result directly; and there are other possible results to be positively feared. If at any particular time I wish children to learn, I must at that time either avoid coercion or I must so use it as not to arouse the contrary set that spoiled, as we have just seen, the most of John's learning."

"But haven't we heard of children who practised piano playing under coercion and later came to love their playing? What about them? And what about holding up standards? Isn't that necessary, and isn't it coercion?"

"That's a good question about the piano playing. I have heard people argue much about it, but they never reached a satisfactory conclusion because they had no way to settle the issue. I hope we shall be more successful."

"I've just come in. I wish you would tell me what you have been saying so that I may go on with the discussion."

"I am glad to sum it up if the others don't mind. We have been discussing coercion and its effect on learning. We A summary of agreed by a kind of definition that the presence the effect of an aroused contrary mind-set is the essential of coercion factor in what we call coercion. The normal and legitimate effect of such a contrary mind-set we concluded is to bring unreadiness for the coerced action and to lessen — in any event — the satisfaction accompanying the successful completion of this action. This unreadiness and accompanying lessened satisfaction would mean, by the psychological Law of Effect, less of learning in connection with the coerced activity. From this we further concluded that if we wish a child to learn best we should as far as is feasible avoid arousing the contrary mind-set."

"Isn't it inevitable that if you force anything on another you do arouse opposition, and isn't this feeling of opposition just what you mean by a contrary mind-set? If this is so, then doesn't coercion, however you define it, necessarily prevent learning? How can one ever learn to play the piano through compulsion, still less learn to like it?"

"Not so fast. You are ignoring certain necessary qualifications to your statements. The typical result of forcing Coercion does conduct upon another is, true enough, to arouse not prevent opposition; but there are many possible degrees all learning of such opposition. Some degrees of opposition are so weak as hardly to mean a contrary mind-set. More to the point, however, we never have said that an opposed mind-set destroys or prevents all learning in connection. On the contrary, human responses are always mixed. We pointed out explicitly in the case of the boy kept after school to work his problems that he had at least two mind-sets, one of opposition to the teacher, the other, much weaker as a rule but still present, to solve the problems. When he succeeds in solving the problems he feels some satisfaction.

This satisfaction may come from either of two sources. He feels satisfaction first at getting out. The more exclusively his satisfaction as he finishes is centered consciously on getting out, the less, in probability, does his success fix any mathematics in his mind. The second satisfaction arises from the success attending his efforts with the mathematics. He may, it is true, have felt his resentment and opposition so keenly that he wouldn't even try to solve the problems. If so, the result is no effort and therefore no chance for success or satisfaction, and consequently no possible learning of the arithmetic. But if he did try at all and did make any sort of success, then there will be some satisfaction and consequently some learning."

"You do admit, then, that coercion can bring learning?"

"Certainly. We have all the time said that coercion might and usually would bring some learning. Our point has been that in so far as coercion arouses and maintains a contrary mind-set, it tends to reduce and lessen the learning we wish."

"Then coercion is merely a poor way to get things learned?"

"It is that, true enough, but it may be worse than that. We have in this whole discussion been ignoring all those accompanying learnings we discussed in our first meeting [Chapter I]. In any actual case Coercion and before us they have to be considered. Coercion concomitants may teach on the side, as it were, many undesirable things. For instance, many boys who have been badly managed in school conceive such a distaste for school that they leave it as soon as the law allows, to the hurt both of their own future and of society at large."

"This question seems to me to grow as we work on it. I had no idea it was so complicated."

"Yes, it is becoming complicated. I fear we shall have to wait till the next time to finish."

"May we not begin then with the piano playing? I am very much interested in that."

"Indeed, yes, if you all so wish."

REFERENCES FOR FURTHER READING

See references at the end of Chapter V (page 73).

CHAPTER VII

COERCION AND LEARNING — *Concluded*

"Will coercion bring success in the teaching of piano playing? That's where we are to begin, is it not?"

"Yes, that's what we agreed to."

"Then, let me tell how it strikes me. I have been thinking a great deal about it. I think I now see how a girl may learn to play from compulsory practice on the piano. Isn't it just like the boy kept in after school — the girl will as a rule give at least *some* attention to her practice, and if she succeeds even a little she will have some satisfaction arising from her success. So she will learn at least a little."

Piano playing under coercion

"Yes, that is exactly the case. Of course the more she puts her soul into what she does, the more likely she is, first of all, to succeed, and also the greater will be her satisfaction in what she accomplishes, and consequently the better will be her learning."

"I find myself confused a little just here. I thought the question was not whether the girl will learn to play a piece from enforced practice. That I never doubted. The question I asked the last time was whether the coercion, if persisted in by the mother, wouldn't result in a fondness for piano playing in the girl. And if this is so, it seems to contradict your analysis."

"You mean, then, to ask whether coercion can create a fondness. And if so, how can we reconcile this with the effect of annoyance, which would be expected to create an aversion?"

89

"Yes, or you might put it, 'Can coercion build an interest?' I should certainly expect from your line of argument that an aversion and not a fondness would result."

"What are the observed facts? Does coercion build fondness or aversion?"

"I think I can answer that. Of course I haven't kept any statistics; but my experience as a music teacher through a good many years is this: if a girl has talent and if she is started right so that she feels herself succeeding, she will learn rapidly. If she does learn rapidly and keeps on growing in her music and if people praise her playing, she will grow more and more fond of her music. But if she has no talent, she won't learn very rapidly and will easily get discouraged. Then when people don't praise her playing, she will begin to look for praise and satisfaction along other lines. For such a girl, a strong fondness for the piano will seldom, if ever, develop."

"But you said nothing about coercion and its effect."

"I don't think much about that with my pupils. It may help or it may hurt."

"I wonder if we haven't now the essential facts before us. If a girl has no talent for playing she will sooner or later find it out. If she doesn't play very well and is normally sensitive to what people say, she will gradually leave off playing for others. In such case the coercion couldn't help, it might hurt. If a girl has talent but doesn't know it, a certain amount of coercion — skillfully applied — may overcome an initial objection to practising until her success, which is probable from her talent, brings satisfaction enough to build a fondness. In such cases the coercion may help."

When coercion can help

"Why say 'may help'? Why not say 'does help'?"

"Possibly you are right, but I must believe in every case that so far as the child feels the coercion to be coercion, the desired learning is lessened. I admit the need for getting the child to put forth the necessary initial effort, but I can not admit that coercion is always the best way to secure this needed effort. Remember that coercion naturally lessens both the chance of success and the accompanying learning. Perhaps some other way than coercion might arouse the effort without at the same time incurring the hurtful effect almost bound to follow in some measure from coercion. In other words, as a teaching device, coercion is always in some measure an evil. In a particular case it may be the best available instrument. If so, use it. But know all the time that it carries with it evil possibilities."

"Do you refer, in speaking of 'evil possibilities,' merely to the lessened learning or to the bad attendant learning?"

"To both. We can never lose sight of either. If we decide to use coercion in any particular case, we must decide only after a full survey of all the probable results."

"You do admit, however, that coercion does sometimes build an interest."

"I must admit it. The facts as well as my own theory demand it as a possibility."

"Would you mind recapitulating your position on this point?"

"I am glad to do so. Building interests is perhaps as important a work as education can undertake. Whether it is feasible to build an interest along any given line depends first of all on the native capacities of the person."

"May I interrupt you? Do you refer here exclusively to some specific talent, such as a talent for music?"

"No, although some pronounced capacity or talent may be the dominating factor. I mean, however, to include other instances where the activity involved includes many different satisfactions as, for example, what we popularly call 'manipulation,' 'inventiveness,' 'social approval,' and the like.''

"Haven't you now so broadened your conception as to take in all conceivable activities?"

"Yes and no. There is practically no activity to be shut out entirely. The Hindu fakir who daily tortures his body has actually built up in himself this repulsive practice as an interest."

"It may be an aside, but would you mind saying a further word about building interests? I mean without special reference to coercion. If I correctly understand you, there are first some necessary prerequisites and then an appropriate procedure."

"I myself reckon two necessary prerequisites for an abiding interest: first, enough capacity for the activities involved to bring continued satisfaction from success; and second, a growing activity. The first may refer more specifically to one dominant talent, as for mathematics or music, or it may contemplate only a combination of more ordinary powers. But there must be the possibility of continued satisfaction from the successful exercise of the activity. The second prerequisite, that of the quality of growing, it seems, is not equally necessary for all people; but on the whole the interest will not be abidingly gripping unless it continually faces at least some element of novelty."

Prerequisites for building an interest

"These I understand to be the prerequisites. Now what about the procedure?"

The procedure for building an interest

"The essential of the procedure is our old Law of Effect, 'Practice with satisfaction.' We must somehow get vigorous action along the desired line and of a kind that brings a high degree of satisfaction. Suppose we say it in tabular fashion:

1. Get the activity going with zest — if possible in the face of obstacles that challenge all but the last reserves of power.
2. See that success attends.
3. If possible, let there be approval from those whose approval is valued.

If the two prerequisites have been met and this procedure can be followed, I believe you will with practical certainty see an interest growing."

"You seem to think that overcoming hindrances is a help to interest. Isn't that contrary to general opinion?"

"Perhaps so, but I am sure of my ground. Granted an initial mind-set in that direction, there are, as Woodworth has pointed out,[1] few things so interesting as overcoming a difficulty that calls for all but the Overcoming hindrances last ounce of available energy. Of course if difficulties of this sort keep on confronting us, we have to be sustained by a belief that the end is worthy of the effort. Approval of others helps just here; it steadies our faith in the end."

"What do you mean by an interest when you speak of building an interest? Your last remark seems to me to imply the presence of interest, but not of *an* interest, as I understand the term. Interest is there, The meaning of an interest but it seems to be fleeting, found only in overcoming and the like. I thought you were to build up a permanent interest in some end that would supply interest to the necessary means."

"Your distinction is well made and properly made. We do contemplate building an interest that will carry its own drive. Unless it results that the end in view, or the working with and toward the end, carries its own drive, arouses an inner urge, is desired for its own sake — unless these things happen, no interest has been built. Now what I mean is

[1] *Dynamic Psychology*, p. 102.

this: If one does put heart and soul with very great endeavor into working for some end, especially for some difficult end; if one sees himself succeeding, if one hears meanwhile the plaudits of those whose praise counts with him — then not only is there interest in overcoming and in being approved, but you may be reasonably sure that an interest will in time be built which will of its own pull carry the person on without plaudits, perhaps even against jeers, without even present signs of success, but with many and varied efforts in a real struggle to achieve the end that is called for by the interest. Such an interest becomes as it were an intrinsic source of effort, capable of lending interest to auxiliary causes."

"From this discussion on building interests I see now more clearly than before how coercion fails. But couldn't we go

Virtues as moral interests

further? Wouldn't these two discussions have important bearings in the field of moral education?"

"Just what do you have in mind?"

"Are we not, in the realm of morals, mainly concerned with building what might be called moral interests? For example, with building up in the child interests in honesty and fair play and consideration of others? If I understand rightly, honesty is indeed the best policy, but the man who acts honestly merely from policy is not really honest. Do we not wish to make him love honesty for its own sake, and isn't this substantially the same thing as the interest you have just described?"

"Yes. We wish these moral virtues and other social interests enthroned in the hearts of each one so that they are, so far as one's feelings at the time go, their own justification for being. Of course we wish more than this by way of understanding the why of them and more in the way of loving our fellow men and so on; but you are exactly right as to their psychological character. They are interests to be built in the hearts of the young."

"And would the same procedure hold for these as for the others?"

"Yes, so far as these are interests, they are to be built in the same way. But some of them are broad generalized ideas and would accordingly demand first the procedure necessary for making such generalizations. That, of course, is another story."

"Would the same limitations on coercion hold in building these interests as hold, say, in building a fondness for piano playing?"

"Yes, and perhaps in effect even more strongly. In piano playing we have the possibility that great natural capacity for music may bring success in spite of the lessened efforts due to the coercion. In this way we have the possibility that the opposed mind-set will disappear under these favorable conditions and an interest accordingly come to be built. There are even good grounds for supposing that strong native capacity and initial interest are usually found together. The coercion might in such cases serve to cut off rival activities. The native ability would do the rest."

"Might not the same thing hold in the realm of morals? Are there not born moral geniuses, just as there are born musical geniuses? I fail to see why the same discussion would not hold unchanged."

"It would probably hold unchanged if we were content to have as many people incompetent in morals as in music. We are for the most part willing — indeed more than willing — to leave the making of music to the gifted few. But everybody needs morals, especially — as the humorist said — does the other fellow. So we must try to build moral interests often in mediocre native ability."

"You mean then that we may use coercion in morals where we don't in music?"

"No. Coercion is just as hurtful in one as in the other. We saw that coercion, if skillfully managed, might in music cut off thwarting interests and give the natural interests a chance to develop. In the same way, skillfully applied, it may help in morals, but we must remember that morals must be built even where there is no pronounced moral capacity to help us."

"I wish you would illustrate this. I don't quite follow all you have said."

"Suppose at home some evening the younger children persist in making so much noise that the older children cannot study and their parents cannot read. What A moral situation should we do and why?"

"That's easy. I'd tell them to stop. If they didn't I'd send them to bed. Coercion or not, I certainly would not allow any of my children to ruin everybody else's happiness, and I'd do it for their own good as well. Spoiling children does what the word says; it 'spoils' them."

"Well, that is what most people would do and for the same reasons. But let's examine the matter a little. There are several ways of sizing up this situation. We may consider the rights of the parents and the older children to reasonable quiet and the attitudes of the younger children toward these rights. So stated, we have an educational situation strongly suggested. The younger children either don't understand or don't appreciate or won't respect the rights of the others. Each of these failures is a matter within the realm of education. A diagnosis should accordingly be made to locate the exact defects, and the proper educational procedure should be followed to correct them. Am I right?"

"You may be right, but you haven't told us what to do. Would you punish the children or not?"

"Certainly not until I had made an educational diagnosis and not then unless I could see in reason that the proposed punishment promised to supply the needed educational stimulation called for in their particular cases."

"Don't you believe wrongdoing must be punished?"

"As you ask it, no. The sole reason the parent can properly have for punishing a child is the foreseen educative effect that is to follow."

"What about spoiling a child? Isn't it a real danger?"

"Yes, but it is brought about by bad education. I understand a spoiled child to be one who thinks his wish furnishes sufficient grounds for getting what he wishes, and who is moreover disposed to make things uncomfortable for others till he gets it. Educational diagnosis and treatment Now both of these attitudes can come in only one way: he has tried them with such uniform success that they have been fixed in him. They can be removed only by reversing the process. He must learn by the action of satisfaction and annoyance that his wish is not sufficient, that others have rights which he must take into account, and that making himself a nuisance is not a socially satisfactory way to secure ends. It may take time and patience on the part of his elders for him to learn these things, but there is no other course available."

"And what is the psychology of the procedure?"

"There are two possible ways of procedure: one is to attach annoyance to the children's wrong behavior, the other is to see that satisfaction attends the right. Of course both at times may be combined."

"You refer in the first to the use of punishment?"

"Yes, and it is best available when the annoyance will be attached uniquely to the wrongdoing. Otherwise there is danger that wrong aversions may be built up, perhaps to the mother for interfering, or to the home as a place where unpleasant things happen, or to the older sister for com-

plaining, or to duty as a disagreeable word that figures
Punishment and its limitations whenever pleasures are curtailed. It is this uncertain effect of punishment, and indeed of all coercion, that makes it so unreliable an agency for moral betterment. If the attendant annoyance happens to be misplaced, mis-education takes place."

"The second possible procedure then is more satisfactory?"

"It promises better in every way, though it is less easy for the unthinking to apply than the 'Shut-up-or-be-sent-to-bed' procedure."

"Do you recognize any proper place for coercion other than those already mentioned?"

"We didn't say explicitly, I believe, that coercion may at times be properly used to prevent the exercise of certain undesirable practices and consequently prevent the formation of undesirable habits. But even here a positive régime of building good interests instead is, if feasible, far more desirable."

"Are there then no other uses for coercion — none whatever?"

"Oh, yes. Coercion may properly be used as an emergency measure to prevent damage to one's self or to others or to valuable property. In themselves these are not educational measures, though we can never forget that they have educative effects, usually mixed, some bad and some good."

"You seem then to count coercion always as an evil, but sometimes as the least of the evils confronting one."

The conclusion "I think it has always attendant evils. Frequently, perhaps usually, these evils outweigh its good. Sometimes the reverse is true. The constant use of coercion, however, is a sign of bad teaching somewhere."

REFERENCES FOR FURTHER READING

Woodworth — *Dynamic Psychology*, pp. 200 ff.
See also references at the end of Chapter V (page 73).

CHAPTER VIII

THE WIDER PROBLEM OF METHOD

"Would not the psychology we have recently been studying affect the simultaneous learnings we discussed the first time we came together? I mean psy- chological set and readiness. We have dis- cussed how these influence ordinary 'main-line' learning, so to speak; but I should think readi- ness and the like would make a great difference in the simultaneous 'side-line' learnings."

The psychology of simultaneous learnings

"I am glad you have brought this up. The wider problem of method has greatly impressed me from the time we first discussed it. I have been thinking about it ever since."

"I too have often thought of how we inevitably face the wider problem of method every time we face a class. In a particular instance I might wish to think mainly of arithmetic, for example, but more than arithmetic is going on — inevitably going on — and I am responsible for all. Inevitable, responsible — these are sobering words to me. I wish I knew better how to meet the responsibility."

The importance of the wider problem of method

"And the importance of the attitudes that are being built! Just think that to these children the attitudes they are building toward life in its various aspects probably mean more for their future than anything else they learn; and we are in good part responsible for these attitudes."

"What do you mean by saying that the children's atti- tudes mean so much for their future?"

"I mean that what anyone does, or perhaps better, tries to do, depends on the attitudes one has built. Perhaps I

How attitudes affect life

am just telling what *I* mean by attitude, but to me my attitude toward anything is what I customarily think about that thing and how I am customarily inclined to behave towards that thing. My attitude toward my friend includes what I customarily think when I think about my friend and what I am customarily inclined to do when the time comes to act in relation to him or her. The patriot's attitude toward his country is different from the traitor's, partly in what he thinks, partly in what he does; but each has his habitual way of thinking about and acting towards his country and his country's good."

"From what you say, attitudes come pretty near to being the stuff of which character is built."

"That's just it, and I mean then that we are helping these children to build characters each day and all the time. And

Character is being built all the time

the building is inevitable. The children must and do build attitudes of one sort or the other, favorable attitudes toward, or unfavorable attitudes against. It can't be avoided. It goes on all the time. They are all the time building attitudes in regard to subject, school, teacher, themselves, ways of going about things. That they build attitudes is inevitable; but what kind do they build? That is where our responsibility comes in."

"And is this what you mean by the wider problem of method? I wasn't here when you talked about that."

The wider problem of method defined

"Yes, in good part at least. The wider problem of method is how to manage myself, manage the schoolroom, the children, everything concerned, so that the children shall grow most and best from it all."

"And the emphasis here is on *all* the learnings combined as a whole?"

"Yes, whether we like it or not, or know it or not, all the learnings will come together. We are responsible for the aggregate, for the combination."

"That's why you call it the 'wider problem,' is it not?"

"Yes, the 'narrow problem' concerns itself with any one or more of the details taken separately; the 'wider problem' considers the aggregate, the whole."

"One thing that struck me before in our discussion is that in such things as attitudes we are dealing with things that we cannot assign as tasks. I mean we cannot say that the children *must* get this or that kind or degree of attitude or else we'll punish them. Imagine a scale of appreciation **Attitudes and appreciations cannot be assigned** of good literature and our saying to the poorer pupils, 'Some of you children are behind in your appreciation of the "Psalm of Life." Those who do not measure up to Unit 14 on the Jones Scale must stay in every afternoon till they have caught up.' That plan wouldn't work."

"I am not sure how well it ever worked even with assigned spelling or arithmetic, but it certainly sounds absurd when you apply it to appreciation of literature. No, it wouldn't work. There are some things that cannot be assigned under penalty for failure to learn. It looks on the face of it as if this were true of all attitudes."

"And if life's decisions spring largely from one's attitudes, attitude building is then about the most important part of education. Isn't it?"

"I see no way out of it."

"Doesn't it seem odd, then — wrong, I mean — to try to run our schools on a plan that cannot take care of what is probably the most important part of education?"

"Do you mean that we are trying to run our schools on the assignment-testing-penalty basis?"

"Yes, I think that till recently this has been the prevailing notion in our country and throughout the world; and probably it is still the position assumed in most curriculum discussions."

Our schools too largely ignore attitudes

"It is wrong, it must be wrong, to ignore the building of attitudes, and we must change our management of children. Our schools must be changed. I think already I see many signs of the change coming. Probably, however, most people haven't seen it yet. I know I had never realized what it meant till we began to talk about it."

"Don't you think if we had some good names to use—*terms*, I suppose our more pedantic friends would call them—it would be easier to get people to see the true situation?"

"Yes, and I have some to propose. I heard them at summer school last summer. The terms as I got them were 'primary,' 'associate,' and 'concomitant.'

Primary, associate, and concomitant learnings

"The word 'primary' was used to refer to all the learning that belongs closely to the enterprise immediately under consideration: If I am making a dress, then the primary learning includes all the learning that comes from the actual making, such as increased skill in planning and cutting.

"The term 'associate' is usually found in the phrase 'associate suggestions,' and refers to all those allied thoughts or ideas that come from working on the dress, but which, if followed up then, would lead me away from my dressmaking. I may thus be thinking whether the dress will wash, and so think about the dye used, and ask myself how such dyes are prepared. This in its place is a valuable and proper question, but I do not need to answer it in order to make this dress, and if I do try to answer it, I must for the time lay aside my dressmaking.

"The 'concomitant' learnings grow (in part at least) out of the dressmaking, but do not belong so closely or exclusively to the dress as do the primary. I may thus say, 'I see it pays to be careful.' I learned this, perhaps in connection with making the dress, but it may and should remain with me as an ideal that will reach beyond dressmaking. In general we may say that the concomitant learnings have to do with the more generalized ideals and attitudes, while the primary learning has rather to do with specific knowledges and skills. The concomitant is, typically, of slower growth, requiring perhaps many successive experiences to fix it permanently in one's character. Prominent among concomitants are personal attitudes, attitudes toward one's teachers or comrades, attitudes toward the several subjects of study (as geography or history), attitudes toward one's self, such as self-reliance or pride or humility. Other important concomitants are standards of workmanship and the like, neatness, accuracy, or the reverse."

"I see what you mean, but why must you introduce more 'terms,' as you call them? If you people who study and read books would only learn to use everyday words, you'd be much more popular and do much more good. And why do you choose such outlandish words for your terms? Who ever uses such a word as 'concomitant'? Why don't you choose a short word? But I didn't mean to offend you."

"You didn't really offend me. I suppose it was another case of 'pride going before a fall.' I was proud of myself that I had made my meaning clear, for I confess I had trouble last summer in getting the idea. And you are in good company in wishing for simpler terms, for I remember the professor said that he felt he ought to apologize for such long words and he

The use of terms

asked us to suggest shorter ones, only we couldn't. But
you, in my judgment, are wrong in objecting to 'terms.'
They help us to think. Why, ever since I got these
distinctions I can see the things themselves more clearly.
In fact I never really saw the things in my pupils until
I got these distinguishing terms. A name, let me tell
you, is the way to hold and spread an idea. When you
talk about a thing and give it its proper name, you
yourself have something to hold to, while other people
begin to ask what is meant and to look for the thing
back of the name. Without terms there would be little
exact thinking."

"I suppose you are right. It sounds reasonable. At
any rate, I can't argue against you. But I wish you would
explain how you actually use these terms 'primary,' 'associate,' and 'concomitant.' "

"Principally they make me critical of my work. I mean
they help direct my self-criticism. I used to be content if
The use of   my pupils didn't miss in daily recitation work
the designa-   and could pass on the term examinations. I
tive terms   thought that was all. Now I know better.
That was being satisfied with the primary only. I never
thought about the associate suggestions, and but little of
what I now call concomitants. It is not that I do not
value the primary now; I do value it, perhaps just as
much as before, only differently, more intelligently, I
believe. But I think a great deal more about the other
two.

"Besides, I used to be impatient if my children asked
questions suggested by the lesson but not on the lesson.
Using   You see my eyes were glued on the course of
associate   study, and I thought of these questions only
suggestions   as evidence of mind wandering. I still am
troubled to keep the class sufficiently intent on the matter

at hand, but I feel differently about the outside questions and I act differently. Now I feel that my pupils and I are really succeeding when these associated suggestions arise. Properly used, they mean growth. We don't yield to the present inclination to follow them up, but we do notice them enough to see whither they invite us. Sometimes we write them down for future use. And I see that a different attitude is already growing up in the class. The children are more thoughtful. Associated suggestions noted in the past come up again in their right places, and James or Mary is proud to have foreseen the point. They feel differently toward me too. We seem to be working more sympathetically, and we really enjoy thinking things out together and connecting them all properly. I find that I respect my pupils more; and, really, the advance connections they see are remarkable. My pupils think more connectedly now, instead of less connectedly as I feared. Their organization is much better. You see I was beforetimes repressing rather than encouraging their natural inclinations to think.

"And as for the concomitants, I am now much concerned about them, particularly as to what attitudes are being built and how I can help forward the better ones. I see now that I always valued those Using concomitants things, the ideals and attitudes of my pupils; but I didn't concern myself consciously and specifically about them. I somehow trusted to luck about them. The pupils who were going to have good ideals were going to have them, and that was all there was about it. I scolded sometimes and I criticized a good deal, but I now think that in so doing I did more harm than good. Now I know that each ideal and each attitude has a life-history of its own; each is built up just as truly as is any fact of knowledge or any skill."

"It seems to me that you are now contradicting yourself. Earlier you were speaking of these attitudes as being built incidentally. Now you talk as if you seek them directly. Which is right?"

Are attitudes sought directly?

"So far as the child is concerned they are principally built incidentally, that is, in connection with other purposes of his. I as teacher, however, must be conscious of what he is doing and steer his various activities so that the proper ideals and attitudes shall actually grow up. I consider them consciously; he achieves them — for the most part — indirectly. But at times we do talk matters over, because clear consciousness is often an important factor in building ideals."

"I understand you now on that point, but I wish to ask further. Do you then judge each thing the children do under these three heads of primary, associate, and concomitant?"

Is each act to be judged in these terms?

"Typically, yes. Each study period, each recitation period, and each recess is in its own measure going to result in primary learning of some kind, well or ill done; in few or many, rich or poor, associated suggestions; in good or bad concomitants. As teacher, I am in some measure responsible, and in so far I must know what is going on and adequately appraise the results. In the light of the results — so far as I do or could influence them — am I to be judged."

"Isn't it different now? If I understand you aright, we examine and promote almost if not entirely on the primary learning, and disregard the other two."

The primary is now too much stressed

"Yes, I think we do. You see we can test the primary learning so much more easily than we can the others. The new scientific tests and measures of achievement even reinforce the tendency to pay exclusive attention to the primary, because they are so far for the most part confined to the more mechanical skills and knowledges. I sometimes fear their first effect will be to fasten the merely mechanical side of school work even more firmly on our schools."

"Well, you certainly surprise me now. You have always been eager for each new advance of science, as I have heard you say, and here you are decrying what you must admit is at least one of the most scientific steps yet taken in the study of education. I didn't expect it of you."

"The new tests are indeed a contribution of the very first value, but what I say is still true. So far as they measure achievement they are up to now largely confined to the more mechanical aspects of learning. A superintendent gives a series of tests in spelling, arithmetic, or reading. Sooner or later the teachers learn the records of their classes, and unless the superintendent is wise they will find themselves rated according to these records. If the superintendent could as satisfactorily measure the teacher's success in building ideals and attitudes, so that all the educational outcomes could be weighed, the situation would be different. But as matters now stand the superintendent is in danger of taking the teacher's attention away from the 'imponderables,' the ideals and attitudes and moral habits that cannot yet be measured in wholesale quantities, and of fastening that attention upon a part only of the educational output and that the most mechanical."

"Don't you think this a fanciful picture? Is there really any danger?"

"Indeed it is not a fanciful picture. The danger is very real. Such considerations as this make me look earnestly for the day when we shall be able to measure the whole gamut of achievement. I believe that day will come and a great day it will be. Till then, however, I should advise

superintendents and supervisors to consider carefully how
they use the tests. Let them use the tests, but with a
clear sense of their limitations and dangers. In the meanwhile there is the greater reason for urging attention to the
wider problem of method. We must make everyone see the
value of the concomitant learning and of the associate suggestions. Every recitation period, every school exercise,
must be appraised under all three heads of primary, associate, and concomitant."

"If you made your expression even stronger, I should
not object. When I consider that while we are stressing
arithmetic, for example, our children are forming at the same time the very warp and woof
of their moral characters, I shudder to think of
the consequences if our teachers see only the arithmetic
and ignore the life-attitudes being built. Fortunately,
there is no necessary opposition between the two, rather the
contrary; but nothing can excuse us for failing to consider
those other outcomes that inevitably accompany every
school activity."

The greater need to study method

"You seem to connect the wider problem of method in
some peculiar sense with the problem of life. Am I right?"

"Yes. The wider problem of method seems to me now
to be almost the same as the moral problem of life itself.
As I see it, our schools have in the past chosen
from the whole of life certain intellectualistic
tools (skills and knowledges), have arranged
these under the heads of reading, arithmetic,
geography, and so on, and have taught these
separately as if they would, when once acquired, recombine
into the worthy life. This now seems to me to be very far
from sufficient. Not only do these things not make up
the whole of life; but we have so fixed attention upon the
separate teaching of these as at times to starve the weightier

The wider problem of method is the problem of life

matters of life and character. The only way to learn to live well is to practice living well. Our highly artificial study of arithmetic and geography and physics has too often meant that the child lived but meagerly in and through the school studies. The practice of living that has in fact counted most for him has often been what he and his like-starved fellows could contrive for themselves apart from their elders. Educative indeed has this been, but not always wisely so. There is no cause for wonder that American citizenship disappoints. Democracy demands a high type of character. Our schools have not risen to the demand upon them."

"Do you mean that the wider problem of method especially concerns building for citizenship?"

"That is exactly what I mean. It has always been so. Without clearly distinguishing what they did, or rather how the results have been attained, each long-abiding type or ideal of civilization has con- Each type of civilization has used its peculiar method trived its answer to this wider problem of method in such fashion as to mold the type of character correlatively needed to perpetuate itself. The Spartan and the Athenian of antiquity differed from each other quite as much by reason of different methods of education as because of the different contents of the curriculum. The proverbial 'hardening' of the former was sign and result of the treatment accorded their youth. The slave of every age has by well-contrived processes been made lowly in spirit in order that he might the more contentedly bear his hard lot and lowly station. Civilizations have differed much as to whether the individual man should think for himself. Those opposed to such thinking have always contrived such methods of treating their young as early habituated them to acquiescence in the officially approved opinions. Prussia, old China, Mahomet, the Jesuits, the older military discipline, all represent various efforts along this line. These have differed among themselves almost *in toto* as to the primary learning they have sought to inculcate; but they have been agreed markedly in the methods of inculcating the concomitants, the desired attitudes."

"Does this have any lesson for this country?"

"Indeed, yes. We in this country must study anew this problem of method in order the more adequately to devise the proper treatment of our young so as to fit them for democratic citizenship. The beginning of this wisdom, I believe, is to recognize the fact that the child learns many things at once. On this rock of simultaneous learnings shall we by proper effort rear the needed structure of an all-round character."

To America its appropriate method

"Don't you think we ought to study more about these simultaneous learnings? Wouldn't our psychology help us?"

The psychology of simultaneous learnings

"Yes, our psychology will help and we ought to bring it to bear on the problem. I should like nothing better than to follow it out."

"First I should like to ask how your S → R formula fits what you call simultaneous learnings. S → R seems rather simple, single as it were, while these simultaneous learnings seem complexity itself."

"That's a good question. To help answer it let's borrow from James two terms that he in turn had borrowed from Lloyd Morgan, *focus* and *margin*. As they used them, the thing we are mainly thinking about at any one time is at that time in the *focus* of consciousness. We are here discussing and thinking about these terms; they are accordingly in the *focus;* but while they are there the janitor opens the door and comes in to shut the windows. He was closing the windows

Focus and margin of attention

before any one of us thought much about him. The kind of thinking by which we were aware of his coming in (yet continued to give principal and direct attention to our discussion) these writers called *marginal*. At any one time we are giving focal attention to one thing, while on the side, as it were, we may be giving marginal attention to one or more other things. For certain purposes it is interesting to note that one's attention is frequently shifted; what is now marginal may in a moment become focal, and what is now focal may then be marginal. When the window stuck and the janitor had to make serious efforts in order to lower it, we all began to watch. He and his window efforts ceased then to be marginal to us and became focal."

"Doesn't this mean that there are many things on the margin, but only one in the focus?"

"Yes, there are many marginal stimulations and, if you watch closely, also many marginal responses. While we are here thinking of focus and margin, which is our focal response, we are also responding by sitting rather than lolling or falling out of our chairs. We are turning heads and directing eyes now to this speaker and now to that. Some are taking notes. As one leaves the room, the others turn mechanically to let him pass. There are, during any extended period of attention to any one main focus, a host of marginal stimulations and a host of marginal responses."

Many marginal stimulations and responses

"Do not the 'concomitants' come in here?"

"Yes, precisely. They are — speaking generally — marginal responses. We are pleased or displeased with this or that line of thought. This weighing or valuing, the accompanying likes and dislikes, as now this and now that meets approval or disapproval — all of these are typically marginal responses."

"Isn't it true that almost no one can give focal attention to one thing indefinitely? I think I have heard so."

"Yes, there is normally a shift, possibly due to fatigue. The well-ordered mind comes back to its undertaking, but some people just hop from one thing to another **The shift of** in succession. Of course they are not so **focal attention** efficient."

"Then the efficient person will during a considerable period of time have a principal focus of attention. From time to time his attention is drawn off, but he comes back. This principal focus guides and directs his steps."

"It seems to me that you are now merely describing with a new set of terms a mind-set and how it works. The efficient person is one who is capable of holding **Mind-set and** one end in view, more or less continuously, till **principal focus** it is attained or until he finds out he cannot reasonably attain it. Your principal focus seems to be about the same thing as the end upon which the mind is set."

"Yes, I think you are right. But some one else has a question."

"I was going to ask if the marginal stimulations we are all the time receiving do not attack and jeopardize, as it were, the focal mind-set?"

"Yes, and any one of these marginal stimulations, if the mind-set be not strong, may dislodge the present focal object and itself become focal."

"Isn't that exactly what happens when street noises distract the attention of a class? They are certainly side **How distrac-** stimulations, and if they find the children not **tions may** interested in the lesson, they certainly dislodge **become focal** it. Long division or prepositions or the Missouri Compromise easily give way to a brass band. I am on a street where every procession comes by, and nearly every procession becomes focal for my pupils. Have I got the idea?"

"Exactly, and your illustrations are apt."

"But isn't it hard sometimes to tell the difference between suggestions that distract and tear down and suggestions that bring up new and constructive ideas? Are both marginal?"

"You are quite right in distinguishing the two kinds of suggestions, and the line of demarcation may well be hard to draw. Both may be suggested by the focus. One would lead attention away and so bring another object into focus. The other makes the old focal object grow. The rival thought suggested by the focus is what we called above an 'associate suggestion.' The suggestion that makes the focal object grow belongs to the primary learning."

"The word 'efficient' was earlier used in connection with those people whose attention remains true to one object, who fasten their fortune to one focus. Are there limits to this? Suppose a coal pops out of the fire and I am too absorbed in writing to notice that the rug is burning, am I really efficient?" *Too great and too little fixedness alike bad*

"You mean that a person ought to be reasonably alert to marginal stimulations. Indeed, yes. We call the other kind 'absent-minded,' and often laugh at their queer ways. Common sense seems to suggest a kind of middle ground between being scatter-brained and being absent-minded."

"Do not certain moral considerations enter here?"

"What do you have in mind?"

"Well, imagine a person anxious to make a trip. I have seen people who, once having got this idea into their heads, could see nothing else. The work left behind undone, the resulting inconvenience to others, costs — none of these things got any consideration. Once the trip had gained the focus, it held on *Morality and marginal suggestions* against everything else. The person seemed to have become blind and deaf to every other consideration. I should call this selfishness."

"If I understand you then, a person facing a situation ought to be open to a great variety of questions besides the bare one of how to effect the end in view? Otherwise he may act wrongly."

"Yes, before the end is accepted all its significant bearings ought to receive attention: Is the proposed enterprise wise and right? Is the cost reasonable? And even after it is accepted there should still be marginal sensitivity to new considerations. New evidence may demand a revision of judgment."

"Well, isn't this just another way of saying again that there must be a just balance between the shut-mindedness of overmuch persistence and the open-mindedness which is too ready to take up new leads."

"This all sounds good and true, but haven't we forgotten the simultaneous learnings we started out to discuss?"

"Not a bit. We needed the notions of *focus* and *margin* to help us with simultaneous learnings. Take this last question about the preliminary consideration of right and wrong and the like, might a person so act as to increase his persistence or his sensitivity in such matters?"

"Assuredly he might. Take persistence, for example. If he does persist this time more than usual and it turns out well, what has psychology to say?"

How persistence may be increased   "I see, you mean 'Practice with satisfaction.' If he practices with satisfaction a new persistency, this new and stronger persistency will grow to be habitual with him. Is that right?"

"Yes, only we must not say that he will necessarily be equally persistent along all lines. His new persistence is likely to be limited pretty largely to this one line."

"Might his persistency grow too strong along one line?"

"Indeed, yes; and it will probably so grow if there is no annoyance to rise up and check it. Your *Persistence* selfish man may be an instance." *may be too great*

"Does this mean that he has learned to disregard the marginal responses that should warn him?"

"It probably means that. If the warnings come and he disregards them and is satisfied with the results, he will in time almost certainly learn not even to hear or see such warnings. If, however, he obeys the warnings and is satisfied with doing so, then he will likely increase in sensitivity to such warnings."

"It seems then that all depends on how it works, whether he is satisfied or not with the results."

"Exactly so. This is nothing but our Law of Effect at work. Two things are necessary if one is to improve: The right and good must stand out from the wrong *How sensi-* and bad, so as to be seen and known, and one *tivity may be* must be pleased with the right and troubled by *increased* the bad. If these conditions are met and one acts accordingly, growth in sensitivity to the right will come as a plain matter of fact."

"Sensitivity to all right things?"

"Indeed, no. Sensitivity along this one line and in some measure to other allied lines."

"Is this the way that the proper balance is built up? I mean the balance between overmuch shut-mindedness on the one hand and a helter-skelter scatter-brainedness on the other hand?"

"Yes, in just this way; and here is where the teacher comes in, to help build the proper sensitivities."

"Isn't this our problem of method seen from another point of view?"

"What do you mean?"

"I mean this, that what a person sees in any situation depends partly on what there is in the situation to be seen, **Method and** but possibly just as much on the person himself, **the building** the sensitivities that he has built up so as to see **of sensitivities** the elements in the situation. We have seen how sensitivity is built. Now isn't method, the new notion of method, just an effort to take care of building the proper sensitivities?"

"That sounds interesting, but I wish you would say more about it. I don't quite see."

"Why just this. We have already discussed how a person is stimulated marginally while he is paying main attention focally; he is inevitably so stimulated in many ways. We also have seen that there are many other elements in the situation that might and would stimulate us, at least marginally, if only we were sensitive to them. Isn't method just an effort to give larger opportunity and encouragement to building up sensitivities and attitudes in our young people, especially along these marginal lines?"

"Why say 'especially' along these lines? Are the marginal responses more important than others?"

"I say 'especially,' partly because they are very important, partly because they are now so largely overlooked."

"It seems to me that we are now in the heart of the question of method, that is, the newer conception, the wider problem of method."

"Do you mean that it is our method of dealing with children that largely determines their marginal responses?"

Method and "That's exactly what I mean. And it is the **marginal** marginal responses that build centers of interest **responses** and stimulation."

"I thought I agreed with you till you said 'centers of interest and stimulation.' Then I got lost. What do you mean?"

"To answer, let's separate 'centers of interest' from 'centers of sensitivity,' though we'll see in a minute they are but two ways of describing the same thing. What is a Possibly the word 'center' is a stumbling block. center of Let's look at it first. You agree that we may interest? build an interest?"

"Yes, I know as a child when I first heard of collecting stamps I thought it too silly for words. Later on I built so strong an interest in it myself that to this day it makes me notice and desire any unusual stamp. It is almost a nuisance, as I don't really wish them for myself and I have no one else to give them to."

"This interest that you built was composed of S → R bonds?"

"I suppose so; it must have been if our psychology is right."

"One S → R bond or a lot of them, an aggregate?"

"Why I suppose a kind of organized aggregate centering about keeping unusual stamps."

"Now that is exactly what I mean by a 'center of interest,' an aggregate of S → R bonds so organized as to center about some one thing as an interest."

"Where does the sensitivity come in?"

"That's clear enough with my bothersome stamps. I can't help seeing the things. I am very sensitive to the sight of any unusual stamp."

"Yes, and if we think a minute, sensitivity goes with the interest. It always does. Whatever you are interested in, you are keener to see."

"Isn't this just what we said about mind-set and readiness?"

"Exactly so. An interest is but the abiding possibility of a mind-set, and a mind-set always means readiness along that line."

"Then to go back; if I understand you, you mean that we build interests and their accompanying sensitivities largely through paying attention to our marginal responses and that the problem of method is mainly then the problem of how to stimulate the right kind of marginal responses. Am I right?"

The problem of method

"Yes, but not only to stimulate the right kind of responses. We must also give opportunity to respond accordingly and under such conditions as will select the good from the bad and give satisfaction to the good and annoyance to the bad."

"You never lose a chance to emphasize 'such conditions as select the good from the bad' or 'give satisfaction to the good and annoyance to the bad.' You surely lay stress on them."

"Indeed I do, and I do it because they form the foundation of all learning."

"I am surprised that you as teacher wish to hand out satisfaction and annoyance. Are you not afraid that you will antagonize the pupils?"

"I do not wish myself to apportion satisfaction and annoyance. I am afraid of just what you say. I wish as far as possible that these be inherent in what the children do. Otherwise I should fear lest I defeat my own method by stimulating the wrong marginal responses. I refer to emotional responses against me and against the things I approve."

"Do you mean that method is especially concerned with the marginal responses and not the focal?"

"Method is concerned with both, but I here stress marginal for the reasons stated before. They are very important and we have too often neglected their method effect."

"Does method working through marginal responses seek to build anything else besides interests and sensitivities?"

"These are general terms; I have in mind every variety of interest, attitudes, ideals, standards, appreciations. All of these mean structures of $S \rightarrow R$ bonds capable of bringing about significant mind-sets and their appropriate readiness."

"I am sorry that we must stop thus in the middle of things, but there is too much ahead for us to go on now to the end."

"Won't you say one word in conclusion?"

"If I am restricted to a brief statement, it shall be this: We must depend upon method working upon marginal responses to build centers of interest."

REFERENCES FOR FURTHER READING

See references at the end of Chapter I (page 18).

CHAPTER IX

The Wider Problem of Method — *Concluded*

"Can we go on from where we left off last time? I am very anxious to learn more about method and marginal responses."

"By all means. What question do you raise first?"

"Is there not a very wide range of stimulation? Some seem very obvious and impelling, others very delicate. I suppose every degree lies in between."

The range of marginal stimulations

"You are quite right. The most obvious and impelling will bring a focal response willy-nilly; the others shade off to those that we just barely notice."

"Could you illustrate? It isn't quite clear to me."

"In ordinary life you can hardly avoid hearing and noticing a thunderclap. It is too loud not to be heard. Or better still, if someone sticks a pin sharply into your arm, the stimulation will immediately become focal. You can't help it. Similarly in an ordinary schoolroom there are some stimulations more impelling than others. The word of command of the teacher is the principal means relied upon to secure voluntary focal attention. This works because the children have built already certain attitudes of obedience. The doings of fellow students, street noises, heat or cold — these if emphatic enough will produce focal attention, displacing the teacher's tasks from the focus.

"So much for the stimulations to focal attention. The most immediately impelling stimulations to marginal responses are perhaps the tone and manner of the teacher, and the observed responses of the other pupils. These come

at the outset of any new undertaking. Later on, the success
or failure of what is undertaken brings very impelling marginal responses."

"Do you mean that the tone and the manner of the
teacher stir to approval or disapproval?"

"Yes, and to like and dislike. As I see it each child is
building all the time centers of interest (whether of like
or dislike) regarding the teacher, the school,
the subject, the way of doing things, the pupil's
own self-esteem in its various degrees of self-
confidence or conceit or abasement, a liking
or disliking for the pupils he works with, etc., etc. Each
of these is a center both of sensitivity to receive impressions
and of expression to give out responses. What results from
the responses is of course determined by the laws of learning."

"But these are not the only environmental factors that
stir to marginal responses, are they?"

"Indeed, no. One consideration, very important but less
obvious perhaps than the foregoing, is whether the general
scheme of school life, both of curriculum and of management,
does or does not satisfy the 'natural' aspirations of childhood and youth. Such aspirations of course are very
varied. If the 'higher' aspirations are stimulated and
granted satisfactory expression, the 'lower' are likely to be
inhibited. This one question of expressing childhood and
youth is big enough for much study and many books. The
felt adequacy or inadequacy of the available self-expression
creates in the class and school a popular mind-
set which by its attendant readinesses and unreadinesses determines in turn, for the adoles-
cent at any rate, almost everything else about a school."

"I hadn't thought of it in just these terms, but I can see
what you mean. Will it not, however, be true that this

Centers of interest always being built

School spirit

adequacy or inadequacy as the pupils see it will vary
greatly with the times? If they don't expect too much,
won't they more easily be satisfied?"

"Yes, and that creates one of our very difficult problems,
but we can not, I fear, go into it now."

"What are some of the least obvious or least compelling
environmental influences? Would you, among these, name
the pictures on the wall?"

Least compelling stimulations "Yes, both their esthetic value and the
stories they tell may stimulate marginal re-
sponses. Many children, of course, escape both. The
cleanliness of the schoolroom and yards is perhaps a bit
more obvious. The school architecture, too, must have
some effect."

"Now you are getting mystical. I'd like to know what
effect on my depraved youngsters architecture can have. I
An opposed opinion must say right here that I think you are going
entirely too far with this method business and
these marginal responses. School isn't run to
please children. There are certain things they have to
learn. We are here to see that they learn them; and I, for
one, propose to see to it that my pupils do learn them.
Furthermore, I believe in assigning lessons, tasks if you
please, and I test too. I can't afford to be squeamish about
what you call marginal responses. I assign lessons and I
expect them to be learned. We know what is good for our
children. They don't. It isn't my business whether children like me or not, or like school or not, or like books or
not. Some day they'll thank me, if they don't now. I
am going to do my duty, come what may."

"Do you mean that it makes no difference whether we
build in our children an interest in school, let us say?"

"I say that it's not my business. I teach the sixth
grade. The course of study tells me what I must teach

and what my children must learn. I propose to see that
they learn it. Beyond that is not my concern."

"You don't care then whether or not your children stop
school as soon as the law allows. It's nothing to you
whether or not they go on to the high school?"

"That's not my business. I am here to teach the required course of study. It's for others to say whether it is
good or bad. I do my duty and leave the results where they
belong."

"Well, I am sorry you look on teaching in that way. I
am sorry you don't see that your duty includes the welfare
of the child. Surely there can be nothing more important
than the attitudes and ideals the child builds. It is equally
certain that he must build them by his own responses. If
I as teacher can help, I must help. No duty could be
more sacred. How best to help is not always easy to tell,
but surely study of these things will help. If you think
the school architecture is not a factor with all children you
are probably correct. But certainly there are some for
whom it has some effect."

"Isn't this best seen in a great cathedral? My church
doesn't have cathedrals, but there are certain great and
beautiful cathedrals which I cannot enter without feeling their effect. It stirs me to awe and
worship. The height and the beauty enter, as
Plato said, 'into the innermost recesses of my
soul.' If at the same time I can hear the organ, the effect
is greatly increased. I do not myself care for ritual, but I
can well understand the combined effect, particularly on
those who have been taught to revere it from youth, of the
great building, its marvelous beauty, the grandeur of the
music, the color of robe and vestment, the incense. If
these things had no effect to stir man they would never
have been cared for, or would have died out long ago.

Method
effect of
edifice and
ritual

You may disapprove if you wish, but how you can deny
their effect is more than I can see.''

"Do you mean that beauty and grandeur of building and
ceremony can build character?   I don't see for my part how
moral character can be built apart from moral
Effect on
character conduct.   What becomes of all our discussion
about 'Practice with satisfaction,' and 'We do
not build where we do not practice'?   I think you are
inconsistent?''

"I have never claimed to know either how or whether the
morally desirable character can be built either in part or in
whole from worship.   A character for action I am satisfied
can be built only from action.   All I claimed was that edifice
and ceremony do arouse marginal responses.   What character
changes result from such responses depend upon what is done
about them and in connection with them, and, of course,
upon what satisfactions and annoyances accompany?''

"To turn aside slightly, don't you think that the consciousness of heroes in one's family or nation may stir
marginal responses in one?''

"Now there you go again.   What kind of responses?
Of contentment that one has inherited so great glory or of
stimulation to add to the glory?   Generally of
Historic
glory contentment, I say.   Surely it makes a great
difference which.''

"I agree that it does make a great difference which is
stirred, and there are, I think, both possibilities.   But if
there are both possibilities, then there follow both opportunity and duty for parent and teachers to direct the stirring wisely.   In any event, we have another method effect
and another reason for studying the problem of method.''

"This whole thing begins to open up to me as never
before.   It seems then that anything that one has experienced, or even heard about, may have, as you call it, method

effect. In my own case, while yet young, I heard from my older brothers of a certain very difficult problem in arithmetic which they had solved. As I in turn approached that problem, this knowledge spurred me to equal them. I was determined not to fall behind them."

"Yes, and an illustrious past may stir the young patriot to maintain the record. The world has known this from all time."

"This may be a fall from the sublime to the ridiculous, but many Europeans think the great size, the abundant resources, and the prodigious **The size of a country** material success of this country have registered themselves in the characters of American tourists."

"Made them braggarts, you mean?"

"I am not saying. I doubt that it has had any one effect on all, but that the consciousness of all this does have an effect I don't doubt. I have even heard the opinion expressed that in many Texans the size of the state has influenced the character, giving it perhaps a certain big openness of attitude."

"May not the opposite influence also be observed? I have seen a child handicapped by some family disgrace either shrink mortified into **The influence of disgrace** the background or, worse, try to brazen it out. Under such circumstances can the child avoid being hurt by the sin of his elders?"

"You have certainly broadened my conception of the problem of method, but I don't quite see something that was said earlier about a democratic method. As I recall, Prussia had its method, and we should **Democratic method** have ours. May we discuss that further?"

"Yes, do. I remember Dr. Thomas Alexander's statement[1] that he visited over three hundred *Volksschule*

[1] *Prussian Elementary Schools*, p. 277.

classes before he heard a single child ask a single question. Would that illustrate the point?"

"Yes. The Prussians wished positively to form the habit of accepting authority and commands from others; negatively, they did not wish these children to get the habit of questioning. If they should form a questioning habit, they might question the monarchical and military system under which they were being suppressed. But these things are not confined to Prussia. I heard a young student at an American university say that while he was acting as a foreman of a labor gang at a coal mine the preceding summer he was told by one of the managers, 'Don't explain to the men what they are about; they will get the attitude of asking why.' "[1]

"What, then, would you advocate in our schools different from what is now found?"

"Nothing startling. We are already far more democratic in our school procedure than are most European schools. But we can improve on what we have. I'll ask you two questions to indicate my thought. First, what are the characteristics of the good citizen in a democracy? Second, what kind of growing and practice will lead from and through healthy, happy childhood *continuously* up to such a democratic citizenship? What do you say now to the first of these?"

**Character-
istics needed**

"Taking the hint from Prussia and the coal mine, I should say we wish citizens able and disposed to think for themselves, not the kind to be led submissively about by bosses, whether political, industrial, or religious. That's one thing."

"You mean they are to think about social matters? That means they must also be intelligent and informed about such matters, doesn't it?"

[1] Reported to me as a true incident. — W. H. K.

"Yes, and I should add they must also be able and disposed to accept responsibility, and to put the common good ahead of everything else, and to subordinate to it all mere private or personal advantage — in particular, to believe in the rule of law and order."

"Suppose we sum all this up by saying we want citizens who are open-minded, yet critical-minded, who are informed and intelligent, who accept the rule of law and responsibility for the common good. What then do we wish in our schools?"

"If we believe that 'Practice with satisfaction' is the rule for learning, we'll want our young people to practice these things with satisfaction to themselves as much and as far as is feasible, and to have them begin such practicing as soon as possible."

"Are you not afraid of overdoing this independence? Children easily get out of hand and become pert and spoiled and selfish."

"There are dangers and we must be careful. That's why I said 'as much and as far as feasible.' There are limits, but that's no reason why we should refuse to go as far as we feasibly can. It is for experiment to tell us how far we can go; and it will certainly be much further than used to be thought possible."

"This sounds very good, but it seems to me you have got off the track. I thought we were discussing marginal responses and method in relation to them. This is nothing but curriculum content."

"Content perhaps. It is in a sense just that, since we are describing what we want. But ask how it is to come, if at all, and you'll see, I think, where our method comes in with its emphasis on marginal responses. Did you notice how large a part the word 'disposition' played in our statement? This is just what the older method disregarded."

"Do you mean that heretofore we have largely sought textbook knowledge and trusted to that?"

"That's part of what I mean. Let's look at it squarely. The old way, the way in which most of us were brought up and the way still largely used, has been, first, to put into a course of study what the children should be taught; second, to assign this to them for learning; third, to test them to see if it had been learned. Now this meant, it was obliged to mean, that pupils were held accountable for learning only and exactly what could be assigned and tested, and teachers were accordingly held accountable for teaching only and exactly what could be assigned and tested."

Attitudes too much ignored

"And you mean that open-mindedness, critical-mindedness, and regard for the common good, all of which are dispositions as you called them, could neither be assigned nor tested?"

"Yes, I mean exactly that and, furthermore, that practical school people, superintendents, supervisors, and teachers have ordinarily given their official attention to information and skills that could be assigned and tested with, at best, some further attention to intelligence, for the intelligent use of some things can be assigned and tested; but that all interests, ideals, attitudes, appreciations have been slighted if not ignored."

"Is it a sign of the same thing that pupils are promoted usually on their achievements in these assignable-testable things?"

"I think it is."

"But I still don't see the marginal responses. I hope you don't think me either stupid or stubborn, but I thought we were discussing method in relation to marginal responses. Instead you talk about assignment and testing."

"I don't think we have got far off the track. We stated

the desirable characteristics of a democratic citizen. Upon examination they are seen to consist as truly of interests, attitudes, and habits as of information and skills and the intelligent use of information and skills. The old way was to assign and test. This — so far as it was followed exactly — left out all appreciations and dispositions, all interests, attitudes, ideals."

"Your point then is that the marginal responses can not be assigned and that it is these that must build dispositions, interests, ideals, and appreciations, if such are to be built at all?"

Marginal responses can not be assigned

"Yes, that is what I mean; and I further mean an about-face of method so as to care for these marginal responses and what they can build."

"And that means?"

"It means that we stress activities, enterprises, experiences which enlist the heart and soul of childhood and youth. In connection with these we *can* get needed information and skills; from them and from them only *must* be got such marginal responses as will build the attitudes we wish."

The need for activities

"Then the good method as you see it is such a managing of school, of both equipment and children, as will enlist childhood and youth in wholehearted, purposeful activities?"

"Yes, for out of them we can best get not only whatever primary learning we need, but also the most numerous and the most useful associate responses, and at the same time the most wholesome concomitants."

"You don't mean that all ages can purpose with equal clearness or wisdom?"

"Assuredly not. But each for his own age can put heart and soul into his sort of activities. Each by exercising whatever degree of development he has will best carry himself forward to the next stage."

"You don't mean to turn children loose?"

"By no means. My way needs teachers, and good teachers, just as much as does the old, if possible even more so. Only they act at a different point. In my notion they should help children to help themselves. People learn open-mindedness by having a chance to practice open-mindedness and under such social conditions as call for it. So with critical-mindedness. So with accepting responsibility for the common good."

"Do you mean that we should expect young children to accept responsibility for the common good of this whole country? That seems like a 'big order' for young children?"

Building interests in the common good

"Not in the sense you seem to have in mind. Any notion of the common good must be built gradually. Have you seen two boys riding one sled, one pushing off while the other steers? Have they a common good?"

"Yes, though they don't name it that way."

"Quite right, then I should wish many opportunities in child life to have 'common good' experiences; and I should hope that these experiences would involve joint responsibility for the common good and some inherent and intrinsic difficulties in meeting them. When any child failed to accept and render his share of the responsibility, I should hope all concerned would trace the shortcoming to the right place, namely, to him and his failure. I should further hope that he would see clearly and regret keenly his shortcoming, and I shouldn't object if the others helped him regret it by showing disapproval of such conduct. Only I should know that too great a disapproval might provoke angry resentment and so distract attention from the original fault and so fail to teach the proper lesson."

"Would this be 'Practice with satisfaction' or 'Let annoyance attend the wrong' as the case might be?"

"Yes."

"But this is a long way off from the common good of the country or of humanity."

"Yes it is, but we must be patient. We must begin in small ways and grow only gradually. First, small joint enterprises, then larger. First, affairs close at hand, then some at a distance. The Junior Red Cross enterprises belong here. After a while conscious generalization will help. It too must begin small and grow gradually, and generalization must always be joined with actual behavior responses lest we build sentimentality. It is indeed a slow business and requires great patience."

"Just where does method come in here? I am a bit confused."

"Method comes in helping along such common good enterprises as this double sled-riding, and in helping, if need be, to insure that shortcomings are duly seen and regretted. This means the sensitivities that How method we discussed a little while ago." helps

"But this is out of doors. Can we have such things in the schoolroom?"

"Indeed, yes. It is a part of good method to help along gripping and fruitful indoors enterprises, both individual and group."

"Where now do the marginal responses enter?"

"All the time some sort of marginal responses are going on. We wish the healthy and wholesome kind. These are, other things being equal, most likely to attend those wholesome activities into which the young people put their whole souls."

"This takes us back to purposeful learning as opposed to coercion, which we have already discussed. But as I now see, our discussion was largely restricted to the primary learnings. Could you now say a word about the associates and concomitants?"

"The plan as here proposed is that we seek to have our children engage in enterprises that, psychologically, meet two conditions: first, that stir wholesome interests already present so as to rouse strong mind-sets; second, that once begun reach out beyond the limits of what the children now see and know and can do. If strong mind-sets are stirred we shall have endeavor — the strong inner urge — and readiness for whatever helps to the end in view. If the enterprises, for their successful execution, reach beyond the present powers and knowledge of the children, then we have conditions that call for growth. New things must be learned."

Conditions favorable to growth

"Is this just the same matter that we considered in discussing mind-set and learning?"

"Yes, only here we have added that the enterprises should reach beyond present attainments."

"But I still don't see the marginal responses or the associates and concomitants. Why don't you tell it right out? Why beat about the bush?"

Attendant learnings

"There are too many things involved to tell them all at once. We have to go slowly. But now for marginal responses. Do you recall our discussion on mind-set and readiness?"

"Yes, we saw how the girl who was eagerly making a dress was ready to think dresses, to see dresses, to talk dresses, in short to do anything that had to do with that on which she was set."

"Ready all over?"

"Yes, that's it."

"Is there any connection here with marginal responses?"

"I hadn't thought of it before, but I see now. Readiness means easier stimulation and more likelihood of responses. Any hint would more easily stir ready bonds. Yes, I see."

"And do you see any connection with associate suggestions?"

"Yes, I see; readiness means that the marginal responses are more likely to occur and so are more numerous. Some of these lead directly into better making of the dress, and so help swell the primary responses; but others would, if followed, take attention away from the dress; these you called 'associate suggestions. Yes, I see how readiness through the avenue of the marginal stimulation would bring more numerous associate suggestions. That's clear, but how about the concomitants?" *Associate suggestions*

"Just what do you mean by concomitants? I am a bit confused."

"They were the responses that accompanied whatever was primarily going on; overtones, you might call them, of feeling; judgments that are going on along with whatever one is doing: 'This is fine,' 'He is a ninny,' 'I am getting it, hurrah!' 'I hate to do this,' 'School is a bore,' 'The teacher isn't fair.'" *Concomitants*

"I don't see the marginal in these."

"You don't! Don't you see that while the girl is making her dress, or the boy his bird-house, or the class is planning an excursion, they are primarily (focally) intent on dress or bird-house or excursion, and all the while other things are intruding (marginally)? Especially are the children responding emotionally (that is with like or dislike or valuing) to each thing that comes up, so that each child is building (and fastening) dispositions or attitudes out of these likes and dislikes, fastening them in himself toward teacher, school, subject being studied, going to college, our country, being honest, etc., etc. In strictness each thing we do helps to build three things: a motor response of skill in so doing (or of not doing), a memory connection, and a disposition toward (or away from) doing it. The disposition to do (or not to do) is but one aspect of the whole act, but it is an aspect that may grow. When it has grown sufficiently, it takes its part along with others like it in determining what one will do in general. These accompanying aspects are what we call concomitants and they are exactly accompanying or marginal responses to focal objects. Concomitants are thus built up around each object that gets implicated through marginal responses with what one does."

"What have 'set' and readiness to do with this?"

"Almost everything. The set and readiness enter into the determination of the marginal responses. A set against How set and is likely to mean a response of dislike. A readiness favorable set is likely to mean a response of enter like. Of course success and failure enter in as we have previously discussed."

"What is your conclusion of set and concomitants?"

"That when children work successfully at purposeful activities which challenge their powers, they almost certainly build favorable attitudes (concomitants) toward everything that entered helpfully into the success."

"Is this the way to build an interest in literature, for example?"

"Yes, speaking generally, this is the way to build an interest in anything."

"What is your conclusion about method?"

"Simply this, that the wider problem of method has to to do with all the responses children make as they work, Conclusion and its concern is to help children build the total of these responses into the best possible whole. The narrow problem concerns itself with how the children shall best learn this or that specific thing, generally named in advance. The wider problem concerns itself with all the responses being made. Since the older education limited itself to the narrow problem, the newer education stresses the wider problem without, however, overlooking the other. In particular the wider problem is much concerned to build attitudes and appreciations. In so doing, it builds the heart of the child; and out of the heart are the issues of life."

REFERENCES FOR FURTHER READING

See references at the end of Chapter I (page 18).

CHAPTER X

INTEREST

"Why have we said so little about interest? I thought it was admittedly one of the main factors in modern educa-

Interest and
modern
education

tion."

"Haven't we been discussing interest all the time? It seems so to me."

"We've hardly mentioned the word, I think. How can you say we've been discussing it all the time?"

"What is interest?"

"I'll tell you what interest is and you'll see that I for one don't believe in it. Interest is the best known device for

An adverse
view of
interest

spoiling children. To go around hunting for easy, interesting things for children to do, to be forever trying to amuse them, to be forever asking what they'd like to do, and whether it pleases them to do this rather than that — this is what interest means and, I repeat it, it is the best way yet devised for spoiling children. I haven't agreed with all that has been said here from time to time, but I have been thankful that so far no one has advocated this wishy-washy, namby-pamby 'doctrine of interest.' I think it is the worst educational doctrine I know."

"If interest is all that and just that, it *is* pretty bad; and I shouldn't blame you for objecting to it. But is that the doctrine of interest?"

"I thought it was admitted that a child, anybody in fact, learns better when he is interested; and I have read that fatigue, mental fatigue I mean, or at least what commonly

136

passes for mental fatigue, is largely boredom, lack of interest.   Are not these things scientifically proved?   If so,
how can the doctrine of interest be so bad as we have just
been told?''

"Do you deny that children can be spoiled?   Have you
never seen a spoiled child?   And can you think of a better
way to spoil a child than always to be trying to amuse him
and encouraging him to do only what interests him?   I am
in earnest about this thing.   I believe that the whole question
of vigorous moral character is at stake, and therefore I am
dead against the whole doctrine of interest.   It's vicious.''

"We don't seem to be talking about the same thing
exactly.   Can't we get together as to what we mean?''

"Isn't the fact that the term is misunderstood one reason
why we don't hear so much about interest as formerly.   I
heard a lecturer say he seldom used the word 'interest'
unless he had ample time to explain what he meant, because
so many people misunderstand.''

"Suppose for the sake of getting together we agree — at
least tentatively — that there are two uses of the word, a
good use or meaning of interest and a bad use
and meaning of interest.   Perhaps later we can   **Two notions**
get the two meanings closer together.   Can't   **of interest**
we bring in our psychology?   For surely if interest has any
meaning we can state it psychologically.   Let's take clear
cases at first.   What are some good instances of interest and
what do they mean psychologically?''

"Washington was deeply interested in establishing the
new government.   How will that do?''

"That's a good instance.   Now let's have another.''

"Mary is deeply interested in making a doll's dress.''

"Again, good.   Now another.''

"A man of many interests is more likely to be com-
panionable than one of few interests.''

"This last brings up a distinction. Do you notice it has the noun 'interests,' 'many interests,' while the others are both verbal in form, 'was interested,' 'is interested.' More precisely the first two are instances of interest now active, now in operation. In the last case the man *has* 'many interests,' but we do not necessarily think of any of them as being just now active. Just as tennis is one of my interests, but I am not playing it at present nor is my interest in tennis now aroused or active. Does this bring to mind any psychology?"

"Isn't it the formula $S \rightarrow R$? We have many such bonds and carry them about with us, but they are active only as stimulated."

"So far so good, but I was thinking of mind-set, which is of course based on $S \rightarrow R$. To have tennis as an abiding **Psychologi-** interest means to have built up already in the **cally, interest** past within one an aggregate of tennis-regarding **is mind-set** and tennis-acting $S \rightarrow R$ bonds such that when this aggregate is properly stimulated we have and feel right then and there a mind-set on tennis, and when this mind-set is so aroused, the person is at that time actively interested in tennis."

"If I understand you then, interest is psychologically the same as mind-set. The abiding but now unaroused interest means the possession of an appropriate aggregate of $S \rightarrow R$ bonds. When this aggregate is stirred so that the mind is now set on doing something about this thing, the interest is active."

"Exactly so. Interest to me is simply another way of naming and describing the psychology of mind-set and readiness."

"To you, then, the doctrine of interest in education is nothing but the doctrine of mind-set and learning. Am I right?"

"Yes, practically that."

"Where does readiness come in?"

"When one is interested, actively interested at the present time, as the little girl is in making a doll's dress, is there any readiness?"

"Surely, she is ready 'all over,' as we said once before when we were discussing mind-set and readiness. But this only confirms the idea that interest and mind-set are the same thing."

"Is this why interest is a favorable condition for learning?"

"Exactly so. We could if we wished repeat under the head of interest our whole discussion of mind-set and learning and this in all its applications to primary, associate, and concomitant learnings." *How interest is favorable to learning*

"Does this mean that there is no such thing as spoiling, that we have nothing to fear under that head?"

"Not a bit of it. I think we can accept pretty much everything that has been said here to-day against indulgence and spoiling."

"Now I am getting confused. At one time the doctrine of interest is the same as the doctrine of mind-set and readiness and is all good. But now we seem to hear that the doctrine of interest is a doctrine of indulgence and spoiling and is, therefore, bad. Which is it? Good or bad?"

"Not quite so fast. Are all mind-sets good or may some of them be bad?"

"Some may be bad."

"And interests, are they good or may they be bad?"

"Of course, they may be bad, but that is not quite the question. It is the 'doctrine of interest' we are asking about. What is the *doctrine* of interest? I understand a doctrine of interest to be some position or opinion as to how interest should be used. Now what is *the* doctrine of interest?"

"It seems to me that we find advocated two doctrines of interest. They overlap perhaps, but one is carelessly conceived and the other carefully conceived. One is clearly indefensible. The other stands on quite a different basis."

"How do you state the two?"

"The indefensible position is the one we heard about at the outset to-day. It says that since interest is the condition favorable for learning, one must, therefore, strive to interest children; amuse them; cajole them; do anything so long as they are interested. This doctrine is bad. It easily leads to, and could hardly fail to lead to spoiling, to forming all sorts of bad habits."

A wrong kind of interest

"But are you not forced logically to this position, I mean to this doctrine of interest, if you start out by saying that a state of interest is desirable? If it is desirable, why not get it, and get it any way you can?"

"In order to answer, let's get the other doctrine of interest before us. Interest is the name this second position gives to that state of affairs in which one is intent on something, in which his mind is so set on some activity that he is striving to go ahead with the activity. It may be a child who is intent on making a doll's dress; it may be a poet intent on expressing adequately his deepest insight into life. Each is interested. This kind of interest inspires whole-hearted endeavor. Each one finds his whole being unitedly and absorbedly at work upon the object of interest. The essence of this interest is that the self is active and unified as it works. This doctrine of interest says that interest, so understood, is the guarantee of attention and effort; and that such attentive and interested effort best utilizes the laws of learnings, particularly of set, readiness, and effect.

Interest as whole-hearted endeavor

So stated, the doctrine of interest is nothing but the doctrine of mind-set and learning as we have previously discussed it."

"You don't mean to deny that there are degrees of interest?"

"Most assuredly not. There are infinitely many degrees, reaching from those things that we do only under the direst compulsion up to those into which we put our whole souls."

"Then I don't understand your doctrine of interest. Which kind of interest are you talking about?"

"My doctrine of interest, as a psychological doctrine, is that learning conditions are met in the degree that whole-hearted interest (short of painful solicitude) is present."

"Why say 'short of painful solicitude'?"

"Because we are discussing learning conditions, and I know that anxiety or fear may be so great as to interfere with learning. So I wish whole-heartedness of interest short of such fear or anxiety."

"You say that this doctrine of interest is a psychological matter. You seem to mean that there is something else. Is there some other doctrine of interest?"

"There is more yet — an ethical or social aspect to the question. Suppose a bad interest, I mean a socially bad one. If the child were whole-hearted about it, he might, psychologically, learn just as well as *When interests are good* if it were a good interest. We need then some criterion to tell a good interest from a bad one. That is what I had in mind."

"Can you give us such a criterion?"

"So far as I can see, we best judge by the kind of growth that comes from the interest."

"Is this where indulgence comes in? Or rather how we rule out indulgence?"

"Yes, when a child, or grown person for that matter, engages in an interest that merely excites, merely amuses, and so leaves no growth effect, we say he is indulging himself, and we call such interest or activity a worthless one or perhaps positively bad."

"If I understand you, you are now criticizing the other doctrine of interest."

"Yes, that doctrine of interest was content with what it called a 'state of interest' (whatever that meant). It forgot that interest is essentially active. It was willing for children to be always and merely amused. That such treatment of children would be bad no one need question. Instead of leading to growth, it would rather hinder growth."

"Doesn't this connect with what was said the last time we met [page 130] about wishing activities that appeal to the child as he is, but at the same time challenge his power and call for knowledge and skill beyond his present achievements? I may have added a word or two to what was then said, but that was the idea as I got it. This criterion for evaluating interests seems to me to be the same as that."

"Yes, it is the same. Both statements look to growth, to progress in the life of individual and of society. We object to 'mere excitement,' to 'mere pleasure,' to indulgence, because they not only don't lead on, but, even worse, they are likely to set up habits of indifference or of excitement that hinder healthy growth. I think we see such in many card players and theater habitués. They are blasé, bored, cynical. Life has lost its enthusiasms for them."

How indulgence injures

"I understand your criticism of the false doctrine of interest, but is it fair to say that anybody ever held it as a doctrine?"

"Possibly not, at least not in the form in which its opponents state it; but I think probably some have miscon-
ceived the better doctrine and have said or done things
that have brought any notion of interest into contempt."

"You used the word 'effort' a while ago. I have been
hoping we could talk about that. I have been confused
by some discussions I have heard."

"What do you mean?"

"Why, I have heard some say that as between interest
and effort, they would choose effort every time. But
others say that interest and effort go together.
From the discussion so far the latter seems the   Interest and
better statement, but I should like to have the   effort
matter cleared up."

"Do you think the poet we mentioned earlier put forth
any effort?"

"Certainly he did. It is no easy matter to express one's
idea adequately. I have understood that many writers
search weeks at a time for a word with just the right shade of
meaning. Effort, yes; more effort than most people know."

"Now, *I* think you are wrong. For the poet his search,
even though it is long, is such a matter of love — if he is
a true poet — that he doesn't count it effort. To him it is
interest, absorbed interest, that and nothing more. To
call it effort is to degrade both the poet and his interest."

"Isn't it clear that you two have used effort in two
quite different senses? One counts effort to be the steps
taken in the active working out of interest, or
perhaps better, the steps taken in the face of   Two senses
difficulty and in spite of the difficulty. This   of effort
naturally makes effort the correlative of interest, the
stronger the interest the greater — if need be — will be the
effort. The other counts effort to be work done unwillingly,
'against the grain,' as we say. This notion will naturally

oppose interest and effort to each other — the more effort, the less interest."

"Which is the right meaning?"

"Possibly there is room for both, if we are careful to let people know which we are using on any occasion."

"Does this mean that one kind of effort is as good as the other?"

"Not at all. Which is the kind that we most wish?"

"Why, the first kind. The effort that comes from interest. The more of that there is in the world, the more there is accomplished."

"Yes, and not only that; but the more joy there is in life. Successful endeavor after strenuous effort brings keen satisfaction. Happiness comes by that road."

"Do you mean that happiness consists of doing things yourself? I don't think so; I like to be waited on, to have things done for me. I have had to work so hard all my life that I have come to look on happiness as being able to take my ease, ring a bell and have a servant come to learn my wish, buy anything I fancy, have a box at the opera and go as often as I like, buy pictures and old furniture, have an interior decorator to plan my house. This is my ideal of happiness. And other people seem to agree. If this isn't happiness why does almost everybody wish this sort of life?"

Effort and happiness

"Many people do think this way about happiness, or at any rate act as if they so thought. But I am willing to abide by what I said. As between passivity and activity, having things done for one and doing things oneself, there can be no question as to where happiness lies. Happiness is essentially a matter of activity, of such activity as means growth. In the long run anything else fails."

"This all sounds very well. I can't object to what you have said so far. But you haven't said enough, and you are

going off to one side. The practical question still remains.
If you could get whole-hearted interest for all the necessary
efforts of life the problem of education might be simple.
But you can't do it. Some things are not interesting. Life
isn't based on the interest theory. It is full of disagreeable
things, things that simply are not interesting and can't be
made so. Now what are you going to do? If you ignore
this effort side of life, you simply fail to prepare children to
live in this world. I challenge you to answer. What are
you going to do?"

"It is an important question and we must face it. But
let us face it fairly. Why do people do disagreeable things?
If we can answer that of grown people, possibly Interest and
we can tell how to educate children. Do you do the dis-
disagreeable things? And can you name one?" agreeable

"I most certainly have to do disagreeable things. My
friend and I have a kitchenette apartment and do light
housekeeping. Most of it I like, except washing the dishes.
That's just plain drudgery. But it has to be done and I
do it. I surely don't run my life on any interest basis, and
I don't believe in it for children. I do disagreeable things
because I must, and I believe in making children do disagreeable things while they are young, so that they'll learn
to do them when they are grown."

"You say washing dishes is disagreeable. Why do you
do it?"

"Why do I do it? Why! Why, surely you don't mean
that I should leave my dishes unwashed! The question is
absurd. I couldn't respect myself nor ask anybody to
respect me if I let the dishes go unwashed. Besides I couldn't
eat from unwashed dishes. No, I want them clean; that's
why I wash them."

"Haven't you given us just the clue we were seeking?
You wish clean dishes, and wish this so much that you are

willing to go to the trouble of washing them. Isn't this after all the doctrine of interest? Isn't it your interest in clean dishes that makes you do the disagreeable washing up? If you had no such interest to impel you, you wouldn't do this disagreeable thing. And the illustration is typical. Whenever you find any one, except, apparently, an ascetic, doing a disagreeable thing, it is because there is beyond the disagreeable thing some interest that pulls him. He cares so much for this interest that he is willing in its behalf even to undergo the disagreeable matter intervening. You do then live on the basis of interest in spite of your brave words."

"What does this tell us about educating children?"

"Much. It tells us that we should seek for our children challenging interests — not the easy, merely amusing ones, — but interests that grip and stir, yes, and those that involve difficulties also, so that our children may among other things have practice in striving in the face of difficulties. The difficulties must, of course, be adjusted to their strength. It is overcoming that on the whole educates. If our children are to grow in persistence, success is as a rule necessary."

"Do you seriously mean that our children will get sufficient discipline, I mean the right kind of discipline, from working at matters that interest them? Have you sufficiently considered the proportion of uninteresting work in the world?"

Interest and discipline

"If you will understand that the matters of interest shall involve dificulties, then I answer 'Yes.' That is what I mean, and I mean it very seriously. You wouldn't accuse Professor Thorndike of 'soft pedagogy,' would you? Here is something of his that I read the other day:

'The discipline from enduring the disagreeable seems to be far outweighed by the discipline from working with an interested will along lines that fit one's abilities.' "[1]

[1] *Teachers College Record*, 25:143 (March, 1924).

"You make out a pretty good case, I must admit. But there is one question yet: How can we make things interesting? I mean school subjects, really necessary things like the multiplication tables and spelling. They are not in themselves interesting. What shall we do?"

"The question is as good as the answer is difficult. There are many factors involved. First of all, if our psychology of mind-set and readiness be accepted, we cannot really *make* things interesting. Anything is interesting according to the degree that it belongs with an aroused mind-set, either as end or aim of the mind-set or as means felt to be necessary to attaining that end. But for such interest to take place, the aggregate of $S \rightarrow R$ bonds must already be there to be aroused. All we can do is to stimulate what is there."

"Well, you can say that if you wish. But you know as well as I that there is a great difference, say, in lecturers. One man will make a subject interesting (I am obliged to use these very words); and another, try as he will, cannot interest his hearers. The audience may be the same and the topic may be the same. The difference is in what the lecturers do. One makes the subject interesting and the other doesn't. How then can you say that we cannot *make* a thing interesting? It can be done. I have seen it done and so have you. It is done or not done every day. I am not just talking words; I am talking facts, and you know it."

"Yes, you are talking facts, but I stick also to what I said. The only way to 'make' a thing interesting is to give it a chance to arouse some interest already present in the mind or, better, in the nervous system. Go back to our psychology. There must be present in the nervous system the proper aggregate of $S \rightarrow R$ bonds before the stimulus can take effect, i.e., before there can be stimulation to

action. The resulting action is the responding of the R.
The interest, as a matter of S → R structure, must be present
in the nervous system before it can be aroused to activity.
Take your two lecturers. They address the same auditors.
One interests, as you say. The other doesn't. The difference is that the successful lecturer so presents the subject as
to stir what was all the time there to be stirred. The
unsuccessful lecturer does not know how to disclose the attractions of the subject or to organize these so as to arouse
those responses of thought and emotion and action-tenden-
cies which, when aroused and active, we call interest. It is
after all a *disclosing* of attractions, a presenting of stimuli.
And this is essentially what we mean when we speak of
making a thing interesting."

"Does this have any bearing on curriculum construction?"

"It has a very great bearing. The main business of curriculum making is two-fold — first, to know what interests,
native or acquired, lie available in the child
nature; second, to know how these may be
stimulated, guided and directed so as to bring
growing. One main part of curriculum making is to
know and stir interests that otherwise might lie dormant.
We must think of all stirring to action as an appeal to what
is present as S → R in the mind and character of the person.
Most people get into trouble by choosing first what children
should learn, then hunting about for the best way to teach
it. If this subject-matter so chosen in advance does not
correspond to the child's present active powers, naturally
there is trouble. In the older days people said of such cases
that human nature is naturally depraved and that we need
not expect desirable subject-matter to correspond to child
nature. They accordingly reduced their subject-matter to
what could be assigned for learning (mostly memorizing)
under penalty. In that day, school was worse than a dull

Interest and
curriculum

place. Switches were much in evidence. When we examine
the subject-matter of that day, we don't wonder that children had to be whipped. Later there came kinder methods,
rivalry and prizes, and also some modifications of subject-
matter. Much later a doctrine of interest was preached,
but it was still likely to be a doctrine of *making* things
interesting. That is, the old subject-matter was assumed,
and interest was used as a teaching device. That people
learn better when interested was seen to be true. 'Therefore,' it was said, 'interest the children in what they are to
learn.' In this way 'sugar-coating' was offered as a substitute for punishment, and people divided into two camps,
one favoring the 'soft pedagogy' of sugar-coating ('interest', they called it) and the other the hard pedagogy of
coercion ('effort,' they called it)."

"Isn't this what Professor Dewey refers to in his 'law-
suit' between 'interest' and 'effort'?"[1]

"Yes, and then he goes on to say that both are wrong,
and in place of both offers the doctrine that interest and
effort are alike the natural accompaniments of healthy
activity meeting normal difficulties. We use the term
'interest' when we think of the emotional warming up to the
end in view. We use the term 'effort' when a challenging
difficulty has been met, and the self still persists in going
forward in spite of the naturally discouraging effect of the
hindrance. Interest and effort are thus but two aspects
of the same on-going activity."

"This all sounds very well, but I still don't see how we
can avoid spoiling children. Why don't you tell us how to
manage?"

"The answer has in good part been given. We get our
best discipline 'from working with an interested will along
lines that fit one's abilities.' Education is concerned to get

[1] The reference is to *Interest and Effort in Education*, Ch. 1.

going in children such activities as (a) evoke work with an
interested will, (b) lie along lines that fit their abilities. To
these I should wish to add a third, or rather make explicit
what was probably implied, (c) that the work, while beginning and remaining within the child's interest, should still
always reach out beyond the past achievement of the child.
If these three conditions are met, interest and effort will
take care of themselves, and growth will ensue."

"But I still don't see how you avoid spoiling. How are
you going to get 'work with an interested will'? I say you
can't start out on that basis without spoiling the child. If
you keep trying to interest the child — to amuse him — if
you continually ask him whether he chooses to do this or
prefers to do that, if you keep forever deferring to his wishes,
you are bound to spoil him. Your start is wrong, and the
result is bound to be wrong."

"If what you say were what I propose to do, I should
agree with you. But you fundamentally misrepresent my
position, and at the same time ignore the essential nature of childhood. Children when awake
are inevitably and incessantly active. They
will set up ends. They will strive to attain these ends.
To do merely nothing is impossible with them. To keep
children from activity, to make them do nothing, is a
foregone failure, and is, moreover, irritating to them in the
degree that it succeeds. We start then not with a child
waiting to be amused, but with one incessantly active.
Only a child already spoiled or already starved into inac-
tion waits to be amused. It is opportunity they crave,
opportunity to receive stimulation and opportunity then to
respond. It is our business to supply or perhaps better
allow both, and then give the more promising of the child's
active stirrings a chance to go ahead. You assume or
pretend to assume that the child is essentially inactive,

**Children al-
ways active**

that he will do nothing, or at any rate nothing good, unless we either coax him or coerce him. This we know is not true. Your essential premise is false."

"Granted for the sake of argument that the child is incessantly active, you still don't show how you will avoid spoiling him. If you allow him to do just what he wishes to do, you will spoil him. If you refuse to let him follow his wishes, you won't get the 'interested will' or the favorable mind-set, and so, on your own account of affairs, you lose what you seek. Take either horn of the dilemma and you fail. Either you spoil the child or, according to your ideas, he doesn't learn."

"No, you are again wrong. What I essentially seek is not that the child shall do what he wishes, but that he shall wish what he does. The difference be- *How spoiled* tween these may not seem very great, but if I *selfishness* act wisely, it is sufficient to prevent spoiling. *is acquired* Let us look more closely at this question of spoiling. What is it? We discussed it once before [page 58]. Spoiling is essentially fixing the habit of selfishness. The child learns to consider only his own wishes. Since all voluntary activity springs out of one's wishes, there is abundant opportunity for any one to become spoiled. What can prevent? Our old rules must guide: 'Practice with satisfaction'; 'Let annoyance attend the wrong.' Each occasion of choice where others are involved is an occasion for learning spoiledness or its opposite, and this holds of you and me as well as of children. I have known some grown men, otherwise and previously good, to be spoiled by indulgent wives. It is simply a matter of deciding with or considering the rights and feelings of others or deciding without doing this. If any one practices ignoring others' feelings and remains satisfied in so doing, this 'practice with satisfaction' will spoil him."

"Do you mean to say that considering the child's interest doesn't lead naturally to spoiling?"

"That's exactly what I mean, or rather that it need not do so. The final question is whether we can give children opportunity to decide things and still not spoil them, not make them selfish."

"If you put it that way, isn't the opportunity of making decisions necessary for acquiring unselfishness? How can a child learn unselfishness unless he practices unselfishness? And how can he practice unselfishness unless he practices choosing, holding before his mind the different alternatives? It seems to me that your opponent's argument in the end turns against him. It proves a boomerang. Isn't it so?"

"Partly so, yes; but we must be fair and face the whole situation. The old way was (in theory) to deny the child the chance to practice choosing. He was too young to choose, they said. His parents or teachers would make all the necessary decisions for him. In so far as this worked he formed habits along two lines: first, of obedience, second, of doing the specific things he was told to do. So far as this was all, he practiced neither selfishness nor unselfishness of choosing, since he didn't really choose (except that acquiescence is a limited kind of choosing). However, a negative sort of good was accomplished. He did fail to practice outwardly selfish acts (as obedience to another is not selfishness and as his elders presumably directed courses not selfish for the child), and in so far he was shut off from the chance to build outward habits of selfishness. But the inner attitude could not be constrained and he may have been building inward opposition to much of what was commanded."

How the old way avoided selfishness

"But what about the boomerang? I still believe that the argument recoils. In their commendable zeal against spoiling, the advocates of the old way cut off the chance to build unselfishness. Isn't it true that if children don't practice choosing, they cannot be building intelligent unselfishness? I can't see it any other way."

"Yes, I think you are right. But isn't there still another side to this question? Suppose we take your words used a while ago, and agree on the policy that children shall 'wish what they do,' don't you think we shall make them soft? People, if they can, always choose the easy course. Where then does discipline come in? I recall what you quoted from Thorndike, but I just don't see it. People don't choose the hard, they choose — if they can — the easy. Then what becomes of strength of character?"

"There are two things to be said. First, young people do not choose merely what is easy to them. Have you never heard boys daring each other to do this **People do not** or that dangerous or difficult or even painful **always choose** thing? Why they like nothing so well as to **the easy** undertake something that has hitherto baffled them. Speaking generally, I believe that all strong, vigorous people, especially the young and ambitious, are more attracted to experiences that challenge their best than they are to the easy and certain lines of action. That's one thing. The other is that any interest worthy the name is almost sure to involve difficulties. The determination to attain the goal in view will carry one through great difficulties. And if the hindrance be not too great or too monotonously prolonged, its very difficulty is a challenge. It actually serves to increase zeal. In both these ways people do, because of their very interest, face difficulties."

"Then you conclude that your doctrine of interest does not lead naturally to spoiling?"

"I most certainly do. There is danger of spoiling in it, just as any sharp tool is more dangerous than a dull one, but a sharp tool will accomplish more. So my doctrine of interest has in it possibilities of character building not otherwise to be secured."

"You claim then that your doctrine of whole-hearted, interested endeavor makes rather for than against strong moral character?"

Whole-hearted interest makes for strong moral character "I most assuredly do. The argument is on our side. Strong moral characters practice inhibitions, but these are best acquired in connection with strong positive interests. Mere inhibitions never built a strong character. Strong character is mainly positive."

"If you stress child decisions so much, why have a teacher? Have you left any place for a teacher?"

"I most certainly do have a place for the teacher, a definite and an abiding place. The teacher guides first in the making of choices and second in the pursuit of the aim. Of course if need be the **Place of the teacher** teacher will command or refuse as occasion demands. But stimulation and guidance are the teacher's more constructive functions. I like to think too of the teacher as a builder of morale. Each school **Place of morale** can have its morale, and, well built, it is a most precious heritage. So also is there a class morale and there is an individual pupil morale. Morale implies both habit of outward conduct and inner attitude towards this. I should like many habits and attitudes built that put the common good above mere individual interest, and others that demand persistence as long as it is wise to persist."

"How are these things to be built?"

How morale is built "There are no ways but the old ways: 'Practice with satisfaction,' 'Let annoyance attend the wrong.' The children must practice, outwardly and inwardly, putting the common good above mere selfish interest. If they fail, then regret for such failure should attend. But note you: It is practically impossible to get the right practice and the right satisfaction or annoyance except through interest."

"Yes, and there's the rub. You can't build interest without practice and you can't get practice unless you already have the interest. So you are caught; either you already have what you want or you can't get it. That's where I say your interest doctrine breaks down. You have to call in the parent or teacher to issue a command, else the children never take a higher step."

"Not so fast. Let's see if we are so hopeless as you say. Is it not true that interest in an end will to some degree extend itself to means?"

"I don't quite understand. Illustrate it."

"Imagine a mother with a child dangerously ill. Is she interested in railway time-tables or other plans for a trip?"

"Not at all, if she is the right kind of mother. You couldn't persuade her to leave home." How interest extends itself

"Oh, I am not so sure. Suppose the doctor recommends a change of climate for the child. If so, she will at once be interested in where to go and how to get there. Her interest in her baby will make her interested in the trip necessary to his recovery."

"Is the mother of a well baby interested in any other things for the baby's sake — things she used not to be interested in?"

"Indeed she is. I have seen many a young woman made over. Before the baby came her interests were only dancing or cards or the theater; now you can hardly get her to leave home, and she studies food values and the sterilization of bottles, not to mention infants' clothes, go-carts, or rattles. Yes, anything that affects the baby is interesting to her."

"Then interest in end does extend itself to means?"

"Indeed, yes."

"And does she practice new things?"

"Yes. I knew a young mother who could never bear to sew for herself or anyone else; but when her baby came, it was different. She sewed for him as if she were born for the work."

"And did she become interested in sewing?"

"This particular woman did. She found out she had more of a gift than she had thought. As her husband, being merely a college instructor, had a small salary, she made most of her own clothes thereafter and was proud of her success. In fact she became a kind of authority on the subject in her young circle."

"Let's see now if we can not find a kind of progression in this."

"Nature gave this woman a potential love for babies and sufficient abilities to enable her to learn to choose food values, sterilize milk bottles, make clothes; but up to marriage none of these possibilities were realized. Am I right?"

"Yes."

"And the coming of the baby awoke her mother love, and that, apart from any interest inherent in them, made her study and learn food values and practice scientific care of milk bottles?"

"Yes, and made her make baby clothes."

"It was her interest in baby then that made her practice making baby clothes?"

"Yes, that's true; and success with baby clothes showed her she could sew. Success and a desire to economize made her try to make her own clothes. First she made over some of the clothes she had when she was married, and from that she branched out into more ambitious schemes."

How interest and practice mutually build each other

"It seems then that first of all nature supplies a potential interest. Then some exigency of life stirs this to activity. The pursuit of this aroused activity involves new allied lines of practice. This practice in turn builds (arouses and fixes) new interests, which in their turn lead to more practice and more interests — and so on indefinitely. Am I right?"

"Yes, that's the way of life."

"Then we are not caught by the fact that interest depends on practice and practice depends on a prior interest?"

"No, I see how it worked in this case. But suppose you had no interest to begin with. In that case I don't see what you would do."

"Nor do I. Show me a person who has no interest to begin with and I'll freely admit I shouldn't know where to begin with him. But where ever was there a normal and healthy child who was not full of interests?"

"I now see why you insisted that children are always active. It gives you the starting point."

"Exactly so, and there is no other."

"Do you mean that education is exactly a succession of interest, new practice, new interest, still further practice, still new interest, and so on forever?"

"That's just what I mean — that, with wise teacher guidance."

"And you wish in developing such a succession to stay always within the realm of interest?"

Education a succession of interest, practice, and interest

"That's what I wish, and I believe that in the degree I can stay always within the realm of interest, in that same degree do I secure conditions favorable for learning."

"Doesn't the fact of indirect interest help us here?"

"You mean that it increases the range of interest? Yes, that is a very good idea. You are quite right."

"I don't understand. What do you mean by indirect interest? Is there a direct interest, and if so what is the difference?"

"By direct interest we mean the condition that exists when a person is really interested in a thing without asking or thinking why he is interested. The mother Indirect *vs.* direct interest is interested in her baby's health in this way. She just is, that's all there is to it. In like manner is a little girl interested in playing with her doll. There is no why about it. But when the physician recommended a change of climate, then the mother became interested in mountain resorts and railroad schedules, *because* these things had to do with her baby's welfare. Her direct interest in the baby so extended itself as to give an indirect interest in these other things. Things uninteresting in themselves become interesting (indirect interest) because of their bearings on things that are interesting in themselves (direct interest)."

"Then you mean that around each direct interest there is a wide region of possible indirect interest?"

"Yes, get the direct interest going strongly and it will reach out, often far out."

"And this is the enlarged interest range?"

"Yes."

"May not an interest that begins as an indirect interest end by becoming a direct interest? The young mother who became interested in sewing as discussed above is an example of what I mean."

"Quite so; and, in fact, each new practice begins normally as an indirect interest."

"May we now have a summing up of what we have covered?"

"There is not so much to be said. Interest and effort are normally and properly but different ways of describing A summary action that is going forward under a definite mind-set. We call it *interest* when we think of how the person warms up to the object upon which the mind is set, how he feels about it, how he values it. We call it effort when we think of the tendency of the set mind to push ahead in spite of hindrance. So much for definition.

"We value interest and effort then just as we value mind-set. Each term indicates a condition of the organism favorable for efficient action — success is more likely to result; favorable also for that complicated kind of action which demands learning — learning is more certain to be called for; and favorable finally for the learning process itself — learning of a higher kind and degree is more likely to take place.

"With interest, just as with any keen-edged tool, for those who know not how to use it, there are dangers; but without it only bungling work can be done — no masterpiece of teaching is possible.

"The criterion for judging good from bad interest is as always whether fruitful growth takes place. To exercise an interest and yet not grow is to yield to indulgence. For best growth three things should concur: a gripping interest, a challenge from the situation for the best effort that in us lies, and eventual success. From these three come growth. Social situations and wise guidance are necessary if the growth is to be along best lines.

"All these put together make up what we may call the doctrine of interest."

REFERENCES FOR FURTHER READING

DEWEY — *Interest and Effort in Education*, pp. 16–60.
WOODWORTH — *Dynamic Psychology*, pp. 100–104.
THORNDIKE — *Principles of Teaching*, pp. 54 ff.
JAMES — *Talks to Teachers*, Ch. 10.
DEWEY — *Democracy and Education*, Ch. 10.

CHAPTER XI

INTEREST — *Continued:* THE SELF AND INTEREST

"Ever since our discussion last week I have been wondering about something I read in Thorndike — that the 'mere decision to accept certain work as interesting

The self and interest improved it.'[1]"

"I don't see anything strange about that. It fits exactly with what we have been saying. Readiness and set will explain the better learning."

"Yes, I see that; but I was comparing this statement with certain statements of Dewey's to the effect that in interest 'the self is concerned throughout,' that genuine interest means that a person has identified himself with a certain course of action.[2]"

"But I still don't see the difficulty. All these statements seem to me to tally exactly with all we have been saying. If one has a sufficiently unified mind-set, one will feel himself identified with the course of action in which he is interested."

"It is the *self*, the notion of the self involved in it all that concerns me. The self is concerned throughout. The self accepts certain work as interesting. In interest one identifies *himself* with a course of action."

"You are right, even if the others don't see it. There is a question here about the self. In any case of interest the self is involved. It is hard to understand, but it is there. In class last summer I ran across the same insistence on the

---

[1] *Educational Psychology*, Vol. II, p. 353. The statement is quoted from Ebert and Meumann.

[2] *Interest and Effort in Education*, pp. 15, 43.

self. Coercion was said to be choice 'external to the self' and there were many other things like this. It was interesting though. I remember a discussion by the class as to whether this 'identification of the self' in interest is a literal or figurative use of the word identify. There was a keen division. I thought 'literal' won out."

"Well, I must be stupid or otherwise wrong-minded, but I don't see what you are talking about. *Self* and *identify* seem to mean something quite different to you from what they do to me. Suppose a little girl is interested in a doll, does she identify herself with it? How can you say she thinks she is the doll or is the same thing as the doll? To me it's nonsense."

"I wouldn't say she thinks she is the doll or the same thing as the doll. That would be nonsense. I say she identifies her *self* with dressing the doll or with whatever else she wishes to do with the doll."

"That's not quite so bad, but I am still puzzled."

"Couldn't we take up this question of the self and see how interest is related to it? I believe it would help us straighten out some other things."

"I should be glad to do so, but we must remember at the outset that a single word like 'self' when standing alone may trouble us more than whole phrases like 'identification of the self with,' or 'choices external to the self'."

"I wish I could follow you people. Any notion of 'choices external to the self' is beyond me. What can such a phrase mean?"

"I think I understand that. Suppose a boy **The self and** **choosing** has planned with other boys to go fishing on Saturday and his father, who is old-fashioned in his management of the boy, says: 'No, you must stay at home and weed the onion patch.' And when the boy demurs, the father, being, as was said, 'old-fashioned,' replies: 'You'll stay; it is for you to say whether you will also get a whipping.' Suppose now the boy decides to stay without the whipping, will you say he chooses so to stay?"

"I hardly know what to say. In one sense he chooses. In another he doesn't."

"Now that's the uncertainty of meaning we wish to clear up. I heard an interesting discussion last summer on that point. The words *hope* and *fear* were used to mark off what is 'internal to the self' from what is 'external to the self.' "

"Your meaning is a bit hazy, but I think I understand it."

"Let me see if I understand you. As we face the future and its possible happenings, we *hope* some things will happen, we *fear* others will happen. If it is a question of choosing, we choose those we hope for, and we reject or choose not to have happen the ones we fear."

"Yes, and those we choose in hope are thus 'internal to the self,' and those we reject in fear are 'external to the self.' "

"That seems all right, but what about 'choice external to the self'? That sounds like a contradiction."

Choices external to the self　　"Contradiction or no, it expresses a fact. Go back to the boy with his fishing plans and the onion patch. The fishing plan was 'internal' to his self?"

"Yes, that's clear. He hoped to go."

"And the weeding the onion patch on that Saturday morning was 'external' to his self and so also, of course, was a whipping. But as between weeding without a whipping and weeding after a whipping he chose the former as the lesser of the two evils."

"Yes, that too is clear."

"Then by the phrase 'external choice' or a 'choice external to the self' we mean where one does choose the lesser of two evils both of which are external to the self, both of which one if left to himself would reject."

"The words 'if left to himself' tell the same tale, do they not?"

"Yes, and so do the words 'identify one's self with.' One really identifies one's self only with those activities which one chooses in hope. In such a choice the willed activity seems in a very true sense to be 'internal' to the self, somehow a part of the self."

"Then if I understand you, coercion, if effectual, means in fact an 'external choice,' a choice external to the self."

"Yes, that's the way I understand it."

"I have heard a person say he was 'torn within.' What does that mean from this point of view?"

"It, too, fits in here. Let us illustrate. Suppose John has joined a poultry club and his broilers are coming on finely. He is tremendously interested. There is no question about it: he has identified himself **To be torn within** with the undertaking. Being, however, a boy and having other interests, he plans in company with other boys to take a fishing trip on a certain Saturday. When the morning comes and he is about to start, he learns to his dismay that roup has very suddenly appeared among his chickens. What shall he do? The fish are said to be biting finely, the bait is all dug, the boys are expecting him. But his broilers — can he leave them even for one day? He is indeed 'torn within.' One interest says 'Go,' the other says 'Stay.' Both are internal. The choice is tragic, but must be made. He decides to stay."

"And you call this an internal choice?"

"Yes, the motivation was within, so we call the choice internal. True enough the roup is 'external,' and for a minute or two John felt so keenly its externality that he was angry with it and almost inclined by association to be angry with the chickens. But this was only for a moment. His good sense at once reasserted itself. Getting angry would do no good. The situation must be accepted. There was no other way out of it. He must accept the situation as a fact and act upon it, else irreparable damage would be done to his chickens."

"It seems to me that you have now brought in the doctrine of *continuity*."

"What do you mean? The doctrine of continuity? I don't recall that we have ever met it before."

The notion of continuity "Perhaps not the word, but you have met the fact often. What I mean is this: Hope and fear perhaps seem at first glance absolutely opposed, with no middle ground between them; and the same with 'things internal' and 'things external' to the self. Before we think closely, everything would seem to be either inside or outside and that's the end of it. So it seemed at first with choices external and choices internal. But now it appears there are degrees. Some choices are more external or more fully external, more internal or more fully or completely internal. Is it not so?"

"Certainly, it is so. If that is what you mean by continuity, then by all means, yes. Life presents such facts and we must recognize them. I should like to begin on it right now."

"How? What do you mean?"

"I mean the notion of continuity. Let's see what it means. Perhaps an illustration will help. Suppose sometime after the roup is conquered John hears of a new-fangled brooder. The principle is novel. John doesn't understand it. He asks his father, who, being old-fashioned in this also, scoffs at the new brooder and intimates that it is merely a city notion, a book-farming affair, which no hard-headed person would consider. John accepts his

father's opinion and next day scoffs when one of the boys
in the club mentions the matter. But the new brooder
won't down. The farm demonstrator explains it approv-
ingly. A boy rival has one and it works well. An intimate
friend makes one and John observes it at close range.
John rigs up a small one for himself. It too works. He
is fully convinced. He remakes all his brooders on this
principle. He is now an open advocate of the idea."

"Do you mean us to see how an idea began as purely
external to John and gradually worked its way in till it
became fully internal? Is this to illustrate
continuity?" Continuity
in choices

"Yes, and the same kind of continuity holds
of choices. They may range all the way from complete
rejections to complete acceptances, from rejections so complete that only fear of the worst conceivable evil could
make us will them, up to desires so strong that only the
worst conceivable evil could keep us from willing them.
Between these extremes of externality and internality our
choices lie."

"Is this after all a matter of mind-set?"

"Yes, psychologically, it is just that. We have in fact
already gone over much this same ground when we were
discussing coercion and learning."

"You used a phrase a moment ago that interested me.
You said John must 'accept the situation,' and you seem
to connect anger with not accepting the situa-
tion. Won't you say a word further about Accepting a
situation
this?"

"It too is a notion that came up when we were discussing coercion and learning. It has much to do with
setting up ends and our attitude toward the ends. When
John was told by his father to stay and weed the onion
patch, we may imagine his mother as saying: 'Yes, I know

it is a disappointment, but I advise you to accept the situation and make the best of it.' And John did. But his acceptance was rather outward than inward. An opposed mind-set remained to keep the choice an external one. The whole affair was from first to last one of coercion. So also later when he faced the question of giving up his fishing trip for the chickens; for the moment he could not 'accept' the situation, and his anger was the sign of rejection. But he soon gave up his anger and 'accepted' the situation, at first not whole-heartedly; but as he found himself succeeding in his efforts with the chickens his 'acceptance' became more and more complete."

"This then is another place where we find differences of degree."

"Indeed, yes; we find every possible degree from extreme rejection to extreme acceptance."

"It seems to me that all we are doing is to say the same thing over again in many different ways; mind-set and readiness with opposed mind-set and unreadiness, internal to the self and external to the self, choices internal and choices external, 'identification of the self with' and 'rejection, acceptance, and rejection.'"

"Well, there is much in what you say. They do in large measure repeat the same notion. But perhaps it gives us different views of the situation."

"What's the good of it all? I thought we were discussing interest. We seem to be mainly introducing more terms. Have you forgotten interest?"

"We are still discussing interest. Much of learning, both primary and attendant, depends on the attitude of the learner. If he works at a thing, feeling that it

Interest and learning

is 'external' to him, foreign to his interests, there is much less of readiness for the work. He accordingly does it less well and he learns less well both

from his successes and from his failures. Moreover, he is
less likely to build favorable attitudes in connection with it."

"Granted all that, where does the continuity or the
matter of degree come in?"

"In many ways. We may think, for instance, of the
members of a class as working at a certain thing. They
will be scattered along on the coercion-interest scale, some
studying under straight coercion, others under a less degree
of coercion, others yet with a mild degree of interest, still
others perhaps with a high degree of interest — in such a
situation we shall see different learning results according to
the place on the coercion-interest scale where the learner is
at work."

"Might one not move up the scale?"

"Assuredly. A girl might begin feeling that she could
not learn a certain thing and would not try. Under coercion she has to try somewhat, and then if she finds that she
is succeeding better than she expected she will be likely to
increase in interest ('go up the scale') and so learn still
better."

"Then you do believe in coercion after all?"

"No more and no less than I have always said. Imagine
a scale to represent what we have been discussing.

$$\text{C} \underline{\qquad\qquad \text{O} \qquad\qquad} \text{I}$$

Let C represent a high degree of coercion and I a high
degree of interest, with O a middle point neither
acceptance or rejection. Pupils who work down The coercion-
interest scale
toward C will learn less or less well than those
who work up towards I. This will be true not only of the
primary learnings, but also of the attendant learnings.
Only, with these attendant learnings, those learned about
C may be as strong as those learned about I, but they are
likely to be unfavorable, while those about I are likely to

be favorable. Around C we are likely to build attitudes against what we are compelled to do; around I we are likely to build favorable attitudes for what we work with."

"But you evade my question. A while ago you admitted that coercion may cause one to move up the line. You are now ignoring that."

"You don't give me time. I say it *may* move on up the line, not it *must* move up the line. Coercion may induce a person to put forth such efforts that he in time builds an interest. If this happens and the good all together outweighs the evil, then good has resulted. Such cases do happen."

"Then you do believe in coercion?"

"I believe in coercion when it causes a person to move up this line towards I and is the best available way of getting him to move up the line. But as a 'steady diet,' so to say, I think it most unfortunate for one to have to live under it."

When coercion is good

"You mean then that coercion cannot be relied upon to make a child study regularly?"

"Yes, I mean just that. A régime of coercion that merely remains coercion is a failure. The same is true of any extraneous motive. As Woodworth says:

'Unless you can get up an interest in a system of activities you can accomplish nothing in it. Extraneous motives may bring you to the door of a system of activities, but, once inside, you must drop everything extraneous. . . . To accomplish anything in such a task [as reading or study] we must really get *into* the subject, absorbed in it, finding it interesting and being carried along by the interest of it.' " [1]

Woodworth on direct interest

"Just what is meant by 'extraneous' here?"

"Anything except a direct interest in the activity itself.

[1] *Dynamic Psychology*, pp. 70, 71.

Curiosity, fear, rivalry, are examples of extraneous interests. Doing this thing as means to anything else as an end is a very frequent instance of extraneous interest.''

"Does this mean that direct interest is the best state of affairs for accomplishment and that we are not to use indirect interest?"

"It means that efficiency of learning or of other accomplishment comes best where there is direct interest in the learning or in the accomplishment."

"I wish we might go back to the self. I want to make sure that I have got the right connection between the self and interest. Do I correctly understand that the self consists of its interests? Is this right?" *The self and its interests*

"From many points of view that is a very useful way of looking at it."

"Is such a self or personality born in us? Or is it built up?"

"Born and built both. We are born with a nucleus of S → R bonds. By experience and the learnings that result we build new bonds and so gradually build up a more complex self. From this point of view the self is thus an organized aggregate of S → R bonds."

"You have brought in the word 'organized.' You speak of an organized aggregate of S → R bonds. Is this meaning necessary? And why?"

"Organization is a very necessary part of our notion of the proper effective personality. Imagine a person whose interests were continually warring with each other, where no decision of his would stay decided. If this were often the case, that person would be neither happy nor efficient."

"Should we aim then at building personality? Is that possible?"

"It is both possible and desirable. Every time a person responds in any way he has in so far contributed in some fashion, for good or ill, to his personality."

Building personality   "When you say 'in some fashion, for good or ill,' you mean he may be tearing down or building up?"

"Yes."

"We ought then to study the kinds of personality that our children are building?"

"Assuredly, yes."

"What does it mean that the self is always active? Haven't I read that somewhere?"

The self always active   "Yes, that is a most useful conception. In the past more than now people seemed to think that children would never do anything unless they were prodded into action or cajoled into it. We deny this by saying that the self is always active; that is, that human nature always wishes to be doing something — we must be occupied. As Thorndike says, mental emptiness is one of man's greatest annoyers."[1]

"Yes, and this is what Dewey had in mind when he said that the coercion-effortists and the sugar-coating people agree at bottom, in spite of their opposition to each other, in taking the self to be inert and static, needing to be pushed or pulled to get it into action.[2] He held, and we must agree with him, that the self is essentially and always active."

The divided self   "I should like to go back to the organized personality, and ask what is meant by the 'divided self.' I have heard that phrase, but I don't quite see how the self can be divided. Might one person have two selves?"

[1] *Educational Psychology*, Vol. I, p. 141.
[2] *Interest and Effort in Education*, pp. 6–7.

"Now you are getting us into difficulties, but I think it will be worth while to face the issue. There have been instances of double selves. This is generally known as dual or double personality. This, of course, is pathological."

"Do you mean that two persons lived in one body?"

"Well, something like that. James tells of such a case. A man forgot all about himself and his past life and began life over again. After a while he forgot this second self and its experiences and became again the other self.[1] But of course we don't usually mean any such extreme condition as that when we speak of a divided self."

"Just what do you mean? It all seems hazy to me."

"Have you not heard of boys that seem very different at home from what they are with the other boys? Jimmy's parents and teachers and all the respectable grown-up world in general see him behaving in one fashion, while his boy friends see just the opposite. We may if we wish call this a divided self. Clearly Jimmy has two more or less distinct organizations of behavior, and he changes from one to the other as occasion seems to demand."

"Such a life seems to include a sham or pretense, a fraud. Is that why you object to it?"

"That is sufficient reason for objecting to it. But there is more besides. Such a life, being split into two more or less diverse organizations, lacks the efficiency of one unified life. It is likely too not to be a happy life; either self is liable to interfere with the other more or less."

"Would coercion tend to build a divided self and is this not another reason for objecting to a régime of coercion?"

"Yes, I think so. For a boy continually to spend his school days paying outward attention to school duties while inwardly he is thinking of other things is to build a divided

---

[1] James — *Principles of Psychology*, Vol. I, pp. 390 ff.
Kilpatrick — *Source Book in the Philosophy of Education*, No. 75.

self. The learning that comes under such conditions is hurt by the division and the boy's character is likely to be lowered in greater or less degree."

"Would you then set up as an aim that we should build in our children unified selves?"

The unified self "Most assuredly. A paramount school objective should be that a child shall not simply grow, but shall grow more and more unified. If we include as we must the social demands on each one, we might almost say that the moral aim of education is summed up in the efforts to build a progressively unified character."

"What is meant in this connection by a 'higher self' and a 'lower self'? "

"It is merely a certain kind of division of self. We all recognize some impulses that lead us on to higher and finer things. In so far as we follow these we are building personalities integrated on the higher plane. This is to build the higher self. But, sad to say, we also recognize some impulses that would lead us downward. In so far as we yield to these and build ourselves about them, it is the lower self we are building."

"Did you get that from Freud?"

"Indeed, no. I cannot say where I first heard it, but long before I had ever heard of Freud, perhaps from the Bible. Plato uses it in his *Republic*."[1]

"Then you always wish the self to be unified on the higher plane."

"Yes, that is what we wish."

"What is meant by the broad self? I seem to have heard that phrase. Is there also a narrow self?"

The broad self "We can contrast the two. The distinction has, as I think of it, especial reference to our attitudes toward other people. Imagine a mother and her

[1] 431A.

sick child. Are the baby and his welfare 'internal' to the mother's self?''

"Most certainly so, if she is the right kind of mother."

"Do you mean that the baby is part of the mother's self?"

"I mean what we said earlier — that all that concerns the baby and his welfare is part and parcel of the mother's self, a dearer part too than her own physical body and its welfare."

"Where do the words 'broad' and 'narrow' come in?"

"Can you imagine a man so selfish that he thinks first of his own bodily comfort and only after that has been satisfied thinks of wife or children? If so, I should say that he has a very narrow self. But the mother who will give her very life for her baby has, I say, a broader self. Her very self is broad enough to include another person."

"Is this the same thing as selfishness and unselfishness?"

"I think it is. I should say that any man is selfish who prefers the demands of his narrower self to the just demands of a broader self."

"Don't you think everybody is equally selfish?"

"I certainly do not."

"But doesn't everyone seek the course that will give him the greatest happiness? This mother, for instance, couldn't get her happiness in any other way than by caring for her baby. She is as selfish as anybody else only along different lines, better lines, I grant you, but still selfish. Everybody is necessarily selfish." What selfish-
ness is

"You ruin the meaning of a very strong word when you make all conduct equally selfish. The distinction I wish to make is one of fact. What does the mother primarily seek? Does she care for the baby because she seeks his welfare or because she seeks her own happiness? Remember that the baby is near to death's door. Does the mother think primarily about herself and does she seek by caring for the baby to secure her own happiness, or does she forget herself and her happiness and seek only the child's welfare?"

"There can be but one answer to that. Any mother worthy the name will forget self in doing all she can for the child, and will think only of him."

"If so, then I say she is unselfish, and that we must not lose this strong term, this most valuable distinction between selfishness and unselfishness."

"Do you mean to say that this 'unselfish' mother, as you call her, is not following the line that pleases her most?"

"I certainly do not. I affirm that she is following the line that pleases her most. And I honor her for having this kind of pleasure, just as I should despise her if she did not so feel. The difference is not that some do and some do not follow out their interests. Everyone does this. The difference is in the kinds of interests. The broad self finds its interests in serving others; the narrow self is indifferent to others. The broad self is unselfish; the narrow self is selfish."

"You were speaking a moment ago of warring interests within, and you said that where this is true a decision might not stay decided."

"Yes; why not?"

"You don't mention will. I have all the time thought that it was my will that made my decisions. You don't seem to think so, but I am not sure what you do think. What "will" Do my interests make my decisions or do my means S → R bonds make them? In either case, where does will come in?"

"Here is where ancient and modern part company. As I see it, will is merely an every-day term to express the fact that a decision has come after a conflict. The interests, the opposing S → R bonds, do finally come together in one 'adopted' line of conduct."

"Has organization anything to do with it?"

"Most assuredly. Will is strong or weak along a certain line according as there is or is not a strong and efficient organization among one's S → R bonds along that line."

"Then will power can be built?"

"Certainly. To build a unified self is to build 'will power,' as you call it."

"Does will power grow from exercise?"

"Yes, it is like all other learning. Exercise with satisfaction will build it — that is, along that one line."

"Now I have caught you at last. You have opposed our making children behave or do things — using coercion, you call it. You have said that compulsion won't work. Now you say that exercising will power strengthens it. I agree and I propose to make my children exercise their wills at whatever I know to be for their good. This exercise of their wills will cause these same wills to grow stronger and in the end they will thank me. I have felt all the time that in making no reference to will you were leaving out the important factor. Now I see that I was right. I remember when I was in college that I found philosophy very difficult. For a while I slighted it and my moral fiber got flabby. Finally I made up my mind that I'd learn that philosophy at whatever cost it might require. It was hard, but I set to work and learned it. My moral fiber grew strong. Now I say I exercised my will and it grew. What have you to say to that?"

Coercion and the exercise of the will

"I say just what I have been saying all the time. Your hitherto varied and contradictory interests came to terms in a decision to learn the philosophy. This coming to a decision was exactly a resultant of the working of all your variously ready S → R bonds. Your 'will' in this was nothing but the action of these bonds in coming to terms among themselves so as to work out a line of conduct. Your practice of this in the study of philosophy brought continued success that satisfied and so made it easier for this particular conduct to take place again and again, each time more surely and more firmly. This, as following your original conscious decision, is what you call increase in will power. I call it improvement in organization of $S \rightarrow R$ bonds or the strengthening of $S \rightarrow R$ bonds. As for coercion, you yourself say *you* made up *your* mind. I agree, and so I deny that it is an instance of what I have been calling coercion. What you say illustrates and supports my contention, not yours. So long as it was mere coercion you slighted the work. It is our discussion of coercion and learning all over again."

"But didn't the coercion help me change my mind? Was it not a positive factor?"

"Possibly so, as I have always said; but the good came after you had so changed your mind that you ceased to act from mere compulsion."

"If I understand you then, you make the self to consist of one's interests and you insist upon organizing these interests so that they will work together better and thus form a more unified self."

"Yes, that is a conception of the self that I have found very useful. Of course there are other things to be said about the self."

"How do you think of moral education from this point of view?"

"In keeping with this, I think of moral education or moral growth as consisting, first, in continually adding and re-fining wholesome interests, and, second, in organizing the new interests with the old in a progressively better and better organization."

Moral growth and will training

"And does this proceed according to the recognized laws of learning?"

"Exactly."

"And is this training the will?"

"The phrase is a dangerous one, I think, but this is the only kind of will training I care to recognize."

"How does the question of incentives enter here? I remember an old book, White's *School Management*, that made much of a scale of incentives and demanded that we use on each occasion the highest on the scale that would work. Is this all out of date or is it still true?"

"My own opinion is that it is still true. As thus used an incentive calls into play an interest, and the incentive ranks high or low according as the interest Incentives called into play is counted high or low. Rivalry is thus placed rather low down in the scale, because it is not the kind of interest we wish to have loom large in child life. From this point of view it, of course, follows at once that we wish to exercise the highest type of interests we can."

"And exercising an interest builds it up? Is that the idea?"

"Yes, as always, 'practice with satisfaction' builds. Exercising an interest with satisfaction makes it come more easily and more firmly to the fore, that is, gives it a larger place in the life of the individual."

"I seem to recall, in connection, a distinction between intrinsic and extrinsic incentives. What are they and how are they related to this discussion?"

"These terms are used when we are concerned as to what induces one to engage in an activity. Suppose an activity is external to the self, then the self will Intrinsic *vs.* not engage in that activity unless by so doing extrinsic it can secure some admitted good that other- incentives wise would be lost or can avert some admitted evil that otherwise threatens to come. In such case the good or

the evil that induces one to engage in the undesired activity
is said to act as an extrinsic incentive to action. Something
outside the activity makes us act. If, however, we suppose
an activity internal to the self, one that we would choose in
and of itself, then the incentive so to act is said to be intrinsic. Something in the activity makes us act."

"Why then should we be told to prefer intrinsic incentives?"

"This question raises anew all our former questions of
coercion and learning. The answers group themselves perhaps under three heads. First, as we quoted

Why prefer
intrinsic
incentives
from Woodworth a little while ago, if we are
to be really efficient at anything we must be
really interested in that thing. Otherwise we shall not
pay close enough or prolonged enough attention to it to
do most with it. Nor shall we get the maximum of learning,
for success will not bring sufficient satisfaction nor failure
sufficient annoyance. Moreover, when we engage in an
activity in answer to a merely extraneous and extrinsic
incentive we are interested not primarily in the activity
but in the incentive and are accordingly likely to slight the
activity at the first chance and in any event to pay as little
attention to it as we can, provided only that we secure our
real end. If we succeed with the activity, the resulting
satisfaction may be located not in the activity but in the
incentive. Whatever learning may result is thus less likely
to be located in the activity itself than to attach itself in
some way to the incentive.

"A second reason for preferring intrinsic incentives is
really contained in the first, but it may well be made explicit for our consideration. It is that we are usually much
concerned to build up in the child an interest in what he
does. If I am teaching history I shall wish to build up in
my pupils an interest in history. This will be the best

guarantee both of present and future study and of future application. But to build an interest one must exercise that interest — it is once again 'practice with satisfaction.' This means that the pupils must practice being interested in history and not being interested merely in winning a prize or in getting high marks.

"The third reason is the idea of the 'unified self' discussed above. Extraneous incentives easily lend themselves to an outward show of pretended attention, while all the time real attention is inwardly directed elsewhere. To live this sort of life is to build a 'divided self,' is to fail to build the 'unified self.'"

"When people speak of 'making things interesting' what do they mean?"

"Many, perhaps most, mean sugar-coating, appealing to some sort of extraneous interest or incentive."

"Is not this likely to result in 'spoiling'?" **Making things interesting**

"I think it is."

"Is the danger of spoiling then a fourth reason for objecting to extraneous incentives?"

"Yes, but I had rather say we have in it two opposed dangers connected with the divided self: one, the danger of breaking or cowing the spirit; the other, the danger of spoiling, of making the child think that his interests alone are worth considering. I should wish to avoid both."

"Might it not be that an activity entered into on the basis of extrinsic incentives could in time come to be sought intrinsically?"

"Yes, as we have several times already seen, this is possible. We may, if we wish, say that this takes place when 'associate shift,' as Thorndike calls it, takes place. We can approve this only if, first, the shift does take place, and second, if this be in fact the best available means of building the interest."

"You spoke of prizes and marks a while ago. Do you put all such under the head of extrinsic incentives and accordingly reject them?"

Marks and prizes   "The question is knotty. Let's feel our way along. As they are generally understood and used, I think I should say, yes. Marks and prizes are extrinsic incentives and should go."

"But do all marks stand on the same basis?"

"I think not. Some of the newer systems so closely measure the success of the activity itself as to be for many purposes the same thing as success in the activity itself. But even here I should wish to say two things: first, I am suspicious, as we shall later see [pages 354–58], of learning even school skills apart from their life use; and second, some people can, even with the closest connection of sign with success, still value the sign and care little for the real success."

"Do you mean to deny that there are natural incentives?"

"I certainly do not, but these I think are inherent and intrinsic and give but little if any support to a system of marks or other artificial prizes and rewards."

"Won't you sum up what we have had to-day? I feel a bit puzzled."

"With pleasure. We have been looking at the two notions of interest and the self from many varied points of view. We have introduced a good many terms,

Summary   some of them a good deal overlapping, because they have proved useful in discussing practical educational problems. Foremost among these notions has been that of the self as active and dynamic, as consisting essentially of its interests, as accordingly dividing the whole world for itself at any one time into two parts, of things internal to it and things external to it. This notion of internality and externality, on the one hand, allied itself

with previous applications of set and readiness with their
opposites and, on the other, allowed us to state, more
neatly, perhaps, certain positions on familiar questions.
The conception of self has thus been clarified. The notion
of the unified self should prove one of very great importance, particularly as an ideal in the moral realm. In
connection with it, 'will' and 'will power' received a new
and more fruitful definition. Finally, the old doctrine of
the desirability of intrinsic incentives was restated so as to
secure new support. In general we seem to have made
progress in connecting psychology with education and
ethics by joining more closely the doctrine of interest and
the psychology of learning with the conceptions of self and
will. If we have succeeded in doing this, surely the gain
has been worth the trouble.

REFERENCES FOR FURTHER READING

DEWEY — *Interest and Effort in Education*, pp. 1–15, 23–27.
KILPATRICK — *Source Book in the Philosophy of Education*, No. 517.

CHAPTER XII

INTEREST — *Concluded:* THE INTEREST SPAN

"I heard a phrase the other day that was new to me — 'the interest span.' I didn't quite know what it meant. Can any of you tell me?"

Interest span defined "I know; I heard about that last year at summer school. It is this way: A young child shifts his interest sooner than an older one. He cannot stick to any one thing so long. His interest span is shorter. For a very young child, a few minutes suffice; for an older one, a few hours; while a still older boy or girl will work at one thing for days or even weeks; and a grown person may have a purpose that extends years ahead."

"What you say is true enough, but I don't see just how you are going to measure such a span. You know I like to be exact in my thinking. Is it the same as the attention span? Or do you count persistence as holding even after interruptions?"

"I don't think it makes much difference how you count provided you are consistent with yourself, but I should rather say it is the endurance of persistence. I like to think of it as the length of time during which a person will pursue a purpose."

"But won't one person pursue different purposes for different lengths of time? Do you mean that a person's interest span is shown by the longest pursuit of the strongest purpose? Or do you mean a kind of average or perhaps a distribution of all one's purposes?"

"Again I say I think it doesn't matter how you count,

provided you follow one method consistently. However you take it, the interest span of a child increases with increasing age and maturity."

"Is it just the length of the span that concerns you? I should think there are other things more important than that."

"There are, I think; but what had you in mind?"

"I was thinking particularly of conscious choice. It seems to me that, in the case of a very young child, things just pop into his head or out of it, I am not sure which to say, and he sets out at once to do them. He doesn't consider; he can hardly be said to choose."

What else varies along with the interest span?

"You think then that with increasing interest span comes an increase in the conscious choice?"

"Yes, but it seems to me that at the very first a child does things without having any aim or making any true choice. The baby puts the marble into his mouth not because he wishes consciously to swallow it or even to see how it tastes; he just does it. The results of his experiment may remain with him, as when he runs across sugar or salt or a hot coal, but he does not mean to experiment. He is simply manipulative. The sight of any small thing stirs him to this kind of action."

"And you think choice can come only after the child has had experiences and knows what to expect?"

"Yes, that's it."

"I once heard Professor Dewey lecture on this very point. So far as I know his remarks have never been printed, but as I recall them he reckoned three stages of choice: first, when the child didn't and couldn't foresee the results of what he was doing, when he simply acted at once upon sense stimuli;

Stages of choice

second, when he knew what he was about and in a general way expected what might happen, but hadn't considered it beforehand, hadn't deliberated on doing it; third, when in the light of experience and expected consequences he chose what he would do. The last only is conscious choice, true purposing."

"If I understand you, you mean that along with the growth of the interest span comes growth in conscious choice, in true purposing; and that this growth follows Professor Dewey's three stages?"

"Yes, that's it exactly."

"What else would change with the increasing interest span?"

"These three stages had to do with ends, setting up ends I mean. Wouldn't a like growth be seen in the choice of means?"

"How?"

"With the first stage, there are no real means — the activity is too simple. There are no real ends and no real means. With the second, there are some steps leading to the end; but I imagine they would come more or less haphazardly. In the third stage, there would be conscious choice of means to attain the consciously purposed end."

"It seems to me that you are merely saying that the child is getting older, becoming more mature. Why all this fine spinning of steps and stages?"

Growing older   "Perhaps we are merely telling how the child grows older, or how he matures; but is it not worth while to see clearly what maturing consists in—for example, in an increase of consciousness in the choice of ends and means?"

"Don't most people fail to look at the inside of maturing and consider instead only the outside?"

"What do you mean by inside and outside? I don't see."

"Most people seem to separate children sharply from adults. Children should grow, of course; but adults are already grown, finished, done, completed. Immaturity belongs to children; maturity, to grown-ups. I wish to look on the inside of what maturing means and see if twenty-one-year-olds (and over) shouldn't go on maturing and still go on maturing as long as they live, at any rate till death comes or senile decay sets in."

"But is this true? Haven't we been told recently by those who measure intelligence that the average person reaches his full mental age at from fourteen to sixteen? How then can he keep on growing?"

Are we mentally grown at sixteen?

"Why not? Anybody but an idiot or moron does keep on growing after fourteen or sixteen. The average boy or girl at fourteen or sixteen isn't equal in wisdom to the same person at thirty or forty. They do keep on growing for a goodly number of years. This I say is a fact, the kind of fact that everybody knows to be true and acts on. Of course people grow after sixteen."

"Must you not say first what you mean by growing?"

"Exactly so, and that's what we are doing. We have found, for one thing, that the 'interest span' grows after the person is fourteen. A man of thirty forms on the whole longer-range plans than does a boy of fourteen. The plans, too, are more complicated and the man sticks to them better. Also, we found that there is increase of consciousness of choice both as to means and as to ends."

What growing means

"Do you think a person can keep on increasing in consciousness of choice after he is thirty-five, say?"

"I see no reason to doubt it. The more we know, the more experiences we have organized, the more we have to take into account in deciding, the better we may have learned that it pays to think."

"Is this the explanation of the old proverb: 'Young men for action; old men for counsel'?"

"There is certainly some connection."

"But may not the young men be right? Isn't there a time when we should cease deliberating and begin to act? I know some cautious old fellows who think so much that they are afraid to do anything."

Deliberation and action

"Yes, depending on the importance and the urgency and our knowledge of the matter at hand, there does come a time when deliberation should yield to action. I should say in fact that deliberation exists primarily to further action."

"Haven't you forgotten what we were discussing? You seem to have left the interest span. I want to know what else changes as the interest span increases. Or have we named all the things?"

"No, there are still other changes that accompany, though most have already been implied. The steps in the typical activity become more and more complicated as age increases. We take these steps more and more in the light of knowledge, and this knowledge gets more and more precise and reliable. Moreover our steps are better planned and better organized. Also, we may and should choose both ends and means in the light of broader and broader ranges of interest."

Other signs of growing

"These changes seem to be but repetitions or enlargements of those that have already been named. They are closely connected both with the greater length of span on the one hand and with the greater consciousness on the other."

"You are right. I said they had already been implied. As stated they are mainly elaborations; but in addition to these will come new types of interests. A small boy whose boat proves top-heavy will learn with interest that lead on the keel will make it stand upright. Later he will ask why and may be interested to study the principle of the lever. Perhaps still later the generalization principle of 'virtual velocities,' as the old books called it, will appeal to him. It is true enough that not everyone develops these more pronounced intellectual interests, but almost everyone goes some way along this road."

"I am interested in the notion of growing. Couldn't we go back to that? It seems to me that what you are really doing is to help us to see what growing is, to see what constitutes the signs or content of growing. Are there yet other things that can be named?"

"There are many other things, too numerous to discuss now. They group themselves largely under two heads; increase in the content of experience and increase in the control over experience."

"Now what are you 'high-brows' talking about? I came in just in time to hear you say 'growing,' 'increasing content of experience,' 'increasing control over experience.' These sound like good 'high-brow' terms. What is it all about? What is the connection?"

"We have been trying to think of the good life as one of growing continually richer and finer as one gets older. This is what we have called growing, and I had just said that growing includes at least the two sides — increasing content of experience and increasing control over experience." *Growth in content and control*

"Let me see if I understand you. By increasing control over experience you mean that it is of no use to know about a good thing unless you can somehow manage to get it. And by increasing content you mean that some people get very little out of life because they don't see enough in life. Am I right?"

"For a beginning, that will do very well."

"Well, what has all this to do with teaching? I have to

teach grammar and arithmetic and history. I don't see any connection that my work has with anything you have been saying. What I want is something to help me teach these very necessary subjects to my very unwilling children. Why don't you people who talk so much about studying education study the real thing? I want to know some good way to teach the use of the decimal point in division and you spend your time talking of growing and increasing content, and increasing control. It reminds me of the Bible saying. I ask for bread and you give me a stone."

"I wonder what the children might think if they only knew. They too ask for bread and how often we give them stones. These unwilling children, are they active?"

"Active! They are as active as cats — if I'd let them be, but not about grammar or decimal points. A few of them like these subjects, but most of them have to be driven. Am I wrong? Oughtn't the children to learn how to use the decimal point? Or don't you people believe in having children learn? Has the verb *to learn* gone out of fashion?"

"Most certainly children should learn. If I have any ccmplaint against the old-régime method, it is that children under it do not learn."

"Then why talk so much about growing? I should say that growing and learning are two quite different things. Trees grow, but people learn. I don't quite understand you."

"Let's see how matters stand. You say trees grow. Very good, and in much the same way do children's bodies grow and also their 'intelligence,' the thing the psy-

Two senses of growing chologists are now talking so much about."

"And is this intelligence the thing that they say is full-grown at about fourteen or sixteen years?"

"Yes."

"Do you believe it?"

"I think in the main they are right."

"But you were talking of another kind of growing."

"Yes, I was thinking primarily of such growing as means more thoughts, more meanings, finer and finer distinctions, better ways of behaving, higher degrees of skill, broader interests, wider and better organizations — all the things that go along with a growing interest span."

"Then growing has two meanings?"

"I think we may say so."

"Does the interest span grow because these added things come, or do they come because the interest span grows?"

"Until a child is fourteen or sixteen possibly both happen. After that time it is mainly (if not entirely) the coming of these new things in their various connections that makes the interest span lengthen out."

"And it is this second kind of growing that mainly concerns us?"

"Yes, in it learning and growing mean about the same thing."

"Is your last statement quite correct? Do you think cramming brings growth of the kind you wish? Yet cramming is learning, at any rate as the psychologists define learning. What say you?" *Learning and growing*

"I know what you mean and I quite agree with you. I think there are degrees of learning."

"And so does the psychologist, but you don't mean quite what he means by *learning*, do you?"

"I think we are concerned with different problems and so tend to use words a little differently. The psychologist is immediately concerned with laboratory conditions. For him, accordingly, learning largely means acquiring the ability to give back, on demand, the skill to do anything when a signal is given. For the laboratory, this is generally sufficient. But I am concerned with life, with remaking life, in the young typically *Two meanings of the verb "to learn"* but also in grown-ups. I wish not merely the ability to respond but also the disposition to respond. For my purposes a thing has not been sufficiently learned unless it WILL be used when the right time comes. CAN is not sufficient."

Will and can both needed

"WILL and CAN — you puzzle me. Won't you explain?"

"Certainly. Take a small child and the lacing of his shoes. Are we content that he be *able* to lace his shoes? I say no, CAN is not sufficient. WILL he do it? I wish learning to go far enough to include both CAN and WILL."

"And what about growing?"

"I say that a thing has not been learned — learned for life purposes you understand — until it has got over into life and to some extent remade it. Then I say the learner has grown by that much."

"What do you mean by remaking life?"

"Take the small boy and lacing his shoes. Heretofore, mother or nurse has laced his shoes for him each morning. Henceforth, he laces his own shoes. His life is, as a result, different in several important respects. Most obviously it is he who now does the lacing, not his mother. But much more, he has now by this much become independent of mother; henceforth, by this much he directs his own life; in this he begins now to decide and act of himself and for himself. Self-respect is modified; feelings of independence are stirred. Ask the mother; she knows. She feels in connection both pleasure and pain, pleasure and pride that the boy is progressing, pain that he is leaving off his dependence upon her. He is ceasing to be her baby. Yes, his life is being remade, reconstructed."

Remaking life

"And is this what you mean by growth?"

"It is an instance of it."

"You spoke earlier of increasing control over experience. That is what we see here in this child, is it not?"

"Largely so."

"You also spoke of the increasing content of experience. I am not so sure that I see it in this instance."

"The increase in content is perhaps not quite so obvious as is the increase in control. Yet it means a richer content to experience when he has learned all these various things from and about lacing his shoe. He sees — either for the first time or in a new light — eyelet holes, the two laces, the even lacing, the over and under movement of lacing. It is, moreover, a new content to experience to feel independent, to decide for oneself, and to feel self-reliant. He now sees times and seasons in a new light. Rising bells, breakfast bells, and such things have hitherto been mainly signals to his mother. It was she who had to obey them. He had only to obey her. Now he has increasing responsibility of noting himself these signals and taking account of the lapse of time. Yes, even in this very simple case, life has added new content."

"Do I understand you to define education in a new way, I mean in terms of content and control?"

"Yes, I should wish to think of education as the process of continuously remaking experience in such way as to give it continually a fuller and richer content and at the same time to give the learner ever increasing control over the process."[1]

"Is this what Professor Dewey meant by saying education is life and not a mere preparation for life?"

"It is part of what he meant."

"I don't quite see why you said so much at the first about the growing interest span. It now seems to me that mere length is the smallest part of the matter."

[1] Dewey—*Democracy and Education*, p. 89 f.

"Perhaps it is, but at any rate it is a good and useful phrase; and I think it gave us a good introduction to this new and richer definition of education."

"I begin to see better what you meant earlier about bread and stone. I noticed then that you turned them exactly about when you replied. You value education as it remakes life?"

"Yes, as it remakes life here and now, I mean the child's life here and now. I am accordingly not so sure as to our **Education is** old formal lessons, whether they best remake **the remaking** life. I fear they too often postpone remaking, **of life** postpone it to so distant a day that present life is starved. The children may be said to be 'active as cats,' but not about their lessons. What I want is to begin with their present child activities as the starting point. If we do this I think the activity will then be on our side instead of against us."

"Is not this notion of education very different from the one that most people have?"

"Yes, and we can only touch on it here; but for a hundred years our best practice has been moving in this direction."

"I should like to go back for a short while to the interest span. Could we not think also of an interest **The interest** range?" **range**

"What have you in mind?"

"I mean that certain things, such as balls and dogs and ponies, are in a boy's interest range; but that some others, such as George Eliot and 'predestination *vs.* free will' are not. It is not so much the length of interest span as it is the content of present interests."

"That sounds very good to me, but do you mean by present interests the interests the boy feels at the moment or all the interests he now has, even though some of these are not now active but are asleep, as it were?"

"It is the latter, I think. I was trying to frame a rule that in directing education — the real education that you have been discussing — we should remain al- Keep within ways within the child's interest range and in- the interest terest span." range

"You mean if we are to keep the child's interest, have it work for us so as to utilize all we know of set and readiness, then we should, as you say, remain always within the child's interest span and interest range. It seems to be a good rule, but of course, in discussing its possible exceptions, we should run into our old dispute about coercion and when coercion is to be used. Under some circumstances, it might be necessary to give up interest and use coercion."

"Yes, that is all true."

"I am thinking about your new rule. How could I, as a teacher of English literature, use it? Does it mean that I cannot teach the English classics because Literature they are beyond the interest range of chil- and the inter- dren?" est range

"If they are in fact beyond the children's present interest range, I should say, yes, that you ought not to require them now."

"But if the children do not reach out beyond where they now are, how are they to grow? In general I agree with you, but I cannot let the present limitations of childhood forever forbid my introducing something better than they now value."

"We seem then to be blocked, to be confronted by a dilemma: For best learning, particularly in the case of attitudes and appreciations, we must have interest, we must remain within the child's interest span and range; but if we remain always within the child's present interest range, how is growth possible? How can he grow if he doesn't reach out?"

"You are right. I see no way out of the difficulty except to compel the child to learn the new material. I think this is one case where coercion is justified."

"But what success can you expect in compelling a child to appreciate a poem? How can you compel appreciation? Some people are cynical enough to say that the best way to kill a book is to use it in the high school. I shouldn't like to agree entirely, but there is some justification for the widespread impression."

Compelling appreciation

"I should like to ask whether we really face such a dilemma."

"What way out do you see?"

"I think I see two very practical ways out, both already referred to in our discussions."

"And what are they?"

"First, that the teacher may disclose interests already present but not evident to the children."

"How? Won't you illustrate?"

"Yes, gladly. The children attack 'Thanatopsis.' They don't see enough meaning in it. They are not interested. The teacher then reads it aloud, commenting here and there. It takes on new meaning. It is now interesting."

"That's good. What's the second way?"

"It is the use of indirect interest. Things in themselves uninteresting may for the time take on a very genuine interest. We can become very much interested in an activity in spite of the fact that it involves otherwise uninteresting aspects."

Increasing the interest range through indirect interest

"I think I see, but will you illustrate?"

"With pleasure. Moving a heavy stone in and of itself may not be interesting. But if some boys are building a dam so as to have a pond, they may get very much interested in moving this very heavy stone into place in the dam. Its very size on the one hand gives it value to them and on the other challenges their efforts. Both give interest."

"You seem conveniently to forget your pious remarks about extraneous incentives."

"Indeed, I have not. Just watch the boys. The original interest in the pond-to-be extended itself sufficiently to include making the necessary dam. It is not necessary to ask how much of their interest in the making of the dam is brought over from the wish for the pond and how much is derived from such native interests as contriving, manipulation, working together, leadership, and all the rest. The point is that the pond-to-be at least was the occasion for the awakening of a very great deal of genuine interest in making the dam. Similarly the interest in making the dam is at least occasion for a like interest in moving the stone. Watch the boys and see. Such activities can be tremendously interesting."

"If I understand you, interest in a piece of literature is not just one thing, but may be very varied. A class might begin working with a poem along one line because of one kind of interest, but the successful prosecution of their work might involve interesting excursions into many other aspects of the poem. Am I right?"

"That is exactly what I mean."

"You say *might* involve interesting excursions. Do you mean it also might not involve such excursions?"

"Yes, there is always chance for failure."

"This is very interesting to me. You insist then that the most educative experiences are those that begin and remain within the child's interest span and range?"

"Yes."

"But, if I understand you, they must in point of experience reach out into new regions?"

"Yes, but still remain within the interest range and span."

"And it is the fact of genuine indirect interest that makes this possible?"

"Yes, and this extending of interest so as to include necessary related activities enlarges for the time the interest range."

"And may this temporary addition to the interest range become a permanent addition?"

"It may well do so. It is a matter of building interests. The conditions here described may be called the natural conditions for building an interest. [See pages 90–93.] They are, I think, the most favorable of all."

"Isn't success a factor in interest building?"

"Yes, generally the main factor."

The value of success in interest building "Then you would wish to add as another item that any activity to be approved for educational purposes should be and remain within the range of success. Is it not so?"

"Quite so."

"This thing grows a bit complicated. Won't some one bring it all together for us?"

"I have tried to say it to myself this way: In order that an experience may be most truly educative it must, first, **When an experience is educative** stay within the present interest span and range, i.e., be and remain gripping in interest, else we lose the advantage of set and readiness; second, it must reach out beyond the hitherto known limitations of insight, attitude, and power, else growth does not take place; third, in this reaching out into new territory, it must still remain within reach of success, else discouragement follows, with loss rather than gain of ground."

"But suppose my pupils simply are not interested in better things. What then? Must I still remain within the interest span and range?"

"So far as I can see, yes. The badness (as you and I feel it) of their present case in literature fixes for you at once your starting point and your aim. You must start where they are; there is nowhere else to start. You must try to move them up the line to something finer."

"Is this starting where the children are and going always no faster than they go an illustration of the continuous reconstruction of experience?"

"It is one illustration of it. Growth as we have been discussing it and the continuous reconstruction of experience are but two ways of describing the same process."

"We have said much about growing and growth. What are the signs that growing is taking place, or perhaps better, what are the lines along which growth should appear?"

Lines of growth

"There are many ways of saying it. I have been trying to say it to myself in this fashion. An experience has been educative when the learner has grown (*a*) in outlook and insight, (*b*) in attitudes and appreciations, and (*c*) in means of control. By growth in outlook and insight I mean that he now sees more possibilities and more significances than he formerly saw. He now SEES better what to do. By growth in attitudes and appreciations, I mean that he has new interests and values corresponding to his broader outlook and deeper insight. He has new things to value. Some old things he values in new ways. Having different interests and values from formerly he WILL now act differently when the time comes. By increase in 'means of control' I have in mind better power of effecting, of doing or getting what one sees and wills. The learner now CAN do more than formerly. I like to say that SEE, CAN, and WILL are the lines along which growth can and should take place."

"Won't you illustrate?"

"With pleasure. A boy goes fishing for the first time and the experience is so managed that he learns from it. Afterward, as he passes a stream, he sees possibilities that before he did not see. And it is not just vague and general. With fishing in mind he now SEES the possibilities of this pool as compared with those shallows. Not only does he see differently, but he feels differently. If occasion require, he WILL act differently. New attitudes and appreciations have been built corresponding to the new insights. Moreover, he now has made a beginning at skill in the matter. He CAN do more. He can better manage a hook and line. He is a different boy. He has grown. His experience has been remade."

"I wish some one would sum up this afternoon's discussion. I feel confused."

"As I see it, we began with the notion of the interest span, and we saw how this increases with increasing age and maturity. We next saw that many things

Summary change as the length of the span increases; chiefly there comes a growing complexity of steps with increase of conscious attention paid to them. There are also differentiations of interests with oftentimes a distinct increase in those of purely intellectual concern. We next took 'growing' as a good word with which to describe the changes we had already noticed. Then we saw that our references to growth and learning were practically two ways of saying the same thing. This led to a redefining of learning and to the definition of education as a process of continuous growth, the continuous remaking of experience in such way as to give it an ever richer and finer content and to give the learner an ever greater control over it. We next considered the interest range and the wisdom of staying always within it. Last we got three lines of growth, indicated by the three words, SEE, WILL, and CAN. Does

one now SEE better what to do?   WILL he more likely do it?
CAN he better effect it?"

REFERENCES FOR FURTHER READING

DEWEY — *Interest and Effort in Education*, pp. 35–45.
KILPATRICK — *Source Book in the Philosophy of Education*, No. 469.

CHAPTER XIII

Purposeful Activity: The Complete Act

"We have many times referred generally to purpose and purposing, but I think we have said little about a phrase I often hear among forward-looking teachers.

Purposeful activity I mean 'purposeful activity.' Just what is meant by purposeful activity and why should we wish it?"

"Purposeful activity is just what it says — activity full of purpose, activity permeated by or directed by a purpose."

"Do you mean any sort of activity, or must it be a manual or motor activity?"

"It means any sort of activity that is dominated by a purpose. Can't one have a purpose that is not manual?"

"Certainly, I may purpose to compose a poem. There isn't much of the manual in that."

"Why are some people so insistent on the manual or motor element here?"

"It is a mystery to me. I cannot answer. All I can say is that the manual element need not be present."

"You don't mean to deny that with the young child manipulation and other forms of motor activity are very frequent, and very proper to be encouraged?"

"Not a bit of it. I agree thoroughly that with children, even with older children, motor activity, physical movement of some sort, is all but essential to any activity that is to prove interesting. But even physical movement, though it includes much more than manual activity, need not be present in any very obvious sense."

"Well, why wish the purposeful activity? Why the purpose? We used to think it sufficient for the child to do as he was told. Has that gone out of date?"

"I thought we had already sufficiently considered why we wish purposing. You recall our discussion of mind-set and learning. Set and readiness seemed to us the keys to learning." *Why wish purposeful activity*

"I wasn't present at the earlier discussions, though I understand set and readiness. But what has purpose to do with set or readiness?"

"Purpose always includes a mind-set-to-an-end and implies consciousness besides. Also it has usually been decided upon after more or less of deliberation. And readiness of course accompanies mind-set — selective readiness, I mean."

"Why say selective readiness?"

"Because in purposing we are ready along certain lines favorable to our purpose and unready along others. This is the effect of mind-set as we saw once before. What we learn depends on this fact."

"You referred to the element of conscious choice in purpose. That is why you say that true, full purposing is hardly to be expected in the very young, is it not?"

"Yes, but if we think of purpose as the opposite of mere dictation and coercion, then we shall wish even the young to purpose as best they can at their stage of advancement."

"And you wish this purposing because you think it best leads to learning?"

"Yes."

"Do you mean the primary learning only or also the associates and concomitants?"

"We mean all, but I thought we had said this often enough already."

"But you do insist on purpose because through the ac-

companying set and readiness the conditions for learning
are best met? Am I not right?"

"Exactly right. This is the main reason. Other things
being equal, the stronger the purpose the stronger the learning that takes place?"

"What other reasons are there for wishing the presence
of a purpose?"

"For one thing, success is surer. The stronger the purpose
the greater the tendency to push ahead in the face of
obstacles and, accordingly, the greater the likelihood of success."

"Are you here desiring success for its educational value
or because you wish to get things done?"

"Both. We are more likely to get things done — and that
is good, if the things are good — but success has great educative effect, besides. The satisfaction of success is a great
factor in fixing learning."

"Won't success build good concomitants?"

"Yes; 'Nothing succeeds like success.' Success builds
concomitants favorable to the succeeding cause."

"Is there still any other reason for wishing the learner to
have a purpose?"

"Yes, the presence of purpose is a powerful factor in organization. The end in view, being consciously held, helps
to direct each step in the process, so that one
part is joined to another part with a conscious
reason. In the end, we see what steps have
been successful and what have not, and we know
what we have done and why. This makes a better unified
whole than we could have where things have been less
consciously done."

"Will an organization so made be useful anywhere else?"

"I should think so. An organization made in its natural
setting is more likely to have natural connections and so is

more likely to be called into use again when a suitable occasion arises. The probable handles, or points of contact, are more numerous. This I think is one of the great weaknesses of the old teaching. It was mostly done outside its natural setting, and had accordingly few handles, few contact points. A person might be learned in that old sense and still find few occasions to use his learning."

"The phrase 'natural setting' seems a good one. Did you invent it?" Natural setting

"Indeed, no. I got it from Charters and Stevenson." [1]

"Do they not prefer it to your factor of purpose?"

"In a way they do. At least I so understand them."

"Why do you insist on purpose?"

"Mainly because I think it is the best single idea with which to call attention to the matter of attitude. I am much concerned to utilize the laws of learning, since learning is the essence of education. The presence of purpose on the part of the learner means the presence of set and readiness. When these are present, satisfaction is attached to success and annoyance to failure. But satisfaction and annoyance are exactly the conditions for best learning."

"Is there any connection between purpose and natural setting?"

"Usually there is, though I should not care to urge it as important. Purposing is not so likely to be present when an enterprise is divorced overmuch from its natural setting. But I have another head under which I shall wish later to discuss natural setting." [See page 357.] The steps in a purposeful act

"What are the typical steps in a purposeful enterprise?"

"I myself reckon four: purposing, planning, executing, judging."

[1] Charters—*Curriculum Construction*, p. 138.
Stevenson—*The Project Method of Teaching*, p. 14.

"I am not quite sure that I see what you mean; won't you illustrate?"

"Imagine a girl — her mother away — who sets out to get dinner for the family and a guest that her father is bringing home with him. She has for some time

Purposing

been wishing a chance to prepare and serve, 'all by herself,' a more elaborate dinner than the family usually has. She feels freer that mother is away; not that she is unloving, but somehow this makes the enterprise more fully her own. True enough she quakes a bit when father telephones that he will bring home the prominent Mr. Marshall; but this is over quickly, as she determines to get a dinner of which she and her father — and her mother when she shall hear about it — will be proud. So far we have the first step, purposing: the girl purposes to serve a good dinner. It seems too to be a whole-hearted purpose.

"With this purpose in mind, she plans her meal: what the menu shall be, how she will set and dress the table, and how

Planning

she will serve the meal. Her course in home economics at school makes her feel surer of herself. In this instance it is necessary that her planning precede the executing. This is not always so; frequently the two overlap. So this is the second step, planning: She plans in advance all that she will do.

"Then follows the third step, the executing. Some last-minute things must be ordered from the grocer. Fortu-

Executing

nately the roast already in the house will do, even for Mr. Marshall. Everything must be prepared, cooked, and finally served, the table meanwhile having been made ready. In this case the executing extends to the end of the meal and even afterwards. All, let us suppose, was done according to plan except for a few minor changes.

"Last comes judging. How well did she succeed? Her guests help her (in more than one way) to judge, but she knows that part of their praise of her success comes from their wish to please her. She tries Judging to appraise it all fairly, for she means to succeed as a housekeeper. So she asks of each thing, 'Did I do what I planned? How well did I succeed?' This I should wish to call the *specific* judging, for there is another kind. If she really means to profit best by her experience she will ask further, 'Now that it is all over, what have I learned? What mistakes did I make? Wherein could I do better next time?' This last I like to call the *generalizing*."

"Do you count then two sub-steps under judging?"

"Yes; (*a*) specific judging, and (*b*) generalization."

"Do you mean that every instance of purposeful activity must follow these steps, all separated like this?"

"No, I do not. The younger the child and the less pretentious the enterprise the less likely are the steps to be so separately distinct as here. But typically, I think, all four will be found logically present if not actually or chronologically distinct."

"Do you mean that two or more might go on simultaneously?"

"Yes, we shall often see planning, executing, and judging intermingled if not exactly simultaneous."

"How are these steps related to each other? How does one influence the other?"

"I think we can answer that. Clearly the purpose is the dominating factor. The purpose either Relations of supplies or is the drive which carries us along the steps to throughout the whole. Then we plan how we each other may attain the purpose; there is obvious correlation here. Similarly the execution is the carrying out of the plan, execution being thus as strictly the correlative of the plan as the plan is of the purpose. Also, of course, the execution is with reference to the purpose. And finally the purpose must test and judge the execution: Does the final result secure and meet the original purpose? If not, was it plan or execution which was at fault?"

"Yes, I see that all four steps are very closely and inherently related."

"Might one person help another take one or more of the steps? Or might one take one or more of the steps for Helping one   another person? If so, would this be good or to take the   bad?" steps   "We often see elders taking one or more of the steps for the young under their care. Shall we approve or disapprove?"

"What do you mean by one person's taking a step for another? How could a teacher purpose for a pupil?"

"How could she? That's what they do nearly all the time. How much purposing do pupils do? I mean as to what shall go on in school. The teachers, or persons directing the teachers, do about all the purposing that goes on in the ordinary school."

"Do we agree?"

"In the case of the ordinary school — yes, I think so."

"Is this good or bad?"

"It depends on whether we accept the general position we have been discussing. If we really believe in purposeful activity, then we must regret to see children having no part in purposing."

"Do you mean that it makes a difference who does the purposing?"

"I certainly do mean that. In fact that's Shall the   the point of the whole matter. If the child is child purpose? to learn best, the child is to do the purposing."

"But surely you do not mean that a child can select as

wisely as a grown-up, as the parent or the teacher, for instance? You can't mean that?''

"As I see it, the word purpose is used in two somewhat
different senses, and we must distinguish them to get the
right idea. Your question uses the word Two mean-
'select' as if child purposing means primarily ings of
that the child, and the child alone, shall select "purpose"
and determine what shall be done; and you seem further to
imply that we expect the teacher to accept the child's
selection."

"Well, what else could you mean?"

"I said there were two senses in which the word purposing
is used. Do you see any difference between a child's doing
what he wishes and a child's wishing what he does?"

"I think I see what you mean."

"Well, our plan is primarily that a child shall wish what
he does, that he have and put soul and purpose into what
he does. If this is his attitude toward what he Purpose as
does, then are set and readiness and satisfaction whole-hearted
and annoyance best utilized for his learning, as acceptance of
we have many times said." what one does

"Then the suggestion might come from the teacher, and
the child still purpose the matter in the sense you most
wish?"

"Quite so. We have, so far, not based any argument on
the child's originating or even selecting (in the sense of his
deciding) what shall be done. So far, all that we have
claimed will be met if the child whole-heartedly accepts
and adopts the teacher's suggestion."

"And is this whole-hearted acceptance the other, the
second, sense of purposing?"

"Yes."

"And you don't care whether the child purposes in the
first sense or not — that is, you don't care whether he does

or does not originate the idea, or whether he does or does not choose (that is, decide and determine) what he is to do?"

Purpose as origination and choice "I didn't say I didn't care. I do care; I care both positively and negatively, care to encourage it sometimes, care to discourage or rather educate it at other times."

"Now I am completely lost. What do you mean, care positively and negatively? Please explain."

"Go back to my distinction between doing as he wishes and wishing what he does. Take the first, 'do as he wishes.' Suppose a child wishes to do wrong; then I **A purpose to do wrong** wish him stopped, caught, redirected, educated in some way, so that (*a*) he shall learn that what he had proposed was wrong, (*b*) he shall learn why it was wrong, (*c*) he shall so regret wishing this particular wrong that hereafter he will less probably wish it again. In a word when he wishes to do wrong, I wish him to learn the error of his way and so to repent of his wrong inclination that he will hereafter not so wish again. Is this wishing him to do as he pleases?"

"No, it is not. At least it is not so when he pleases to do wrong."

"But who is to say whether he is wrong? That's the rub."

"The teacher. That's one thing the teacher is there for. But notice this, the teacher is mainly there that the child may learn. The good teacher will so manage **The teacher is in authority, but must educate** that the child shall best learn, all things considered."

"What do you mean? You have something else in mind."

"I mean this: that if the child purposes to do wrong, it will not usually suffice for the teacher merely to forbid, still less merely to punish."

"You mean the teacher must manage the case so as to educate the child, cause him to grow?"

"Exactly so; the teacher must increase his outlook and insight, improve his attitudes and appreciations. It is again a case of SEE and WILL."

"And you think mere denial or mere punishment are not usually the best means of improving SEE and WILL?"

"Usually they are not, though at times they may be."

"You have discussed the case when a child wishes to do wrong. Suppose he wishes to do right?" *Purpose to do right*

"Then I wish him to go ahead and I pray success may attend."

"Why?"

"Because I believe in practice with satisfaction. When he himself thinks things over and chooses rightly and from right motives, I wish these inclinations better fastened in him; so I wish him God-speed. It is practice with satisfaction."

"I admit your consistency. You wish the child to 'practice the right with satisfaction' and to 'practice the wrong with annoyance.' But have you not overlooked one thing?"

"What is that?"

"This child will grow up and leave you. Do you not wish him to have practice in judging right from wrong? And if so, doesn't that mean that he must have some lee-way for practice? If the teacher interposes the moment that he goes wrong, I am afraid *Practice in judging* he won't get the best kind of practice."

"You are exactly right, and for that reason I wish the teacher to give the children freedom enough to practice choosing."

"Freedom! how much freedom?"

"As much as they can use wisely."

"And how much is that?"

Freedom,
why and
how much "Growing is the test. If they learn how to make better moral distinctions and if they better act accordingly, they are growing, and then they are using their freedom wisely. If not, they are not so using it."

"But may not one learn from his mistakes?"

"Most certainly, and I mean to include that. What I demand is that the child shall grow in the matter at hand."

"Then, if we may go back, in this matter of child purposing, you first and mainly wish whole-hearted purposing of Why child
purposing what a child is doing because the learning results are then likely to be best?"

"Yes, up to to-day that has been our main contention. That is what we have mainly meant when we have hitherto advocated whole-hearted child purposing."

"And this is quite consistent with teacher suggestion, provided the child does whole-heartedly accept the teacher's suggestion?"

"Quite so."

"But now you wish to take a step further and say that a child should, under wise teacher guidance and control, practice choosing?"

"Yes, granted wise guidance, to practice choosing is the best promise for growth in power to choose."

"And in this you would give all the freedom the children can use successfully?"

"Yes, that's it."

"And by 'successfully' you mean that they are to grow in making wise and ethical choices?"

"Yes, growth is always the test. If that is taking place properly, we are on the right line. If not, something is wrong."

"Is this the only reason why you wish the children to practice purposing in the sense of selecting and deciding?"

"Well, I should add another word to selecting and deciding, namely, the word originating. I wish the children to have practice in seeing in any situation its own problem, its own demand. If the teacher always suggests, I fear they will lose this opportunity. This is an important aspect of initiative."

"You think initiative can be developed in any one? I thought we were born with it or born without it, and that that ended the matter."

"Excepting the most unfortunate, all are born with some capacity along this line. Here as elsewhere proper education will develop what nature has given."

"Now, one last question: Do you believe in teachers?"

"Most certainly. We need them on my basis, more if possible than on the old basis." Place of teachers

"And you lodge actual final authority in this teacher with power to command or forbid as may be necessary?"

"As between teacher and child, I certainly do."

"But you wish the teacher to give freedom?"

"Freedom, yes, but not unlimited freedom; freedom for practice, and as much freedom as does in fact bring growth from practice. Growth is always our criterion."

"And you wish the children to assume as much responsibility in matters of choice and direction as is consistent with best growth?"

"Yes, for I think they can grow only as they practice. That is the law of exercise."

"But at times the teacher may step in?"

"Yes, not only *may*, *must* step in, to save the day. But as a rule the teacher helps best by helping the children to help themselves. This again is the law of exercise."

"We've been all this time discussing how the teacher or other person can step in to help or hurt a child in the matter of purposing. It has taken us a long time, and there are yet three other steps. Shall we take them up?"

"By all means, unless you think we have already covered the whole ground."

"What do you mean?"

"I mean that we are to deal with the other three just as we dealt with purposing. We wish the child to practice Practice in all planning, practice executing, practice judging. four steps It is his practice alone that can educate him. necessary And practice is impossible without freedom for practice. So again we wish freedom, as much and only as much as the child can use wisely. And still again, the test is growth."

"It does look as if we have already covered the ground with all four steps."

"I should like to ask about planning. Don't you think that the teacher should often supply the plan. Take a Shall the boy planting corn, for example; think of the teacher waste of land and fertilizer and effort. Science supply the has worked out better plans than a boy can plan? make."

"And in such case you would advocate furnishing the boy with the best plan the teacher could find or devise?"

"Yes, wouldn't you?"

"I think it depends on what you seek. If you wish corn, give the boy the plan. But if you wish boy rather than corn, that is, if you wish to educate the boy to think and plan for himself, then let him make his own plan."

"No matter how much waste is involved?"

"We always have to balance all factors and then decide. In a particular case the waste may cost more than the learning will come to."

"And what about the wealth of material which science has worked out, surely you wouldn't reject and lose all that?"

"Most certainly not. I should hope my boy would consult the books where all this accumulated wealth could be found. But I should hope that *he* would search and *he* would find and *he* would compare and *he* would think why, and in the end that *he* would make his own decision."

"Why do you wish these things?"

"For the reason named: I wish to educate the boy, and I believe that he will learn only as he practices. If he is to be an intelligent user of what science has to offer he must practice finding and adapting what science has to offer to his problem."

"You would use guidance?"

"Yes, just as we explained above. The teacher has authority, but he will try to help the boy to help himself."

"Then you object to the practice which some teachers of agriculture follow of furnishing the boy a detailed plan of how to conduct his home project work?"

"I most surely do."

"Are there no things which the boy should take over bodily from the expert?"

"There are in the aggregate many such, but when teaching is our object we must be on our guard not to hurt the boy by overstressing these."

"Are there other reasons for wishing the boy to make his own plan?"

"Yes; one such is that if he makes it he feels a different degree of responsibility for carrying it out."

"And that increases the whole-heartedness of his purpose."

"Yes, and this means a more definite set with more of appropriate readiness with consequently more of appropriate satisfaction and annoyance, and consequently better learning of all kinds, associate and concomitant as well as primary."

"You say then practically the same thing of all four steps — purposing, planning, executing, and judging. The more fully the child can and will take each step for himself the better, but if there is trouble the teacher is to step in to save the day?"

"Yes, that's what I think."

"When you say 'save the day' is it the success of the enterprise that concerns you?"

Teacher should help the child to help himself "Not primarily. It is the child that primarily concerns me. I do wish success, as we have said before, for the sake of the learner. Failure discourages and otherwise lessens the learning. Success encourages and otherwise improves the learning."

"And the teacher helps best by helping, if possible, the child to help himself?"

"Yes, always."

"I have somewhere heard the phrase 'complete act.' What does it mean?"

The complete act defined "A complete act is one where the learner himself takes each step in the process; he purposes, he plans, he executes, and he judges."

"Then there are all degrees of completeness to be found?"

"Yes."

"And in our ordinary schools few really complete acts?"

"Yes, either of child or of teacher. The teacher tells the child to do what some one has already set out for the teacher."

"You mean that teacher and child are both bound by a course of study?"

"Yes, by course of study and by examinations given from above."

"And you think this bad for both teacher and children?"

"It is at least unfortunate, though the matter is too complicated to admit of an answer in a few words."

"Your definition of a complete act seems to fit only individual enterprises. Can not a group enterprise be a complete act?"

"Certainly, if the group does as a group per- The group complete act form each step with reasonable whole-heartedness, jointly and singly, as the lawyers say, then I should say we have a joint or group complete act."

"You said we found few complete acts in the ordinary school. Where do we find them?"

"I should say they are far more frequently found out of school, in extra-curricular activities, on holidays and in vacation time. They are also being introduced increasingly into the school work of the more progressive type."

"You approve their introduction into school work?"

"I certainly do, just as fast as we feasibly can introduce them."

"Won't you summarize what we have covered this afternoon? I think I have the gist of the discussion, but I should like to know how you see it and say it in brief."

"We have been discussing purposeful activity in many of its varied aspects. Purposeful activity need not be primarily manual or motor. We value the Summary factor of purpose because it promises success, because it organizes the steps in the process or, perhaps better, into a process, and because it so utilizes set and readiness as to furnish the conditions most favorable to all kinds of learning. The four steps in a typical instance of purposeful activity are purposing, planning, executing, and judging. The last includes two kinds of judging, the *specific* as to the success of the result and the *generalizing* as to what general lessons have been learned. These steps mutually imply each other, but may in particular instances go on several at a time. For learning to go on best, the learner should himself take each step in the process. Where this takes place we have what is called a 'complete act.' If a child is about to fail with any step, the teacher may properly intervene to save from failure; for final failure may mean discouragement and lessened learning. But the teacher will help best by helping the child to help himself."

"In it all then you wish the child to carry as much as possible of the whole activity?"

"Yes; if we wish to educate the child, that is the best way."

REFERENCES FOR FURTHER READING

KILPATRICK—*The Project Method*, pp. 8–9, 17.
KILPATRICK—*Source Book in the Philosophy of Education*, No. 27, 265, 512, 513.

CHAPTER XIV

MEANING AND THINKING

"I am interested to see that each thing I pay attention to carries me forward or backward to something else. Is this always true?"

"I don't quite understand you."

"Why, this knife carries me back, or carries my mind back at any rate, to my uncle who gave it to me. This blade, which is dull from use, carries me on to the idea of sharpening it. These words on the blade carry me to Sheffield, England, where the knife was made. This chair I think of as being my father's. Those flowers, I know came from Aunt Sarah. Each thing I see seems to point to something else."

How each thing points elsewhere

"Isn't that merely another way of saying that each thing has meaning?"

"Does 'meaning' mean that one thing points essentially to something else to fill it out?"

"It would seem so."

Meaning

"Does each thing have one meaning or many?"

"Many, surely. This stick is bamboo; that means the far East. Shaped as it is, it means also a walking cane. It was a gift from my uncle in China; it means then his thoughtfulness."

Many meanings

"On one occasion it meant, too, a weapon of defense. You remember when the dog attacked you?"

"Yes, that's true."

"It does seem that each thing has or carries many meanings."

"You mean that each thing has many different connections or relations which give to it its meaning or meanings?"

"Something like that seems to be true."

"What then does 'meaning' mean?"

"That sounds like an odd combination of words. If you answer the question, are you not using in your definition the name of the thing to be defined? And is that good logic?"

What 'meaning' means

"It wouldn't trouble me, but suppose I change the question to this: What is the situation in which the word 'meaning' fits?"

"That almost makes it worse for me, but I should say that a meaning is present and is put to use when one thing makes you think of another."

"If I understand you, we have an instance of meaning whenever any one thing makes us look to or think about or expect something else, and the something else is almost, if not quite, a part of the thing. This chair makes me think of my grandfather who made it himself for his library. *This* makes me think *that*. *This* means *that*. This chair is what he made."

"In a case of meaning then there will always be found a *this* and a *that;* the *this* is first present to thought and the *that* then comes to mind; the *that* fills out or completes the *this*. Am I right?"

"Yes, that's the way I understand it."

"And any one thing may have many meanings?"

"Yes, depending on how much experience one has had of the thing or in connection with it."

"I don't quite understand."

"To the baby a milk bottle means food or, rather, taking this food; but to his mother it means food as nourishment for the baby, and the possibility of illness if the bottle has not been properly sterilized or the milk be not properly prepared. The milk, of course, comes from cows and must be properly certified. Certification means a careful examination by suitable authorities. To the baby few meanings, to the mother many, very many, each according to his or her experience."

Meanings come from experience

"Do meanings come then from experience?"

"Certainly."

"It reminds me of the S → R discussion. May we not say that the *this* is an S and that the meaning, the moving from the *this* to the *that*, is the R?"

Meanings and S → R

"That is exactly the way we must think of them, I believe."

"Then meanings are learned?"

"Exactly so. They have to be acquired through experience, and the laws of learning control here as elsewhere."

"Must they be consciously made?"

"Not necessarily with conscious intent, but the more we think about any experience the more meanings will probably come out of it."

"Do you say that a thing *has* meanings?"

"Do you mean to ask where the meanings reside — in the thing or in the person?"

"Yes."

"That's an old question. To many it has been a puzzle. But it seems to me that we have answered it. The S is the thing and the thought response (R) comes, if it comes at all, because an S → R bond has been built up and if the S sufficiently stimulates the bond to act."

A thing and its meanings

"Where do you say that meanings reside when they are not in use?"

"I think there are two answers; first and primarily, in the nervous system in the S → R bonds; second and secondarily, in the thing as a stimulus or symbol. Still more exactly, in the S → R relationship where the S has a bond or connection so built up as to bring the appropriate response as a meaning."

"Might the two ever get separated?"

"Something like this did happen with the Egyptian hieroglyphics. The symbols, the hieroglyphics, remained as cut on the temples and monuments of Egypt, but the knowledge of what they meant had been lost to all men and remained lost till the Rosetta stone was found and used."

"You people make me tired. What is the use of all this palaver about meanings? Why don't you come down to the solid ground and talk about things that are worth while? Why can't you use common sense? To you education seems to stretch out to include very far-away things. I can't understand you."

"Are meanings then of no use? Suppose by some mischance you were to lose your stock of meanings, how would you get on?"

"What do you mean?"

"I mean just what I say. What would you do? You couldn't talk, for language is but one lot of meanings. You couldn't eat, for you wouldn't know food from stones or clothing. You couldn't walk about; you wouldn't know a tree from a hole in the ground or a house from a paved sidewalk. Your thinking would reduce itself to practical zero; you'd have nothing to think with."

The use of meanings

"Would it be as bad as all that?"

"Yes. It is hardly too much to say that you and your world (that is, you as a thinking being and the world as

you use it, as it exists for you) consist of the meanings that
have been built up in you by all your varied experiences."

"And the child thus progressively builds himself and his
world?"

"In a very true sense this is a correct statement."

"And meanings are the stuff of which he builds both
himself and his world?"

"So far as he knows himself and his world **Meanings the**
and builds himself to act on this knowledge, **stuff of ideas**
yes. Meanings are the stuff of which one's thought world
is built, and they exist as the means of the conscious
control of self and the world."

"Wouldn't you say then that the educator should take
account of this fact?"   **Education**
"Indeed, yes. This is one of the reasons **and**
why education is changing so fundamentally **meanings**
nowadays, why we insist on actual experiences and are
no longer content with mere words descriptive of things.
Actual experiences build meanings."

"Doesn't experience also test meanings that have been
built?"

"Most certainly, but I included testing as part of the
process of building meanings. Actual experience is the
richest evoker or suggester of meanings and at the same
time the best and only final means of testing meanings."

"You think then that experience is better than education?"

"Who said anything like that? Why oppose experience
to education? Why not say that experience is the best
educator?"   **Experience**
"Then you don't believe in teachers or **and**
schools? Experience is sufficient?"   **education**

"Again I ask you who said anything like that? Why
oppose experience to teaching and schools? Why not say

that the best school is one that makes the best use of experience? And if you say 'yes' to this, then I'll say that a teacher is necessary to help pick the most educative experiences and to help steer each experience to its most fruitful outcomes."

"Where would the race experience come in?"

"I could almost say everywhere. You can't live here on this earth without living on, in, through, with, by, and from **Race expe-** the race experience. It is everywhere and all **rience and** pervasive. But, in addition, the intelligent **education** teacher will use the race experience as a basis for choosing among the possible experiences while also using it as a basis for steering any actual experience to its best outcomes."

"Do you mean to limit our children to what may be called first-hand experiences? Have you no place for vicarious experience?"

"You strike now, to my judgment, a more significant question. When it comes to the learning process our own **First-hand** first-hand experiences have a vividness and a **vs. second-** touch that the reported experiences of others **hand expe-** almost certainly lack. In this sense, experience **rience** is the best teacher. If vividness and definiteness of learning were the whole story, we might say that we should use only first-hand experiences. But there are other factors to be considered. First-hand experiencing may be very painful, for this reason too costly to use. We do not advise that a child learn by personal experience that a sharp knife can cut an artery, or that arsenic is a poison, or that a leap from the housetop would probably kill. Still again, to use only first-hand experiences is a long process. If we did not somehow shorten the process, each individual would have to start where the race began and there could be no progress in civilization. What combination then to make of first-hand

and second-hand experience depends on at least these three factors and how they interact in any given instance."

"I don't see the three factors. Which are they?"

"I mean vividness and definiteness of learning to be the first, cost in pain or sorrow the second, cost in time the third. The more first-hand experience the more vivid and definite the learning, but it is likely to be costly of time and pains."

"Would you not say that there is a sort of irreducible minimum of first-hand experience which is necessary if the second-hand experience is to be assimilated?"

"Yes, I should. If a child has never seen a zebra I can tell him that it looks like a striped mule, and if I take proper pains he will get some idea of a zebra. But if the child has never seen a mule and I have to tell him what a mule is like in terms of horse, then his notion of zebra is less definite. The further we get away from first-hand experience, the hazier our ideas are likely to be."

"So you would have early education take pains to provide a great variety of first-hand experiences?"

"Indeed I would, much concrete experiencing with things, leading on to more and more precise thinking about things."

"And what about the education of older children?"

"Always and everywhere there should be experiences that bring meanings, experiences so selected and so guided that the stock of meanings is continually en- Meanings riched and better organized. More and better and first-hand meanings, better and better organized." experience

"Could you define education in this way?"

"On its intellectual side, yes. What I just gave would be such a definition."

"What is the connection between meanings and thinking? Are they not closely related?"

"Yes, almost as closely as wings and flying."

"What do you mean?"

"I mean that meanings, when appropriately put into action, constitute thinking, just as wings appropriately at **Meaning** work constitute flying."

and "Meanings are the stuff we think with?"

thinking "That's another way of saying it."

"Would you say that meanings are structure and thinking is the functioning of structure?"

"I think that is just what we have been saying."

"What then is the essence of thinking?"

"For practical purposes thinking is a going from a *this* to a *that*. It is expecting something else from this **The essence** thing at hand. When I say, 'This cloud means **of thinking** rain; we had better hurry,' I am thinking. I am seeing this cloud, but I am going beyond the mere cloud. I am, from and because of the cloud, expecting rain."

"Then the practical essence of thinking is a look into the future?"

"Yes, an expectant look into the future."

"That is why some have called thinking an adventure?"

"Yes, in its practical essence thinking is an adventure into the unknown future."

"I can see the future about it — I mean the **Thinking an** element of futurity in it — but why say 'ad- **adventure** venture' and 'unknown'? I should think many meanings are so well known and fixed as to have lost any element of uncertainty they may once have had. This chair, for instance, is something to sit in; I have sat in it so often and so satisfactorily that I know pretty well what to expect. Where then is the adventure into the unknown?"

"We can well agree that there is a wide range in this matter of adventure, of certainty and uncertainty. Even your familiar chair may unexpectedly break down, or may conceal a pin that has somehow got hid in its cushions.

Suppose we think of a scale from a state of very great uncertainty (U) reaching up to a state of very reliable certainty (C). Any instance of thinking will belong

U   C

somewhere on this scale. We might say our wish is to move our thinking about any specific thing as far above U and as near toward C as we can."

"Would you say then that your thinking on that point has increased in reliability?"

"Certainly. It is now more to be relied upon." _{Reliability of thinking}

"If I understand you, the thinking you are talking about tells you what to expect as regards a certain matter?"

"Yes."

"And this expectation since it depends on human fallibility in a very complex world is more or less uncertain as to its outcome?"

"Yes."

"And for this reason thinking is to be counted as an adventure into the unknown?"

"Yes."

"Are there ways of increasing the general reliability of one's thinking?"

"To be sure there are."

"Are you not now assuming what has been called 'formal discipline'?"

"No, I think not; that is, not in any unwarranted sense. If a person forms such a habit as 'stopping to think,' which can be so formed as to hold in many more or less novel cases, his judgments are thereby carried up this scale of reliability. There are still other habits that may be formed for the examination of _{Increasing the reliability of thinking}

the situation, the collection of data, the testing of suggestions, and the like. All such tend to raise the reliability of
one's thinking."

"And you think that if these habits are formed one's
improvement in thinking will be equally good in every line
of thought?"

"I did not say so. One must form such habits in a limited
field of experience, since he is finite. The habits thus formed
will then carry over to other fields only as there are common
elements between the new and the old."

"And by 'carry over,' you mean that one will think to
use these thought habits in the new field?"

"That is mainly what I had in mind."

"But after one has become familiar with a field his
thinking in that field has on the whole increased in reliability?"

"Yes, he has accumulated the results of his past thinking
in that field. The bad thinking of the past has been in good
part eliminated; the good remains. His accumulations are
the thoughts that have stood the test of experience."

"Then you say we can improve the reliability of our
thinking partly by accumulating the tested results of past
thinking and partly by building good thought habits?"

"Yes, that's it."

"I once heard an interesting discussion on whether words
convey thought. What do you say? Do words convey
thought?"

Do words
convey
thought?
"I don't see anything debatable in that. Of
course words convey thought. Otherwise how
can I tell anybody anything?"

"That's just the question — how do you tell anybody
anything? Or perhaps better, what exactly does take place
when you tell a person something?"

"I still don't see the difficulty. I just tell him. That's

all I see to it. I convey my thought to him by the words I use. Where is the difficulty?"

"Let's try. Choose some color that you know and that I don't know. Then tell me what the color is so that I will know."

"All right. Will gamboge do? Do you know that?"

"No, you have made a good choice. Go ahead now and tell me."

"I'm not sure that I can make you get the exact shade I have in mind, but I'll try. Gamboge is a yellow verging on brown in deep masses."

"Now I think you have answered our question as to whether words convey thought. You say: 'I am not sure I can make you get the exact shade I have in mind.' And then you tell me about yellow and brown. Don't you see that you are using meanings that you and I have in common (yellow and brown) to try to make me think certain things that you think?"

"Yes, I see that, but that's just what I said. I just tell you. I convey my thought to you by my words."

"But that is just what you don't do. You didn't convey your thought of gamboge to me; you didn't even try. You went at the matter by a roundabout way. You *How words* talked of yellow and brown, trying to make me *stimulate* 'get it' you said. I repeat, you didn't convey *thought* your thought; you didn't try to. You tried to stir me to think something like your thought. You thought if you talked about yellow, I would think yellow. Then if you said 'verging on brown,' you thought that my thought would move out in the direction of gamboge."

"You're quibbling now."

"Indeed, I am not. I think a most helpful notion of style, whether oral or written, and an excellent lesson in punctuation will come out of the distinction I am making."

"Well, I don't follow you. Won't you try again?"

"With pleasure. Suppose I have a long fishing pole and I see a frog not far away. I think he is of the kind that can make a long leap. I wish to see him do this. How can I convey my thought to him that I wish him to leap?"

"Nonsense. You don't try to convey your thought to him. You don't even wish to convey any thought to him. You take your long pole and stir him to action. You poke him. He leaps. It is an S → R bond affair. You stimulate him. He leaps. Why does he leap? Because he has by nature the right S → R bonds. That's all. But it's different with the gamboge."

Stirring
a frog
to action

"Is it different? On the contrary, isn't it exactly the same thing. Let's illustrate with a speaker. He wishes his audience to think and feel certain things. He chooses his words, his intonation, his gestures, all as stimuli to stir his auditors to think certain thoughts and feel certain emotions. While he is doing this he may be thinking that the room is hot, that the crowd at the door is noisy and may hinder his efforts, that his auditors are not yet ready for his full thought and must be prepared, that they are now a little sleepy and had better be stirred by an amusing story. Does he really try to *convey* his thought?"

"You mean to ask whether *convey* is a good word to describe what he does or rather what he tries to do."

"Exactly so, and I think it isn't. In a sense he may be said to convey his thought; but psychologically, no, he *stirs* thought. He uses symbols to rouse meanings."

We stir to
thought, not
convey
thought

"And both must know the same symbols and they must be joined with like meanings?"

"Yes, that's it. That's what language is."

"But the speaker uses more than words — he shrugs his shoulder, he frowns, he sneers. These, too, are symbols and have meanings."

"Quite right, and they are language too of a kind. At any rate they all illustrate my point that, psychologically, we do not directly *convey* thought. We stir it. We stimulate it. We use S's that are connected with like R's in both speaker and hearer. We speak the S's, the hearer makes — more or less accurately — the R's that we hoped for."

"How about that punctuation lesson you promised?"

"It is the same. I don't punctuate — or I shouldn't — merely to use, repeat, illustrate some rules on punctuation. Some people do; they are mere pedants. I *Punctuation* say to myself, 'I wish my readers to think *to guide* thus and so. If I use a comma here will they *thought* more likely think this or not?' I punctuate then pragmatically, to affect my readers and to effect in them certain desired thoughts, to make them think the things I wish."

"And that gives you a practical criterion with which to judge the success of your punctuation?"

"Exactly, yes. I like the phrase, 'success of my punctuation.' You have got my idea. A pedant seeks criteria to judge of the 'correctness' of his punctuation, and he means by correctness mere conformity with established rules."

"And you think your notion here will help one to punctuate more successfully?"

"Indeed, I do think so. It will help the individual as matters now stand and, still more, will gradually help the literary world to reduce the number of senseless conventions in this field."

"And what about style? You said, if I understand, that your idea of stirring, not conveying, thought *Successful* would help the writer or speaker." *style is*

"Yes, and I repeat it. If I, as writer, under- *successful* stand fully that I am trying to stimulate people *stirring* to think, I have a real criterion with which to judge of my own success."

"Some people have cynically said that words are to conceal thought. Does that come in here?"

"I think it does. If I believe that I can directly convey my thought, it will be easier for me to be content if I can see my thought in my words. In such case my words will probably conceal my thought. But if I have to consider the other person and the effect of my words on him, I shall not be content that my thought lies concealed in my words. I shall ask myself very explicitly what thoughts my words are likely to call forth in my readers or hearers, and I shall keep experimenting till I can make words stir the exact thoughts I wish."

"It has been an unusual discussion we have had; I should like to hear it summed up."

"As I see it, we have discussed two main things, meanings and thinking. Meaning we found to consist in the fact that a *this*, present to thought or sense, suggests or points to a *that* as filling out or completing the *this*. Thinking we saw is exactly the name we give to the movement from the *this* to the *that*. That is, thinking is a meaning appropriately at work. From this relationship we saw that education is greatly concerned with having children get many and exact meanings as the basis for thinking. We saw too that practical thinking is essentially a foretelling of what to anticipate or expect when one faces a situation. In this sense, thinking is to be considered as an adventure into the unknown future. From this fact, education gets a principal task of increasing the reliability of thinking—in general by developing certain rules to guide the process, and more specifically by accumulating in any field the successful thoughts pertaining to that field.

Summary

"An interesting application of this conception of meanings and thinking was that words do not, psychologically, convey thought, but at best act as symbols to arouse in the hearer or reader the thought desired by the speaker or writer. This conception gave a practical criterion for punctuation and for speaking and writing: How shall I so say this as to stir the precise thought I wish?"

"I am coming to see that there is more in the work of education than I had thought."

"So am I, and I am glad."

REFERENCES FOR FURTHER READING

DEWEY — *How We Think*, pp. 6f., 26ff., 30ff., 39ff., 63ff., 116ff., 125ff., 129ff.

DEWEY — *Democracy and Education*, Ch. 12.

KILPATRICK — *Source Book in the Philosophy of Education*, No. 29, 531, 532.

CHAPTER XV

THE COMPLETE ACT OF THOUGHT

"Do you recall what we agreed upon last time as the essence of thinking?"

"Yes, it was the movement of attention from **The essence** something at hand to what it means." **of thinking** "Before you begin on that, I wish to ask as to what is meant by the word 'essence' as you use it here."

"Essence is an old word, not so often used now as formerly. As here used, it means thinking stripped, as it were, of all surplusage, thinking reduced to its lowest terms, so low that it would not be thinking if it were carried any lower."

"As I recall we discussed the essence of practical thinking, but not of thinking in itself."

"Yes, because thinking is used in a number of senses I thought if we said 'practical thinking' we should be less likely to go astray."

"And what was that essence? I wasn't here when you talked about it."

"The essence of practical thinking we found to be the movement of attention from any given situation to what to expect from it, or expect to do about it. The **Thinking an** baby is crying; I think he is cold and needs to **adventure** **into the** be covered up. Such thinking looks essentially **unknown** to the future and involves an adventure into the unknown."

"I don't quite see."

"The baby is crying. This is an event in a situation. I face it and think: He is cold and needs to be better covered.

232

Whether he is cold and whether covering him more warmly will accordingly meet the situation involve for me essentially a leap into the dark, not total darkness to be sure, for I know somewhat of babies and their cries, but it is still a venture, a surmise, an hypothesis. I test my hypothesis, my surmise, my mental leap, by trying it out, acting it out, acting upon its consequences: If the baby is cold, covering him will probably meet the situation."

"I am a bit troubled. You say 'future' and yet say '*is* cold.' The future is clearest when you set out to try the idea of covering the baby. This seems, too, more clearly or more surely an adventure."

"Our words nearly always join us to the past and its ways of thinking. '*Is* cold' is perhaps an instance. I myself like to think of the whole incident as involving for action the future element, and this you have well brought out."

"Is this another reason why you said 'essence of practical thinking'?"

"Yes, I had in mind the kind of thinking that takes place typically in action in connection with practical events. Take this baby. Probably the deepest reason why you say '*is* cold,' is because that is your first step in clearing up the situation and deciding what to do about it. The whole thing looks to doing something about the crying. That crying indicates a situation to be remedied. We must do something. Now the whole thinking process involved is one of wisely meeting the situation. The doing, what we are to do, necessarily lies in the future. And we don't know whether we shall succeed; it is an adventure into the unknown future."

"Are you not discussing what Dewey calls the 'Complete Act of Thought'?"[1]

"Yes, exactly that."

[1] *How We Think*, Ch. 6.

"I have heard a good deal about the complete act of thought. Just why is it important?"

"It happens to have been one of the most influential conceptions given to the educational world in the past few decades. It has been gradually remaking American teaching ever since."

"Might we not study it? I tried once, but somehow the class never got anywhere. I know it is important, but I never felt that I had reached the bottom of it."

"Yes, do; let's study it."

"I shall be very glad for us to discuss it, but it will take close attention if we are to get out of it what is in it."

" 'We are game; let's go to it,' as the boys say."

"First let us be clear that we are discussing not just any or all thinking, but the *complete* act of thought."

The complete act of thought

"Does that mean a very complicated instance of thinking?"

"Not necessarily complicated, but one exhibiting all the steps necessary for completeness. A simple instance might suffice. What the necessary steps are we shall see as we go."

"Won't you give us a preliminary notion?"

"Willingly. Keep in mind two things. First, practical thinking means following along a practical meaning; this

Thinking a forecast

thing which is now happening tells us something else to expect next. This dark cloud now lowering makes us expect that rain will soon follow."

"But may we not be mistaken? Will the rain certainly come?"

"Certainly, we may be mistaken. That's why we say that thinking is an adventure, that it involves a leap into the dark, a surmise as to the future, an hypothesis as to what will happen."

"You said there are two things to keep in mind. What is the other one?"

"The second grows out of the uncertainty. Since we must leap, the second tells us to make the leap as reliable and trustworthy as possible." Reliable thinking

"Why?"

"Why? On account both of the present situation and of the future. We wish to do the wise and right thing now: If it is going to rain we wish to go to the house; if it is not going to rain we wish to continue our walk. So much for the present, but we are also concerned about the future. If we can use this present instance to help us hereafter to fore-tell more accurately which clouds do mean rain and which do not, then on future occasions we shall more surely know what to do. For the sake of the present we wish to judge as carefully now as we can, using all pertinent past experience to help us. For the sake of the future we wish to test our present judgment that we may know wherein it was justified and wherein not, so as hereafter to judge better in the light of present experience."

"You have said so much I am a bit confused."

"You asked about the complete act of thought. Just plain thinking tells us what to expect next. The complete act of thinking is to make surer of our thought by taking the steps necessary to give greater reliability."

"What are these steps?"

"Let us consider each step one at a time. What is the situation calling forth the thought? The baby cries; we must do something; we don't know what to do. The situation Or more generally: A situation calls to action, calling for but we have no response ready; we must act, thought but we do not know what to do. Two things I should like here to emphasize, the call or drive to action, and the lack of a suitable response certainly appropriate."

"Is this lack what Dewey calls the difficulty and is that the cause of the thinking?"

The difficulty does not impel   "This lack is what Dewey calls the difficulty, but let us be clear, the difficulty does not impel us to action."

"But it does impel us to think, doesn't it."

"I cannot agree with you. A difficulty as such does not impel. The drive to thought comes from the drive to action. We think because that is the only way, seeing that we face a difficulty, in which to secure action. I should say the difficulty, the lack of the behavior pattern, is the occasion but not the cause of the thinking. The thinking comes because the organism still struggles to continue the action."

"Do you call this one step or two?"

"I like to say that these constitute the first two steps: First is the drive to action; second is the presence of a difficulty, the lack of an appropriate response or lack of appropriate behavior-pattern."

"What is the third step?"

"To answer this, ask what the mother will do when the baby cries. She will notice the kind of cry and consider the situation so as to see what is probably causing the cry and this in order that she better may know what to do. More generally: The third step is an examination of the situation to narrow the task for thought, to locate and define the problem, so as to facilitate the arising of appropriate suggestions for solving the problem."

Examining the situation

"This step will sometimes take a long time, won't it?"

"At times, yes; at other times a moment or two may suffice. There is every gradation."

"And is the fourth step the arising of suggestions for a solution?"

"Yes, exactly that; in theoretical terms, the arising of hypotheses; in practical terms, the coming of suggested behavior-patterns.   Psychologically and logically, they are both the same." Suggested solutions

"And what step is the testing?"

"Testing gives us two steps: fifth, elaborating the implications of the hypothesis; and sixth, trying out by actual test one or more of the implications."

"You are wading in deep water now. I am lost completely. I don't believe I do anything like your fifth and sixth steps when I think; John Dewey may, but not I."

"Oh, yes, you do. Consider this mother. She is, let us say, not sure whether the baby cries because he is cold or because he has colic. She listens intently to the Elaborating kind of crying and notices the baby's move- the ments; she concludes tentatively that he is cold. implication This listening and noticing make up step 3, the tentative conclusion that he is cold is step 4. Now she says to herself: 'I'll see; if he is merely cold, more cover better tucked in should warm him in a few minutes.' This thinking *if* etc., *then* etc., is putting the tentative conclusion to work as an hypothesis; and this is what we called 'elaborating the implications of the hypothesis.' If the baby is cold, covering him more warmly is the practical implication."

"You mean that you take the hypothesis or suggested solution and ask what it tells you to do or to expect. This is what you mean by 'elaborating the implications,' is it not?"

"Exactly so."

"And then step 6 is testing to see if what you are told to do or to expect, is really the right thing?"

"Precisely."

"And how do you test?"

"If the implications tell you something to do, you do it and see if the trouble is relieved. If the implications tell Testing is   you something to expect, you look for an in-
trying out the stance and note what happens. If what was
implications foretold does happen, then it looks as if the hypothesis is correct."

"Can you illustrate the latter?"

"Yes. Before the planet Neptune had been seen, it was noticed that the outermost planet Uranus (outermost so far as then known) was leaving its (supposedly) proper orbit. What could be the cause? (Step 2 of the thinking process.) Closer examination (step 3) confirmed the general fact and gave details. Thereupon certain astronomers formed the hypothesis (step 4) that there was another planet further out from the sun than Uranus which was deflecting Uranus from its otherwise proper path. They then calculated where such a planet would have to be (step 5) thus to pull Uranus out of its path. If the calculations were right, they would know where to look for the new planet. They did look (step 6) and sure enough the new planet was found and later called Neptune. Later careful calculations of both planets (steps 5 and 6 repeated) have confirmed the conclusion thus reached. The difficulty of the wandering of Uranus is explained. The once hypothetical planet is now a known fact (Neptune)."

"Suppose covering the baby more warmly does not stop his crying?"

"Then the mother may take up the colic hypothesis (step 4), make some deductions from it (step 5), try these out (step 6), and observe the results. If the baby then stops crying (and didn't stop for the warm covering), presumably it was colic and not the cold that was troubling him."

"Do you think the mother of a crying baby is going to be concerned to follow these steps? I don't believe it. I think she will do just what mothers have always done, try first one thing and then another till she finds something to stop the crying."

"There are several things to be said in reply. Incomplete thinking First, I seem to think more highly of mothers than you. Most of the mothers I know do think whenever and wherever baby is involved, and more in these days than ever before. Second, I have nowhere said when anyone will think or that anyone *will* think. All I have said is that if one does think sufficiently his (or her) thinking will show essentially these steps."

"Do you mean that the steps must always follow each other in this order?"

"No, I do not so think. Dewey himself explains that he does not mean us to understand a chronological order."[1]

"What I think happens is this. If the baby Steps logical, not chronological cries a little, the mother will 'guess' that he is cold and call to his older sister to see that he is properly covered. If no more crying, well and good; no further thought is given to the matter, and we cannot say that there had been a complete act of thought. If, however, crying continues, more careful thought is given till the household has exhausted its resources. This may well have included all the steps of a complete act of thought. If still no solution and the baby still cries, then the physician is called in and he repeats the steps on a more professional scale. If still there is no satisfactory solution, higher experts may be called in and the process carried out with all the refinements known to science."

---

[1] "In speaking of 'steps' it is perhaps natural to suppose that something chronological is intended, and from that it is presumably a natural conclusion that the steps are taken in a temporal sequence in the order taken above. Nothing of this sort, however, is intended. The analysis is formal, and indicates the logical 'movements' involved in an act of critical thought." *Journal of Philosophy*, 19:29.

"And you think it is essentially the same process repeated over and over again?"

"Yes, with ever increasing consciousness. At the first, there is so little conscious thought that the steps are aborted and run, as it were, together. With increasing conscious consideration the steps emerge with increasing definiteness."

"I heard an old farmer say, 'It can't be a coon, for those are not coon tracks.' What step was he using?"

"Clearly steps 5 and 6 'telescoped' together, thus rejecting the hypothesis (step 4) that it was a coon which had committed, I suppose, some depredation."

"And you think if we look closely we can see in any thinking worthy the name these six steps?"

"Yes, that's what I think."

"One thing troubles me about the mother and the crying baby. I agreed that the difficulty was practical, namely, what to do, but I thought the problem would be not what *is* the matter with the baby, but what to do when a baby is cold or has the colic. You seemed to assume that the mother knows what to do if only she knows what the trouble is."

"I quite see your difficulty. I did assume that the mother knew what to do if the baby were merely cold. Under other circumstances the problem might, as you suggest, be elsewhere or it might even lie in both places. In the last instance I should prefer to say that one practical situation involves two problems, first, what is wrong, second, how shall we remedy such a wrong. Each problem would then repeat the same six steps."

"I notice you were careful earlier not to say that the solution was proved to be correct. You qualified your statement each time—'it looks as if,' 'it might be presumed.' Was this intentional?"

Difficulty of final proof

"Yes. Final and complete proof may be a very difficult thing. It is wiser to be cautious."

"I don't see it that way. If the solution works, doesn't that prove it? What more do you wish?"

"It often happens that two or more hypotheses will work equally well in a great number of specific instances. For a long time the hypothesis that dew falls from the sky was accepted as true. It seemed to work: dew is not found under trees or other cover, nor on cloudy nights. But after a while instances were found where this hypothesis would not work and eventually a different hypothesis was formed that so far explains all the present known facts."

"I notice even here you are cautious. You say 'so far explains' and the 'present known facts.'"

"You are right. One should be cautious. The future may at any time upset our present thinking."

"You said earlier that this Dewey analysis had greatly influenced American teaching. I do not care to dispute your statement, but I fail to see in what has been so far said any good reason for expecting so far-reaching a result. Won't you explain?"

Influence of the Dewey analysis

"Do you know that some years ago most normal schools followed the Herbartian Five Formal Steps in their teaching methods?"

"Yes."

"And do you know that these are giving way and largely to teaching through problems?"

"I have noticed something like that."

"I think the more you notice the more you'll agree. Well, I am myself in no doubt that much of this change is due to this analysis and its allied theory."

"You give it credit for the problem method of teaching. Do you think it deserves similar credit for what I hear called the 'project method' of teaching?"

"Yes, it and its allied philosophy."

"I still don't quite see why teaching should be so much

concerned. Won t you explain? Why is a problem better
than the five formal steps?"

"In order to answer suppose we list the separate steps
in the complete act of thought and see how
learning is fostered by using them.

The steps in the complete act of thought

1. A situation arouses an impulse or tendency
to pursue a certain course of action.

The baby's crying stirs the mother to seek to relieve him.
Unexpected movements in Uranus stir the astronomer to
try to explain these movements.

2. A difficulty appears: how to continue the given course
is not known; there is no appropriate way of responding
known or immediately available.

The mother does not know what to do for the baby. The
astronomer has no satisfactory explanation for the movements of Uranus.

3. An examination of the situation is made to locate and
define the difficulty more precisely.

The mother listens to the baby and considers his movements. The astronomers measure carefully the deviation of
Uranus from what had been expected and consider all
possible interfering causes. Each is meanwhile considering
all the facts with reference to possible solutions.

4. Suggested solutions arise: hypotheses are formed,
behavior patterns are suggested.

The baby is cold or perhaps has colic. Uranus is attracted by some hitherto unknown planet yet more distant
from the sun.

5. Implications (one or more) are drawn from each suggested solution, each hypothesis.

If the baby is cold, covering him more warmly will relieve
his discomfort. If a planet is attracting Uranus, we should
see it in such and such part of the sky.

6. Actual trial is made to see whether the deduced implications hold.

> Does the baby stop crying when covered? Do we find the new planet where we were told to look, and is it such as to explain the aberrations of Uranus?

7. A solution is accepted in the light of the tests made.

Of course there is no problem till the second step leads on toward the third, but let us ask how the problem guides the process after that. In step 3 the problem as a conscious formulation is emerging into definiteness, but even so the presence of the felt difficulty thus seeking to define itself more narrowly guides the thought process. The mother's anxiety (felt difficulty as to what may be the trouble and what she should do) causes her to consider all the signs of discomfort shown by the baby and to bring to bear all she knows about such. The search to define the problem and the accompanying preliminary search for possible solutions each goes on in the light of the problem as thus far seen. Data are sorted out, the more promising from the less, and the more promising are given further consideration. All of this means that the whole situation is considered in the light of its bearing on the problem. Consciously to reject any data as not pertinent means a relating (in a negative sense) of these data. Consciously to accept any data as pertinent is to organize all such about the problem."

How the problem guides the thought process

"If I understood you then in the third step the problem actually guides the examination and organizes the whole situation in its varying relationship to the problem and probable solution. Am I right?"

"Yes, that is the way I see it."

"Couldn't you illustrate with a school problem or something more nearly like it?"

"Suppose the question is as to why New York, which
was once smaller than Philadelphia, won its preëminence
among American cities. A class studying this
would have, as step 3, a study of the facts
as to when and how Philadelphia was once
ahead of New York and the facts as to wherein New York
is ahead now and when this came about. While this
definition of the problem was in process there would be a
preliminary study to see what explanations for the change
of status should be considered. This one step 3 would thus
involve a close study and evaluation (from the point of view
of pertinency) of a vast deal of information. Much would
be lightly dismissed as not pertinent to the problem, but
much would be considered as highly significant. A very
considerable organization of data would certainly result just
here, and all by reason of felt relationship to the problem.
The problem is here the guiding and organizing feature."

Illustration from geography

"Yes, I see now, but how about the other steps?"

"Step 4, the arising of suggested solutions, shows a similar
influence of the problem. Any solution to be considered at
all must be a way of looking at pertinent data that promises
to remove the difficulty. The arising of a suggested solution
is then a promising arrangement of data. In the Philadel-
phia-New York problem, if one suggests that New York has
a better harbor, we have at once a relating of harbor to
commerce and this to city size and importance. If the
Erie canal is suggested, at once comes a relating of East
and West, with the mountains as a trade barrier and the
Erie canal as one way of getting around the barrier, with
consequent effect on the commerce of New York. In a
word, any suggested solution worth considering does involve more or less of the data pertinent to the problem
and an arrangement of these that at least promises to
solve the problem."

"It seems then that again the problem acts to select pertinent data and to organize such into some connected point of view."

"Yes, the problem again selects and organizes. Thinking is thereby directed along both these lines." *Again the problem selects and organizes*

"And does the same hold of steps 5 and 6?"

"Yes, in much the same way. The elaboration of implications (step 5), the opening up of the content of the hypothesis, is to get implications pertinent to the solution of the problem. And the testing of these (step 6) is again as they bear upon the solution of the problem."

"It is interesting to see that in each step the problem selects and organizes."

"What organization results from the whole process?"

"First of all, the accepted solution is an organization of all the facts and features recognized as pertinent in the situation, such a way of looking at all these as takes due account of all the pros and cons in the case. When we are justly satisfied that *The resulting organization of experience* we know why New York outgrew Philadelphia, we have a great deal of data, historical, geographic, and economic, reduced to an orderly arrangement of cause and effect. Second, if the search for a satisfactory solution has led to the rejection of any unsatisfactory hypotheses, then each of these makes its contribution of organization, because we see why it was rejected and thus see more clearly wherein lies the satisfactoriness of the accepted solution. Third, the search to define the problem, the search for possible hypotheses, the elaboration of the implications of the various hypotheses, and the testing of these by actual trial — all these cause a conscious and critical survey of the field in which the problem is located. In this third kind of organization, negative conclusions (that thus and so does not bear on the problem) will be as true an organization of data and perhaps prove as valuable elsewhere as would positive conclusions. All that is necessary to give valuable organization is that the conclusion be as consciously made as possible."

"You spoke earlier of the drive or tendency to pursue the matter at hand. Does much turn on this?"

"Indeed it does. The greater the zeal, the more interest will there be in finding a satisfactory solution, the greater will be the readiness in pertinent neurones; and so the greater will be the effort, the readier will thoughts come, the more will satisfaction result from successful connections made, the greater will be the annoyance when promising leads disappoint. In a word, the laws of set and readiness are the better called into play by the zeal to push on with the matter at hand. And then will satisfaction and annoyance work favorably to the matter at hand. What is done will be better done and better remembered."

"I have heard the question asked as to whose problem is contemplated in problem solving, the pupil's or the teacher's? Whose problem is contemplated and what difference does it make?"

"I should think our previous discussions would answer that."

"You mean that it is from the pupil's action that the pupil learns. Therefore it is the pupil's problem that we wish?"

"Exactly so. The more fully the pupil feels the problem and determines to solve it, the more fully do set and readiness, satisfaction and annoyance, help him to succeed and help him to learn from what he does."

"It seems to me that everything we said about mind-set and learning fits here."

"It does, exactly."

Strength of interest

Whose problem, the teacher's or the pupil's?

"And everything about 'complete acts' and purposeful activity."

"You are exactly right. Those discussions throw light here, and our recent discussions of meaning, thinking, and problem solving throw still further light."

"In the 'complete act,' we discussed how it might be hurtful for the parent or teacher to take unnecessarily one of the steps for the child. Would not the same thing hold here?"

The child should himself take the steps

"Precisely, and our conclusion there fits here. As far as feasible the child should consciously take each step himself, but the teacher may step in to save from defeat. In such a case he helps best by helping the child to help himself."

"You have spoken as if there are only individual problems. Might there not be group problems?"

"Indeed, yes. I should, in fact, hope that a good part of the day's work of all the children above the very young would consist of group problems."

Group problems

"Would it not be well to divide a big problem into smaller parts and let a small group work on one of the component parts?"

"I think so, but let them report to the whole group in order that as far as feasible each individual shall in the end at least have thought through the whole work."

"Do you think geography can be taught wholly by problems?"

"Probably so, by problems and purposeful enterprises, but I question whether we shall always wish to teach by cutting out separate pieces of life and considering them separately as distinct subjects. I think that as life seldom if ever presents geography by itself, perhaps it should accordingly not be taught by itself."

Teaching subjects by problems

"Do you think we have time to go into that now?"

"I do not, but we must return to it after a while."

"How would you sum up what we have considered to-day? I am afraid I may lose some part of it if we leave it like this."

Summary "We have been discussing the complete act of thought. Ordinary practical thinking consists essentially of inferring from the situation at hand an expectation of what it means. We can do this only because of the **The complete act of thought** meanings we have previously formed of the like things. Such thinking involves a step into the future and accordingly is liable to error. The complete act of thought is the full logical process by which one takes pains to make his thought reliable. Such an act of thought typically arises when a tendency to action has been hindered because no customary or tested meaning or procedure is available. The thinking is thus the effort to find a satisfactory meaning or plan of action. The measures for increasing reliability involve first the effort to get the best possible suggestions as to the needed meaning or plan of action and second the effort to test the suggestions thus made. To get the most promising suggestions we examine carefully the situation of difficulty to locate the problem more precisely if that be possible and to arouse promising suggestions. To test a suggested solution (hypothesis) we first ask what would follow if it should be accepted, and second we put the matter to a trial to see whether the predicted does follow. If the predicted does follow from one hypothesis and so far **The greater care in thinking, the clearer the steps** as known from no other, we accept that hypothesis as the best available.

"While these logical steps are to be seen in the degree that care in thinking is present it does not follow that they always appear with separate distinctness or in the order given. And if a given situation of difficulty does not yield to the first informal efforts at solution, we shall frequently find repeated efforts made, increasing in conscious formality as the matter involved seems to warrant the more careful procedure.

"We found the use of problem work increasing in educational procedure, partly because it utilizes better the conditions favorable to learning, partly because it better serves to organize for the learner the field of attention. A favorable set and readiness may be expected from the initial impulse, and this, by well known psychological principles, is likely to be enhanced by the thwarting which sets the problem. Besides both these, a problem itself has a challenge which arouses the alert mind to a peculiar endeavor. From these three factors distinctly favorable conditions for learning are more than likely.

Value of problem solving

"As regards organization, we saw that the urge and the definiteness of the problem guides thinking first to the selection and evaluation of pertinent data and second to the consequent joining of meanings in such a related and evaluated way as to result not only in the definite organization constituting the solution, but also in a valuable mapping of the whole situation studied. The respective satisfaction and annoyance at accepted and rejected relationships, felt according to the degree of interest present, tends to fix these organizations in mind, while the fact that they were made in answer to practical thinking gives them the greater probability of practical application when related demands shall later arise."

"Do you not reckon thought as man's strongest instrumentality of control?"

"I certainly do."

Conclusion

"Do you know any better way to increase one's effectiveness of thinking than by facing and solving many and varied problems felt by the learner to be vital to him?"

"I know of no better way, nor any other that equals it."
"Is that in essence what we have been discussing?"
"As I see it, yes."

REFERENCES FOR FURTHER READING

DEWEY — *How We Think*, Chap. 6.
KILPATRICK — *Source Book in the Philosophy of Education*, No. 27, 529.

CHAPTER XVI

WHY EDUCATION IS CHANGING

"Am I wrong in thinking that education is changing now more rapidly than ever before?"

"So far as I can tell, you are right, not wrong."

"Do you think the sober historian will bear us out?"

"I do. I believe I could quote authorities *Changes to* if there were need." *be seen in education*

"How is education changing? I see larger enrollments and larger and finer buildings, but I am not sure that I see better teaching than formerly."

"According to our best information, we teach better to-day than they taught seventy-five years ago, provided we still believe in teaching the same things."

"Have there not then been changes in the curriculum?"

"Yes, great changes; not so much perhaps in the names of the subjects taught as in the content of what is taught."

"Do you mean that geography now is not *The curric-* the same as geography then?" *ulum is changing*

"That's just what I mean. Practically all the subjects are greatly changed in content."

"Even arithmetic?"

"Yes, it has changed greatly, and ought to change more."

"Why has the content of the school subjects changed?"

"For various causes. Speaking generally, because the present civilization demands a richer content, but an additional reason is that we are studying the question with increasing knowledge and with less respect for mere tradition."

"Do you think that content has changed any more than aim or method? It seems to me that the intelligent teacher of to-day has very different aims from those held by our predecessors, and consequently uses a different conception of method."

"How do aims differ? I teach algebra and geometry, and I am not aware of any specially different aims from what my teachers had."

"It seems true that certain departmental teachers are less likely to feel the changes than others. This is more likely to be true where, as in geometry, the content doesn't change much with the times."

"How are aims different? I repeat my question. I did not hear a real answer."

"I think in those older days teachers didn't so much ask what they were aiming at beyond the textbooks — and these were pretty well fixed by tradition. If the children could recite the content of the textbook even by mere rote memory, and if they kept quiet and were otherwise 'good,' the teachers felt that they had done their duty. Nowadays many intelligent teachers are very much concerned with public questions, with social trends; and they are asking how they can best teach the children in the light of pressing public demands."

"Do you mean by 'public questions' such matters as an immigration policy, the relations of capital and labor, or the tariff?"

"Those are some of the things I had in mind."

"But surely you don't think it is the duty of the school to deal with such controversial matters. Think what trouble we should bring down on us if we attempted to teach children the answers to such questions."

"Teach answers to these questions, no; but to introduce the older children to such questions, make them intelligent with regard to them, get them to feel more keenly what is involved, yes."

"You said a moment ago 'teach children'; I wonder if the difference between the old and new is not pretty well indicated by the contrasted phrases, 'teach Teaching subjects,' 'teach children.' What say you?" children,

"I think the contrast has a significant lesson not subjects for us, but of course we don't teach unless children learn. So teaching children must mean that they learn something. But I quite agree with you that we are properly concerned first with our children that they shall grow, and only second-arily with subject-matter that it be learned. The older view seems to reverse this order."

"And you think that the better education of to-day differs from the best of the past in aim, in content, and in method, all three?"

"I do. I certainly do so think, and furthermore I believe the difference is of very great significance to us."

"Why should there be such a difference? What has brought it about?"

"You are asking a big question. I hesitate to go into it."

"I wish you would. I have heard many express a wish that we might discuss it. What do you think is the main thing that has made the change?" What has

'Science.' brought these

"You surprise me. I thought you would changes have said industry or our many inventions and discoveries."

"I think science lies at the bottom of our discoveries and our inventions; without it they would not have Science, been; and our discoveries and inventions in discovery and turn underlie the changes in modern industry. inventions You have only to mention steam, electricity, and chemistry to see more fully what I mean."

"And all these inventions and their applications change life and the conditions of life?"

"Exactly so; and the change is seen to be the greater when we remember that this country is as yet new, that but recently it was rural, agricultural, even pioneer."

"I see well enough these changes in life; even in my lifetime they have been many; but I don't see the bearings of all this on education and schools. What difference does it make to them?"

"Much in every way."

"How? Be specific."

"Consider first that the child is educated by the home, the church, the community, the larger world without, as truly as by the school. In fact when you take all into account, the 'little red schoolhouse' played a much smaller part in the total education of our forebears than many seem to think."

The school not the only educative agency

"How so?"

"Because most of the population went to school only a few months in the year and for not many years. Many pioneer men and women had even less than this meager schooling."

"Yes, and they had correspondingly little education. They were a crude lot, let me tell you."

"Crude seems a needlessly harsh word. For one thing, they had character — stronger, some people think, than that of their less crude descendants. They conquered the wilderness, and that took not only bravery but resourcefulness. Life for them was hard, but it was hearty and vigorous.

Frontier education

"I should like, too, to deny that they lacked education. Abraham Lincoln was one of them — one of the crude ones if you wish — but he had an education far and away better than most have who now live so much more easily."

"Well, Lincoln was an exception, and he did have access to some of the best English literature. I suppose we may account for his wonderful literary style by his close study of a few great classics."

"Lincoln's style is far from constituting him or his character. I was thinking of much more than that. I should think of Lincoln as well educated even if he had not left us the Gettysburg speech or the Second Inaugural Address." *Lincoln as an example*

"Do you mean that Lincoln had a great heart and a great character?"

"Yes, I mean all that and more. He was not educated in the sense of having acquired the conventional signs of a cultivated and refined life. But he knew life, he knew people, he knew the big issues of his time, he had thought himself through to firm convictions. Moreover he had built strong interests in the things that count — his heart was right. And not only these things, he was capable also — he knew how to bring things to pass. In a word he seems to me to have made of himself the character needed by his times. However great the demands, he rose to meet them."

"Is that what you mean by education?"

"Yes, so far as these things can be acquired. Education means nothing less than all this; and Lincoln had it all."

"But we seem to have got off the track. We were asking whether our forebears were educated."

"So we were, and Lincoln was brought in to show the possibilities of that older education. As schooling, it was at best slight, generally much worse than that; but the life itself educated."

"Do you think the life of that day educated those children any better than the life of the present day educates our children? People laugh at moving pictures, but the 'movies' are a liberal education in themselves. And there is, besides, the radio and all the other modern inventions."

"Time for time, demand for demand, they did better then than do we."

"How so? I don't get your meaning."

"The demands now are greater than the demands then. Life is now vastly more complex in detail, and we are far more tied up with others about us even to our most distant neighbors. Our problems are much more difficult."

Frontier life as an educational agency

"I suppose our times are more difficult; I think you are right there; but our schools are much better. Why say the education of that day was in comparison better? Or did you mean to say that?"

"Yes, I meant just that. I'll put it this way. The demands now are relatively greater, and the opportunities for learning now relatively less. Education suffers accordingly."

"The greater demands of the present I've seen and admitted, but the greater relative opportunities of the past I don't see."

"In that day the home and the immediate community made up almost the whole of life. Food, clothing, shelter — almost everything that went to the making of life — came mostly from the home, or at most from the near neighborhood. The home supplied the corn and wheat; the neighboring mill ground it. The crossroads blacksmith did practically all the necessary iron work. Clothes came from wool or cotton grown at home, spun at home, dyed at home, woven at home, and at home made into garments. Shoes were made at home, near by at the farthest."

Life of to-day relatively less efficient as an educational agency

"I grant all that, but where is the education?"

"Exactly in all this. With all these things going on right at hand the children were early introduced to life itself. They shared with their parents in all these necessary operations for supplying the elemen- **How edu-cation came** tary constituents of life. Not only were skills **from sharing** needed and developed. but insight and attitudes **life with parents** were gained. It required no far-flung imagination to see the closely woven fabric of their immediate social life. Social insight came so easily that it seemed all but instinctive. And with insight came positive response. If any shirked, all saw, and in obvious truth all suffered. The needed social attitudes came almost inevitably, so close and apparent was connection between cause and effect."

"This reminds me of something we said a few weeks ago."

"What is that?"

"That education is such a remaking of life as brings growth, and that growth runs along the three lines of outlook and insight, attitudes and appreciations, and techniques of control."

"You mean that the children of these early days gained outlook and insight?"

"Yes, it was all but inevitable from the kind of lives they lived, but of course they gained outlook and insight only for life as it was then seen."

"And so, too, with attitudes and appreciations?"

"Yes, life was definite in requiring and giving a just appreciation of what was then needed. And of course techniques of control came most certainly of all. **How the** The girl must learn to cook, spin, weave, sew, **girl then** and all the many other things that made up **learned** women's work then."

"That's how she learned household economy in those days?"

"Exactly. She had to; and what is even more, she saw that she had to, and she never questioned it."

"That sounds like coercion, only very effective coercion."

"Yes, so effective it was seldom felt as such."

"And so ceased to be coercion?"

"Yes. The girl did these things of inner choice, only demurring when the task extended beyond her powers."

"So she did learn."

"Certainly she learned. First, she had an inherent motive impelling her to learn — a real set with all its readiness — second, the situation to be met told her and the rest of the family when she succeeded and when she failed."

"Yes, and the same situation supplied satisfaction for success and annoyance for failure. There is no doubt that she learned."

"And her brother?"

"It was the same with him. He helped on the farm. He carried the corn to mill. He held the horse while the blacksmith shod him. He was an active participant in all that his father did."

How the
boy learned

"How about the larger political life?"

"It was simple; the problems were less complicated — partly because less well understood; but the boy heard and saw everything that went on. Local affairs were out in the open. When court week came the boy would go to see any specially interesting case tried. Even the larger political meetings were so important that all attended or at least heard the matter discussed in detail at home."

"But just think what children can see now! How can you ignore that?"

"I don't ignore it, but I still assert that, in proportion to what they were expected to learn, the children of that day learned more, relatively, than do our children."

"Do you mean that just living their lives itself taught

them, whereas our children now do not by just living learn
so large a proportion of what they need?"

"Yes. That's part of it. The children of those early days
participated in the serious life of their parents. The common
run of our city children nowadays are on-lookers.
They may have a few duties required of them, Restricted
but we and they know that they don't feel any of present
special responsibility for the success of the home. family life
Relatively, they are onlookers and feel so. In the city homes
of the well-to-do, children are economic drones and nui-
sances. In that earlier life they were economic assets."

"Do you mean that, accepting their due places as actual
sharers, they were early educated to a sense of responsibility in the family life?"

"Yes; and children now not so sharing are in danger of
growing up with too little sense of such responsibility."

"Do you think any of the present wider social ills are due
to an analogous lack of responsibility?"

"Indeed I do. We have trouble to get citizens to vote.
They won't accept responsibility for matters of public welfare. Our city government is notoriously bad."

"And you think the lives children now lead fail to educate
them to meet these social demands?"

"Yes. Government is too complex, too difficult to see, too
far off. The children can't see it. Their parents even do not
understand it. So children grow up neither
knowing nor caring, still less doing anything Complexity of
about it." present life
an educative
"What about labor and capital?" difficulty

"It is too complicated to say much about, but at least one
difficulty is that the children, whether of the 'labor' group
or of the employing group, see or hear, at most, but one
side of the economic problem. Division of labor, valuable
as it is for production, has divided life, and people with it,

into widely separated parts. Unless special pains be taken, no child will grow up seeing how one kind of work is related to another kind. Under such circumstances it is easy for the demagog to appeal to narrow and selfish interests."

"Does this general line of thought throw any light on the introduction of the various manual activities into the school?"

"Yes. The older life gave children enough first hand contact with things to supply them not only with the personal and homekeeping skills but also with the varied meanings of practical affairs necessary to practical thinking. Now, unless the schools take special pains, many city children would grow up mentally starved so far as concrete things and their meanings go, not to mention the lack of useful skills."

Why our schools are using manual activities

"And working with such things fits the active manipulative life natural to children?"

"That's another way of looking at it and a good way too."

"Do I correctly understand that we are to think of education as all the influences that mold one's life and that just plain natural living in those older and simpler days came fairly close to giving the whole of the all-round training then needed for such a simple life?"

"Yes, that's well said."

"And that now with so many lines of work having left the home for the factory — large and distant factories at that — the home and community no longer supply the same sort of education they once did?"

"Yes. Or you might say it in this way — that the school in that day had but a small part of the total educational work to carry. Now it has a much larger part."

"I don't see why you put all these things on the school."

"For the simple reason that they are not otherwise cared ✓
for. The school is the social institution made to care for all
that would otherwise be neglected. You may
not like it, but it is a fact. The school is the The school
must accept
residuary legatee so far as concerns social duties. duties other
What the others won't care for, the school must agencies
relinquish
undertake."

"Don't you think it weakens the family to have the school
take up so many things that the family should care for?"

"Don't misunderstand me. I am trying neither to impov-
erish the home nor to relieve it of its proper duties. What I
am trying to do is to recognize facts. The present family
faces a different situation from the old family. I would
strengthen the family in any way feasible, but we must not
refuse to do the best possible by all the children. What the
family cannot or will not do, the school must do. Possibly
the rising generation, if better educated to face present conditions, will raise the status of family life in the next generation."

"And are the other educative institutions—the church, the
community, business life—in similar fashion yielding their
former educative functions to the school?"

"No single answer will suffice. Much of business demands
better general education than formerly, but business itself
offers less in the way of apprenticeship. 'No Business as
admission' signs indicate too that childish ob- an educative
servers are not welcome. Putting it all together, agency
it seems fair to say that business on the whole follows
the general trend; it demands relatively more and offers
relatively less. The schools must make good the difference."

"How about the community?"

"I think we have already answered that. Social life is
vastly more complex, which means at one and the same
time that it too demands more and offers relatively less."

"I don't quite see what you mean by 'offers relatively less.' How is this?"

"I mean that the complexity of modern social and political life makes it harder to understand. More of it goes on unseen. So many things happen that each one thing gets less talked about at home. For these reasons young people see less of public affairs and hear less about them than formerly. The community in proportion to what it comprises offers smaller opportunities for the young to see how it works. Relative to demands, the community is less educative than formerly."

"Isn't part of the difference because we see the demands better than formerly?"

"What do you mean?"

More adequate insight now   "I mean that the people of the frontier times saw clearly the situation close at hand and their children got practical skill and character training to fit the narrow range of their daily living, but none of them got insight enough not to waste our natural resources. Look at the school lands sold for a dollar an acre; and, as if that were not bad enough, see how often the proceeds were squandered besides."

"You mean that part of the present greater demand is owing to our greater insight into possibilities and dangers?"

"Yes, that's just it; and I say that the simple life didn't give broad insight then any more than it does now. I've lived in the country and I know."

"I am glad to agree with you that a very significant part of the difference between demands then and demands now is our present better insight into what is needed. It is part of our slowly accumulating stock of knowledge. The world has learned by experience. Your suggestion helps us to see this. I should like, however, to make clear that I have at no time wished a return to the simpler life of those early days.

My sole idea has been to see why our schools now must carry a heavier load than schools were formerly supposed to carry."

"And you still say that the school must make good the deficiency?"

"Yes, indeed; whether the greater demands come from a more complex civilization or from fewer educational opportunities or from more adequate insight, the result is the same. The school must carry a greater burden." **The schools must carry what others leave**

"Does this tell us anything about the problem of the rural school?"

"Yes, it does; but I think we can generalize. Each school should consider on the one hand the educational demands facing its children and on the other hand the total educational possibilities inherent in the lives the children are leading anyhow. With these two things in mind the school can decide on its task. What won't come to the child otherwise, the school must, if possible, undertake."

"Will these considerations mean different curriculums for the rural school and the city school?"

"Properly understood, each curriculum is unique to its own situation. Yes, the rural school must have a curriculum to suit its situation. So with the small city; so with the large city. So with East; so with West."

"The school must always undertake to supply what would otherwise be lacking?"

"Yes, as far as it can."

"What about the church in these changing demands?"

"There are many delicate elements involved here, and people are not so well agreed on the answer. Certainly in some quarters there is a lessening of authority. Many new ideas are pressing for consideration. The outlook is not clear."

"Do you think we are passing through a period of peculiarly rapid readjustment, or is this rapidity of change going to decrease?"

"I should say the contrary."

"What! Do you mean that things are going to change more rapidly?"

"I think they will."

"That's a startling outlook. Why do you think so?"

"What makes the changes?"

"Life must change when we keep having so many new inventions and discoveries."

"And what makes inventions and discoveries? And are they likely to increase or decrease in number?"

"Our scientists make the discoveries and I suppose our inventors, whoever they are, make the inventions?"

"And the inventions mainly depend on the discoveries?"

"Yes."

"So we come back to science and our scientists?"

"Yes."

"And is science increasing or decreasing?"

"Increasing, and increasing rapidly."

"And an ever increasing science makes ever increasing discoveries?"

"Yes, and I suppose that means ever increasing inventions, and that means ever increasing change."

"Yes, that's the argument. Do you see any escape?"

"No, not unless civilization somehow goes to pieces."

"Then you face not only inevitable change but the added fact that the change will itself become more rapid?"

"Yes, I can see nothing else."

"I can't see that all this makes any difference to the schools. If we let you people run on the way you like, we should get clear away from practical school affairs? What possible concern is it of the school that there should or should not be rapid changes in social life?"

"I think a great difference."

"I asked you what difference, not how great. I don't see why we are concerned."

"Do you think the school should so prepare young people that they can take charge of affairs after we go?" Schools must prepare for changing life

"I certainly do. Don't you?"

"If we understand preparation rightly, yes. Suppose we say yes, and suppose you set out to prepare your pupils for that coming day, how can you prepare them if you don't know what that day will be like?"

"Why, then, I couldn't prepare them. How could I, if I don't know what I am preparing them for?"

"But things are changing; do you know what new inventions will be made?"

"Certainly not."

"So you don't know what changes will be introduced into life?"

"No, but some things are fixed and settled."

"And you can prepare for them?"

"Yes."

"And not for the new ones?"

"Not exactly."

"Why say not exactly?"

"I was thinking that I might prepare the children to expect changes; that would be some help, I believe."

"And prepare them to adjust themselves to a changing situation, adjust themselves to change itself, perhaps?" How to prepare for an unknown future

"Yes, I think so."

"Imagine two teachers: one knows exactly what his pupils will face, what they will face and all they will face;

the other knows (or thinks he knows) some things they will face, but he mainly knows that they will face inevitably and increasingly rapid change in unknown directions. Now I ask, should the teachers manage their schools alike."

"I think not. The fixed-civilization teacher will know in advance the answers to the questions his pupils will meet.

Preparation in a static civilization
He can teach these answers just as his pupils will need to know them. But the changing-civilization teacher can't do that. Really I don't know what he can do."

"Teaching for him becomes a different problem, doesn't it?"

"It certainly does. I had never thought of it in just that way before."

"The fixed-civilization teacher can teach his pupils *what* to think, you say, but the other cannot."

"How about *how* to think? I mean how to attack problems? How to judge of difficult situations? Couldn't the

Preparation in a dynamic civilization
changing-civilization teacher do that?"

"And if so the schools would be run differently, would they not?"

"Yes, I see now. I begin to see. As long as people looked on the world as fixed and static, they had children mainly memorize answers to the questions they might expect to meet. Memorization and adjustment to a fixed order, habituation I mean; that's the kind of school we should expect, and that's the kind they did have. It's certainly interesting."

"Yes, and if people face a rapidly shifting and changing world, changing in unexpected ways and in unexpected directions, then what?"

"Why, their education would stress thinking and methods of attack and principles of action rather than merely what to do. Yes, I see it. Such a school would try to make self-

reliant and adaptable people; and are not the better of our
newer schools working just exactly along these lines? This
is all very interesting."

"But we agreed above that even in a shifting civilization
some things would stay fixed. Wouldn't selfishness be one
of those fixed things?"

"At any rate the danger of selfishness is always with us.
Then you would have us prepare against this?"

"Yes, but I don't know exactly how to do it."

"And now we face education for morals."

"I am glad, for I have long wished that we might discuss moral and religious education."

"We shall probably have to postpone that particular
topic for a while, but at least some part must
come in here."

Certain
demands
relatively
unchanging

"What do you mean?"

"Certain human traits, as the tendency to
selfishness, we shall always have with us; and new forms of
selfishness will constantly be possible with the new modes
of living."

"I wish you would illustrate."

"Take the automobile. It is a relatively new invention.
Has it given us any new example of selfishness?"

"I think so. What the newspapers call the 'road hog'
is at any rate a peculiar development with the automobile."

"What is the conclusion of this?"

"That in morals we cannot depend merely on fixed rules,
a set of don't's and do's. We do wish a number of very specific habits; but we also wish to go as far as we
can toward building up conscious unselfishness
as a trait of character in our young. Specific

Intelligent
moralization

unselfishnesses, yes, in so far as we can foretell; but, if
possible and as far as possible, we wish to enthrone the

more general conception of unselfishness so as to take better care of the new cases that are bound to occur."

"You mean, if I understand, that we must teach principles and not mere habits?"

"That's another way of saying it. Any words we use have their pitfalls, but rightly understood, yes, I agree."

"When has a thing really been taught? I am sick of this talking of teaching morals when so many think that if you give orders often enough or require children to memorize rules of conduct you are teaching morals."

"I agree thoroughly with you, and should like to say that we haven't taught till the child has learned. It is just like selling and buying."

"What do you mean?"

"Just this. The salesman hasn't sold unless the customer buys. The teacher hasn't taught unless the child learns. I believe in the proportion:

When learning has taken place   teaching : learning = selling : buying."

"That's very good. I like it. But something still remains. When has the child learned?"

"We had that once before. The child has not learned until he CAN and WILL do the thing. That is particularly our answer in the matter of morals. It takes all three, SEE, CAN, and WILL; but to me 'WILL he do it' is the main one."

"And all this means a new type of teaching?"

"How so?"

"Our older school concerned itself mainly with CAN. CAN this child repeat these words? CAN this child perform these skills?"

"Was that because the school in that day and time could expect the home and community life to teach the SEE and WILL?"

"In good part so, I think. Yes, I agree with you."

"If I understand you, the changing times have changed largely the duty of the school?"

"Yes, that's it."

"And the new duties demand a broadening and enriching of the curriculum?"

"Yes, otherwise our rising generation will Résumé not SEE its duties and obligations and possibilities."

"And it requires, too, a new method because the home and community life has lost much of its former educative possibilities?"

"A new method?   I don't see that."

"I mean that in a former day vital activities surrounded the child on all sides. His life was filled with purposeful activities of real worth and he saw and felt the A new worth. Now the usual home has for the child method few of such vital activities. His life is largely needed reduced to mere play which does not have all the needed educative values. The school as usual must make good the deficit. The school accordingly must introduce activities, purposeful activities, in order to give the child the vigorous living that he needs. This of course is method in the broad sense."

"We have thus a need for a new type of school."

"Yes, but many not thinking deeply and knowing only the schools of their childhood consider the needed new changes as fads and frills."

"So this is why the old three R's no longer suffice?"

"I think so."

"And why we see everywhere signs of a change in method?"

"Yes, there is fundamental need for new aims, new content, and new method."

"So far nothing has been said about a new science of education. That seems to me one of the most potent factors in changing aim, content, and method of education."

"So it has been, but it has come largely as an attendant result of the causes previously discussed. The need for a

The new study of education
different type of school has, as was to be expected, brought consciousness to the problem."

"And this new consciousness of the problem working itself out has given us the new study of education?"

"Exactly so."

"I am surprised that nothing has been said of democracy in connection with the new education."

Democracy and the new education
"Well, for one thing we cannot mention everything at once. Democracy I think has been at work slowly remaking the school to a greater sensitiveness to child nature, and perhaps especially to make us see that we must get our children to where they can and will think for themselves. In both it has worked hand in hand with science."

"But you think the most fundamental causes for a new conception of education have been the new industrial order?"

Summary
"Yes, that and its own underlying cause, science."

"And you think that with a greatly changed civilization has come a shifting in the relative duties of home, school, community, and church in the education of the child?"

"A shifting first of relative opportunities of home and community, and a consequent shifting of relative duties of the school."

"What about those who say, 'What was good enough for me is good enough for my children'?"

"They are simply blind. They know they live in a changed world, but they do not see that the changed world makes new and greater demands on the schools."

"And what about the three R's and 'fads and frills'?"

"As for 'fads and frills,' I should not like to say that teachers have made no mistakes, but I must say that the three R's no longer suffice to do for children what the times demand. We must enrich the curriculum and we must change our methods. To make these changes is no more a matter of fad or frill than is the building of garages. If we live in the modern world we must face its duties."

"Have we already made most of the needed changes?"

"We are not yet well begun."

"Then you look for yet greater changes?"

"I certainly do."

"And they will cost yet more money."

"They certainly will."

REFERENCES FOR FURTHER READING

DEWEY — *School and Society*, Ch. 1.

DEWEY — *The Educational Situation*, Part I.

CUBBERLEY — *Changing Conceptions of Education*.

KANDEL (ed.) — *Twenty-five Years of American Education*, Ch. 3.

CHAPTER XVII

Subject-Matter and the Educative Process

"All these years I have been thinking I knew what subject-matter is, but recently I heard it discussed, and now I don't

The meaning of subject-matter feel at all clear about it."

"Moral: Don't discuss; or perhaps better, don't think."

"Is your trouble that you don't know what subject-matter means as a term or that you don't know what is the most useful way of thinking about it?"

"I don't know which, probably the latter."

"I don't see your difficulty. Subject-matter is what you learn when you study."

"I am not so sure whether it is what you learn or what you study."

"Is there any difference?"

"I think there is a great difference. Sometimes at any rate one studies over a whole area and learns just a little or at the most concludes but little. Subject-matter-of-study seems to me almost always wider than subject-matter-of-learning. What you study contains much chaff along with the wheat. Study seems to be an effort to find the wheat and to separate it from the chaff."

"What you say is true, but I don't just like your figure. The wheat was there from the first and was wheat all the time. Study seems somehow to bring the learning into existence."

"Don't you think this hairsplitting is awful? Why not go on to something practical? I liked the suggestion of seeking the most useful way of conceiving subject-matter. Why not consider that? Only I have no suggestion to make."

"Isn't subject-matter simply one essential factor in the educative process? There must be a learner, a child let us say, and something learned. Without both these two, child and subject-matter, there is no educative process."

Child and subject-matter two factors in the educative process

"I see you've read Dewey's *The Child and the Curriculum*. What does he mean by saying that many so conceive the two as to make them disparate? Only I believe he does not use the word 'disparate.'"

"I think he means that many conceive them as belonging to entirely different kinds of things, without any common ground between them."

Are these factors disparate?

"Well what common ground can there be between a child and the definition of a verb or the multiplication table? A child is a live, wriggling, emotional creature, a young and erring mortal. The multiplication table was fixed before the foundation of the world. It is perfect and timeless. We can't mention life in connection with it; it is neither dead nor alive. I should say that properly considered child and subject-matter are disparate, as disparate as an inch and an hour. And this young, weak, erring child needs exactly this perfect subject-matter to make good his deficiencies, and that I call learning."

"If the two are as disparate as you say, how can you get them together? And what is learning and how does it get in its perfect work? I think you go too far. If they are really disparate, they cannot interact."

"Whether disparate things can interact, I don't know; but don't you think the natural tendency of holding the two as separate and disparate is to reduce learning to mere memorizing, to holding unrelated — disparate — matter in the mind?"

"Yes, I do think so. I believe observation will bear out what you say. For myself I wish to think of child and learning and subject-matter as all having a common denominator, as all belonging together in one single conception."

"Your common-denominator, get-together, one-single-conception idea sounds good, but I can't think of any such. What have you to suggest?"

"I like Dewey's, the conception of experience. The subject-matter of the curriculum is race experience, the
Experience   picked winnings of the race, the best ways man-
as a unifying kind has yet devised of meeting its problems."
conception   "That's all right for subject-matter, but where does the child come in? I thought we were to have a common denominator?"

"It is a common denominator. The child has experience, the race has experience. The child's experience is, of course, childish; but it is merely the small, the beginning, the germ; the fuller form we see in the race experience."

"I get a glimmer of what you mean, but not all. Won't you elaborate?"

"Compare inch and hour with inch and mile. Inch and hour are, as was said, truly disparate. An inch is neither longer nor shorter than an hour nor yet equal to it. The two do not belong on the same scale. But with inch and mile it is different. An inch is shorter than a mile. If we think of a scale of length, an inch will belong on it, and so will a mile."

"What are you talking about? I thought we were discussing experience as a common denominator for child and subject-matter."

"So we are. Just wait. I say that on the scale of life or experience the child, like the inch on the mile, reaches but a small way. His ways of behaving are only beginnings, his language, for example, is limited and full of errors. The race experience, the best ways of behaving that man has yet devised, like the mile, reaches in comparison much longer. But — and this is my point — they both belong on the same scale. The best and wisest among us are in speech but doing better and wiser the same kind of thing the child is doing in his childish talk. There is no disparateness between the two. The greater is but the development to a higher degree of the less. Child-experience and race-experience are but earlier and later stages of the same thing."

"As useful as is the term experience for your purpose, I think you used a phrase even better."

"What was that?"

"Ways-of-behaving. To me this is even a more obvious common denominator to child and subject-matter than is the notion of experience. The child is, if he is anything, a bundle of 'ways-of-behaving.' As you yourself said, the race-experience has pre-served for us the best ways-of-behaving that have thus far been devised. Then child and subject-matter are both alike ways-of-behaving. The child's ways are small, crude, erring, perhaps, when we compare them with the best ways-of-behaving of the best among us; but they clearly belong on the same scale, as you have just brought out." Ways-of-be-having as a unifying conception

"That sounds good, but let's look more closely. The combination $7 \times 8 = 56$ is subject-matter. How is it a way-of-behaving? Did you not too hastily include all subject-matter in your assertion?"

"I think not. Consider a case where $7 \times 8 = 56$ actually belongs. I buy seven eight-cent stamps. I could pay for them separately, paying in at the stamp window eight cents seven distinct times — I mean in seven separate and distinct payments. That would be 7×8. But that is too much trouble. Thanks to The way of behaving $7 \times 8 = 56$

our race experience (for many uncivilized tribes do not know so much arithmetic) instead of seven separate and distinct operations of paying eight cents each I make one paying operation of fifty-six cents. This race experience subject-matter way-of-behaving is much neater and more expeditious."

"I had never thought of that before. And do all the things that we teach our children show the same thing? How about geography?"

"It too, properly considered, consists of ways-of-behaving. I was in Detroit and learned to my regret that a certain train

Geography as ways-of-behaving

upon which I was relying did not, on account of the change to daylight saving time, get me into New York soon enough to meet an engagement. No other through train passing Detroit would do as well. Then came my geography. How about the Lake Shore road? Many trains between Chicago and New York pass that way, and the distance from Detroit down could not be great. There must surely be a road that would make the connection. Search disclosed such a connecting road with a satisfactory schedule of trains. A fast train to New York was caught and the engagement met. Here geographical knowledge actually meant a way-of-behaving. It told me where to look."

"Would you be willing to say that all subject-matter in the curriculum really works this way?"

"I am quite willing to say that all *ought* to work this way; that anything which does not so work has no place in the

Ways-of-behaving and the curriculum

curriculum."

"This is one way then of criticizing a curriculum?"

"Indeed it is, and trenchant criticism it gives too. Much curriculum content I fear could not stand it."

"You would have to interpret behavior rather broadly,

would you not, in order to include all desirable learnings under the head of ways-of-behaving?"

"No more broadly than behavior properly extends. To me behavior is as broad as life; it specifically includes all ways of reacting in life to life situations. So far as I can see that will include all we need."

"A moment ago you used this conception as a criterion for criticizing the curriculum. I am wondering if it is equally valuable as a criterion for judging learning."

"What have you in mind?"

"I mean so as to decide whether a thing has been learned. We have said this in several different ways before. I should like now to say that nothing has been learned *When learn-* until it has been made over into an actual way- *ing has taken* of-behaving. Much school learning seems to *place* me to be merely for show purposes, chiefly for show on examination day. To me this is a degradation of the notion of learning, a prostitution of it. Nothing has been learned till it is there ready and disposed to serve as an actual way-of-behaving."

"Wouldn't that condemn many schools and teachers?"

"I think it would, but it is no less valuable for all that. In fact I think our schools are often off the track. They seem not to know what they are about or why. If everybody saw that subject-matter is good only and because it furnishes a better way-of-behaving and that learning means acquiring actually that way-of-behaving — if every one saw these things, we should have, as we ought to have, a different kind of schools."

"Does this have any bearing on education as a preparation for life?"

"This conception helps us to understand one previously discussed, the continuous reconstruction of experience. To learn anything as a new way of behaving is of course

to reconstruct experience.   If we demand that the way-
of-behaving be got only as it is immediately needed, we
shall have the continuous remaking of experi-
Education
as the re-   ence; and this of course is life itself, living now
construction   — the opposite of education as a mere prep-
of experience   aration for future living."

"And you really mean that you wish everything the child
learns to reappear soon as a new way of behaving?   Everything — arithmetic, geography, history, spelling?"

"That is exactly what I mean.   I should wish each thing
to be learned when and because it was needed as a way-of-
behaving right then and there.   If it comes into the child's
life because it is thus needed, I think it will sooner and
more frequently and more vitally be called on to serve again
in that child's life."

"Do you mean there should be no variation from this,
none whatever?   Remember how many inferior teachers
we have."

"I told you what I should wish.   In this world we often
are compelled to take less than we wish."

"Somewhere I have heard the phrase 'potential subject-
matter.'   Does it not fit in here?"

"I think it does.   Take an illustration that we have used
once before.   A child sets out to learn to lace his shoes.
Potential vs.   While he is working at this, everything that he
actual sub-   studies in connection is, I should say, *actual*
ject-matter   subject-matter-of-study.   A year ago this activity was far ahead of him and of his abilities.   Even a month
ago it was too much for him.   To-day it is actual subject-
matter.   Now a year ago, and more so a month ago,
his mother knew that if all went well the time would come
when shoe lacing would thus become actual subject-matter-
of-study.   She saw it then as potential subject-matter to the
child, possible in the future but as yet not actual."

"Then you have by contrast defined for us two terms, actual subject-matter, potential subject-matter."

"Yes."

"What do you call anything after it has been learned, well learned? To him who has learned a thing in the past it cannot now be called actual subject-matter, still less is it for him potential subject-matter. What name do you give it?"

"So far as I know there is no good name to give it. I have sometimes by contrast called it 'once-was' subject-matter; but that sounds odd."

"You spoke of the boy's lacing his shoes. I wish we might go over that again. I should like to see more clearly the various steps in the educative process and particularly how the notions of study, learn, and subject-matter enter. We have touched on various parts of this already. I should like to see it all brought together."

"I am glad to do so, though it is not easy. Let us take the boy's lacing his shoes. I like to think of this as typical of practical out-of-school learning. I should like to emphasize here the two terms 'practical' and 'out-of-school.' " Practical out-of-school learning

"You mean then that not all learning takes this form?"

"Yes, that's what I mean. I think this is the most significant learning. I know there are other kinds, but I find it difficult to draw lines of demarcation. Certainly this shoe-lacing instance is typical of a very important class of learning. I reckon five steps, which I propose to number and discuss:

"1. The boy starts out to do something, here to lace his shoes. This he has never done before 'all by himself.' He has seen mother or sister or nurse do it, so he knows more or less about it, at least enough to make a beginning.

"2. He meets a difficulty. The activity is brought to a stop. Now, as we saw once before, this difficulty arises because he lacks a certain way-of-behaving (as the behaviorist psychologist says, he lacks the appropriate behavior-pattern). He has many habits and skills, many ways-of-behavior, many behavior-patterns, but he lacks this particular way-of-behaving; namely, the behavior-pattern of lacing his own shoes. True enough he already has parts of the needed way-of-behaving; he knows eyelet holes, he can put lace point through eyelet hole, he can pull on the string, he can even tie a knot; but as one whole operation he cannot. He lacks it. And the difficulty is that he lacks it. Lack, difficulty. No lack, no difficulty.

"3. He tries again and again, his mother helping him. He pays attention to all the promising elements in the situation. He notes the order and arrangement of lacing. He watches how his mother does it. He looks at her finished result. He tries again and *studies* as he goes.

"This attention to promising elements in the situation in order to make good his lack is what I call study. Study is thus the studious effort to acquire a needed new way-of-behaving.

"4. Eventually (we will suppose) he gets the 'hang of the thing' — he finds, gets, and applies the needed new way-of-behaving. He can and does lace his shoes.

"Learning appears here as getting the needed behavior-pattern, the lacking new way-of-behaving. As we said earlier, learning (this kind of learning) has not taken place until the new way-of-behaving is so built up in the learner that it becomes in fact to him a new way of behaving.

"5. The new behavior-pattern (way-of-behaving) now being available and applied, the difficulty is gone. The activity is resumed and carried to its conclusion. The shoes are laced."

"I see where *study* and *learn* come in. They are clear, but I don't see the subject-matter. Where is it?"

"Curiously enough it appears more complicated than we had beforetimes carelessly thought. We may define subject-matter as what we study and what we learn from the study. If so, we find the first How subject-matter enters part of the definition in step 3, the things to which attention was paid, those promising elements; and the second part in step 4, what was learned."

"Most people, it seems to me, do not see these two parts in the conception of subject-matter."

"Yes, and some who have got the new point of view doubt the wisdom of continuing to use the old term; but I am not yet convinced that we should give it up."

"You speak of the new point of view. Have you not in fact introduced us to new conceptions of study and learn as well as of subject-matter?"

"Before we answer that I should like to recall that this boy who yesterday could not lace his shoes and to-morrow and thereafter does lace his shoes is a different The reconstruction of experience person. You remember when we were discussing the reconstruction of experience [see page 190] it was brought out that henceforth this boy is more independent, more a self-directing person. He not only can and does lace his shoes, but he now is called upon to consider hours and bells in a way and with a responsibility new to him. Having greater responsibility he has more chance to meet responsibility and of course also more chance to shirk. The moral world thus opens a little wider to him. He is in sober fact more of a person. Moreover he feels it. Right or wrong, good or bad, he feels his growing independence, his new responsibility; and through this his personality again grows more complex. And not only he but his mother feels it all. She rejoices that he has gone forward; but her mother heart has its corresponding pang, he is now less dependent on her, is now less her baby.

He has taken a step forward on the road to manhood with its admittedly separate personality and self-control."

"And this you think of as the reconstruction of the child's experience?"

"Yes, this is true education, true living."

"I like your phrase 'step forward.' Would you say that each instance of learning is in so far a 'step forward'?"

"Yes, a step forward at least toward a more complex and generally distinct personality, not necessarily a step forward toward a goal ethically good. A step forward in the first sense might be a step backward in the second sense."

Subject-matter properly means a step forward in the child's life

"And subject-matter as something learned is thus both the occasion and cause of stepping forward in the reconstruction of experience."

"Yes, I like so to think of it. In this sense subject-matter has not been properly brought into the child's life unless he does, because of it, step forward in the reconstruction of his experience."

"You have said nothing about teaching in connection. Was there no teaching here?"

How teaching enters

"Almost surely, yes. The mother will help the child to learn. To my mind that is what teach means. But I always wish to use 'learn' in the full sense of actually acquiring new behavior-patterns, new actual ways-of-behaving."

"You repeat then your proportion:

teaching : learning = selling : buying?"

"Yes, I wish always to keep that in mind."

"It seems to me that you have defined *study, learn, teach,* and *subject-matter* as if they belonged to life, not to school. Is this intentional or have you other definitions that apply to school?"

"Life has been foremost not only here but everywhere else when we have sought the better education. To me education is of life, for life, and by and through life; and life is of and for education. So the saying is true that education is life." Education and life

"You spoke of new conceptions of study and learn and subject-matter. What differences do you see between the old and the new as regards these?"

"Chiefly this, as it seems to me. The old conception, seldom found within the past seventy-five years one hundred per cent pure, was this. Childhood is, in itself and apart from adult activities, a waste period. Education as a preparation for adult life is thus a good way of utilizing this otherwise wasted period. To do this we (a) study adult life and see what it needs. After laying aside the things that will be learned without our consideration we take the remainder and organize them into an order suitable for learning. This is a curriculum. (b) We divide this curriculum into suitable portions of 'subject-matter' ('lessons') and assign these (under a penalty) for learning. This with the testing named below constitutes 'teaching.' (c) The child undertakes to avoid the penalty by getting to the place where he can show that he has learned. The effort to get to this desired place or state is 'study,' and the typical way is to memorize a printed page. (d) When the child can avoid the penalty by answering our tests, chiefly 'reciting' what he has memorized, we count that he has learned. (e) If we carry the matter far enough we hope that the child will keep what he has thus 'learned' in the 'storehouse of his memory' till the day of need arises, and that he will then look within, choose what he needs, and apply it."

"The whole thing then has in the past been based on an extreme notion of preparation for future living."

"Yes, so it seems to me."

"Did our word 'recitation' come from re-cite?"

"Exactly. It meant the time when the child repeated for us to hear what he had memorized from the book."

"And originally this was *verbatim?*"

"Yes, indeed. A favorite method was the catechetical, question and answer method. History and geography and science, for example, used often so to be written."

"Is this older conception entirely dead?"

"It certainly is not. Most people seem still to think of education in this fashion."

"I have been contrasting the two ways in which subject-matter enters into life in these two conceptions. In the new

Two con-
trasted views
of subject-
matter

conception, the subject-matter is brought in because it is needed to carry on some activity already under way. In the old, the subject-matter is simply set out to be learned, which as you say generally means mere memorizing."

"I don't get your full meaning."

"Well, take an illustration. Imagine a boy at home making a wireless outfit. Some of the older boys have

Intrinsic
learning

succeeded at this so well that they could 'pick up' almost all the stations. This boy would like to do as well. He starts out, meets a difficulty, studies the books and all the apparatus he can see, finds out where his difficulty lies, and remedies that. This done he starts again, after a while meets a new difficulty, again studies, again succeeds in overcoming the difficulty. And so on through the whole thing. In the end he too can hear distant stations."

"I see what you mean. It is the same analysis we had before of out-of-school learning applied again and again."

"Did he study?"

"Most certainly."

"And learn?"

"Assuredly."

"Was the subject-matter that this boy learned pertinent to his life as he himself saw and valued life?"

"It certainly was. It was inherent in what he was doing, part and parcel of it, intrinsic in it."

"Let us then say that this was a case of 'intrinsic learning,' and let us call what was learned 'intrinsic subject-matter.'"

"And is there extrinsic learning with extrinsic subject-matter?"

"Let us see. Imagine a typical boy in the upper grades of school studying bank discount. Is bank discount necessary to carry on his life as he sees and values life or is it rather outside his life?" Extrinsic learning

"I should say outside."

"I am not so sure about that. It is part of his real life to avoid difficulty in school. I have seen boys study their teachers almost as hard as the boy we have mentioned worked at the wireless. I should say that learning bank discount is not outside but inside his life."

"To settle the matter if we can, let's ask two questions. First, is the decision to study bank discount an internal or an external choice as we used those terms earlier?"

"If he is a typical boy, I should say external. I can hardly think of a boy's hoping in school that he would get a chance to learn bank discount."

"Very good. Now the second question. Does the bank discount learned by this boy enter his life primarily as bank discount? Does he use it for actual discounting purposes, or does it enter primarily as something to give to the teacher on demand? Which?"

"Clearly not as bank discount but as something to be got because the teacher or the curriculum demands it."

"Then I should say that for this boy to learn bank discount is a case of 'extrinsic learning,' and for him the bank discount was 'extrinsic subject-matter.'"

"Then most learning in most schools of to-day is extrinsic?"

"I didn't say so, but certainly much of it is."

"Are there degrees in this as in other matters?"

"Assuredly. I like to think of a scale extending from the

E————————————————————I

most extrinsic of 'extrinsic subject-matter' at E to the most **The extrin-** intrinsic of 'intrinsic subject-matter' at I. Few **sic-intrinsic** schools would fall at either extreme." **scale**
"Would more be nearer to E or nearer to I?"

"I surmise, nearer to E."

"What has history to show? Has there been any movement in the past hundred years?"

"Indeed, yes. There has been for a century a general trend away from E in the direction of I."

"And our most progressive schools?"

"I should say they are moving decidedly towards I."

"Do you believe a school could be run at I? Or is that just an ideal to be held in mind but not to be sought seriously?"

"I think Dr. Collings's school was run approximately at I."[1]

"Was it a success? I have heard that these **Collings's** experimental schools do not succeed." **experiment**
"Read and see. On ordinary subject-matter tests it somewhat surpassed the national norms, while in attitudes and the like the results were truly remarkable. Success? Indeed, yes, a great success."

[1] Collings—*An Experiment with a Project Curriculum.*

"Can you say that this success was owing to the use of intrinsic subject-matter? May it not have been due to Dr. Collings's enthusiasm?"

"How much was owing to intrinsic curriculum and how much to enthusiasm I cannot tell. But I do know two things: It was run on the intrinsic basis and it was a great success. Dr. Collings thinks, and the facts seem to me to bear out the contention, that without the intrinsic curriculum no such measure of success would have been possible."

"Why should you expect intrinsic learning to be superior to extrinsic learning?"

"We have implicitly answered this question already several times. Recall all that has been said *Why intrinsic* about set and readiness, interest, complete *learning is* acts, purposeful activity, the complete act of *preferable* thought. If you look closely you will, I think, see that all of these contemplate and even demand 'intrinsic subject-matter' and oppose mere 'extrinsic subject-matter.' "

"In a word 'intrinsic subject-matter' provides the conditions most favorable for learning?"

"Exactly so."

"Do you refer here to primary learnings? Or also to associate and concomitant?"

"All learnings. Dr. Collings, in fact, set out to get mainly concomitant learnings. He got all."

"Are there not definite evils that may reasonably be expected from the use of extrinsic subject-matter?"

"I think there are; but what had you in *Evils of* mind?" *extrinsic*

"Well, for one thing, not all subject-matter *learning* can, under penalty, be assigned for learning. Any régime that relies on assignment-under-penalty will find itself leaving out of account some of the most valuable learnings."

"What do you mean?"

"Exactly this. There are some things we can easily assign for learning under penalty, such as the simpler skills and the memorizing of printed matter. Both of them mainly rely on simple repetition. These we can assign precisely and test easily.

Some valuable learning is slighted

"Some other things cannot be assigned at all under penalty, for example, appreciations and attitudes. As we said the other day, imagine a teacher's saying, 'You boys are deficient in your appreciation of *Nicholas Nickleby*. You must stay in this afternoon and raise your appreciation to 70 or above.' Or imagine the principal's saying, 'If you boys don't like your teacher any better by next Monday I'll have her punish you till you do.' No there are some things that will not be got in this fashion."

"Between these two extremes of things that can easily be got by assignment and those that will not thus be got lie those of intermediate position, such as formal outward behavior, the solving of not-too-difficult problems.

"I repeat then what I said at the outset, a régime that is content with assignment-and-testing-under-penalty will tend to restrict itself to the things that can be so assigned and tested, which means that there will be small consideration for the attitudes out of which are the issues of life. Even if individual teachers should wish to stress the weightier things, they will find themselves judged by the comparative showings of their children in these more mechanical matters of skills and facts, so that they too will in the end almost certainly yield to the pressure of authorities above them and rest content with this starvation diet curriculum."

"I hadn't thought of that in this light before, but I can see where you are right."

"Wouldn't the children's method of study be influenced for evil by the assignment-testing régime?"

"Indeed, yes. Most obviously such a scheme means mechanical memorizing with lessened attention to thought connections. Where examinations are the prin- Children's cipal means of testing we frequently find school method of work reducing itself to cramming. Teachers study is hurt will drill children on old examination questions. In New York state where there is a state syllabus and a very elaborate state examination system ('the Regents' ') we often find that teachers do not even possess a syllabus, but spend their days drilling on old examinations. Such seems to me to defeat largely the purpose of education. Surely in such is a minimum of the reconstruction of experience."

"I have been troubled about the effect on the teachers of the fixed curriculum with emphasis on assignment-testing. I lived once in such a system, and I never saw less thinking on the part of the teachers."

"Yes, how can you expect teachers to think when they are tied hand and foot. To tell a teacher what she shall teach and when she shall teach it, and to count success Teachers to be only and exactly that children shall suc- are not cessfully pass these mechanical subject-matter encouraged tests — all this I say is to treat a teacher as a to think factory operative. Under such a régime a teacher may be a skilled artisan, but an artist and thinker, no. She has no chance. In fact she is not expected to think. 'Hers not to reason why, hers but to teach and dry — up.' That's what I say, and I have seen it happen too often."

"Well, you make out a pretty bad case against treating teachers so. How many will agree with you in it?"

"We'll oftener find it true than we shall get agreement on it."

"I should like to ask about moral character training under such a régime. I say that morals suffer perhaps most."

"There is certainly something in your indictment. We have already seen that certain finer character aspects of

Moral character is hurt

life, the attitudes and appreciations, will suffer in such a régime. We have seen the evil tendency toward cramming. In its extreme form this may be found as cheating. Perhaps most of all is it true that education, to be morally educative, requires that children live as a social group in the school with the teacher as the comrade and social arbiter. But if assignment and penalty be stressed, an opposition between teacher and pupils is all but inevitable. This means that the child spends from eight to twelve years of his life thinking of those in closest authority over him as his opponents. A good part of his efforts will be spent in 'beating the game.' If there can be a worse training for citizenship it would be hard to find it."

"Doesn't a régime of 'intrinsic subject-matter' tend to make an ally of the teacher?"

"Yes, just as 'extrinsic subject-matter' tends to make an enemy of him."

"You have all been pretty severe on the assignment-testing plan of teaching. If it is as bad as you say, why does it persist?"

"There are two answers to be made. One is that it doesn't persist — not in its old strength. It is yielding all along the

Why extrinsic learning persists

line and giving way increasingly to a closer and closer approximation to intrinsic subject-matter. The other is that the general assignment-testing practice lends itself most easily to the authoritative management of teachers. The administrator, because he must succeed as an administrator, almost inevitably seeks a plan that can be mapped precisely in advance, where precise expectations can be laid down, and precise checks made on results, so that responsibility is exactly located.

That this defeats the purpose of education is not usually perceived either by the administrator or by his board or by the parents. Tradition favors this old plan. They are more or less blinded."

"But is it not true that teachers are more alert than administrators to the evils of the extrinsic régime?"

"No one statement is true either of all teachers or of all administrators, but there is some evidence that we find more alertness among the teachers on this point. It comes closer home to them."

"Before we go, I wish some one would give us a summary of what we have covered during this discussion. It seems to me to include a good deal."

"As I see it, we have considered three main items: (a) subject-matter as ways-of-behaving, (b) an analysis of practical out-of-school learning which yielded new conceptions of study, learn, and subject- Summary matter, and (c) the distinction between 'intrinsic' and 'extrinsic' subject-matter.

"As soon as we saw that subject-matter is properly to be considered as ways of behaving, the best that the race has yet found out, it was at once easy to see that a child had not, for life purposes, learned anything until he had made it over into his own actual way of behaving. That this may be possible, many curriculums must be made over. This led once more to the notion of education as a continual reconstruction of experience.

"From the analysis of a practical instance of out-of-school learning, it became evident that study and learn are vital life activities inherently necessary whenever a difficulty is met and overcome. Subject-matter is thus intrinsic in those situations where the individual takes a step forward in the remaking of his own life experience.

"Such intrinsic learning differs radically from mere ex-

trinsic learning. Intrinsic learning is, as said above, a vital
life activity necessary in order that an individual overcome
a difficulty. Extrinsic learning is artificially introduced into
the learner's life by some external authority. It is learned
thus under penalty, actual or implied, and is accordingly
not used then or there to forward life but rather that it may
be presented by the learner to show that he has accomplished
the task imposed. It needed no argument to show that
intrinsic learning utilizes better the various conditions
favorable to learning already discussed. Of a régime of
extrinsic subject-matter, we saw that it tends to restrict the
range of desirable learning, to hurt the child's methods of
study, to lower his morals, and to reduce the teacher to
somewhat less than a full person."

"Don't you think one reason why so many still hold to
extrinsic learning is that textbooks are built on that basis?"

"Yes, and courses of study, and promotion standards,
and school furniture, and — most of all — people's conceptions."

"Do we have to change all these?"

"Yes."

"Where shall we begin?"

"With whatever is nearest to hand."

"Must all be changed together?"

"Probably so."

"Will it be a difficult task?"

"Yes."

"Is it worth the trouble?"

"Indeed, yes."

REFERENCES FOR FURTHER READING

KILPATRICK — "Subject-Matter and the Educative Process,"
Journal of Educational Method, 2:94–101, 230–237, 367–376
(Nov. 1922, Feb. and May 1923).

KILPATRICK — "How Shall We Select the Subject-Matter of the Elementary School Curriculum," *Journal of Educational Method*, 4:3–10 (Sept. 1924).

KILPATRICK — *Source Book in the Philosophy of Education*, No. 467, 468, 473, 475, 477.

DEWEY — *The Child and the Curriculum*.

COLLINGS — *An Experiment with a Project Curriculum*, pp. xvii–xx, 48, 317–335.

MERIAM — *Child Life and the Curriculum*, Ch. 8–12.

BONSER — *The Elementary School Curriculum*, Ch. 1–8.

DEWEY — *Democracy and Education*, pp. 193–200, 212–227.

CHAPTER XVIII

Psychological and Logical

"What do these terms 'psychological' and 'logical' mean? I know what each means when it stands alone, but when they appear thus contrasted, they seem to have specialized meanings. Am I right?"

Meaning of psychological vs. logical

"Yes, I think you are right. As contrasted terms they were introduced, I believe, by Professor Dewey."[1]

"I know it; I found them in reading him. But I wish we might talk it over. I believe it would help me, at any rate."

"The clearest idea I can get is to think of the 'psychological' as the order of actual experiencing and the 'logical' as the way we arrange what we learn from the experience."

"I don't quite understand. Won't you please explain?"

"Suppose we illustrate. Take government, for example. When did you first begin to learn anything about government?"

"Do you mean at the very first, when I was a child?"

"Yes."

"I can hardly say. The earliest occasion that I recall is when I wanted to go on a picnic with my older sister. My mother wouldn't let me, and I cried. I think she punished me. At any rate I learned that there were some things I couldn't do without my mother's permission."

How ideas are gradually built

"Suppose we take that as a beginning, though it certainly was not your very first occasion. You had in this

---

[1] See *The Child and the Curriculum*, pp. 25–28; *How We Think*, pp. 61–63; *Democracy and Education*, pp. 256–261.

294

an experience of being governed and you learned something from it."

"Yes, and the next time I knew better what to expect."

"You mean that what you learned grew out of one experience and prepared for a succeeding experience along the same line?"

"Yes, that's true, though I hadn't said it to myself in just that way before now."

"And is this always true, that each experience leaves some result of learning and that this resulting learning in turn prepares, in part at least, for the next experience?"

How "result" and "experience" succeed each other

"You have in mind a succession of experiences along any one line, like government?"

"Yes, and I mean to ask whether in such a case there always is a succession of experience and result —

$$E_1 \ R_1 \ E_2 \ R_2 \ E_3 \ R_3 \ E_4 \ R_4 \ . \ . \ . \ "$$

"I believe you are right. If I understand you, E_1, E_2, E_3, etc., mean successive experiences of government, and R_1, R_2, R_3 refer to the successive results learned respectively from these experiences."

"Yes, and each R grows out of the E preceding and prepares you in some measure for the E succeeding."

"I am getting lost. You are going too fast for me. I see the different experiences all right. Every time mother or father or the teacher made me do something, or set up a rule, or punished me for breaking a rule, that was an experience of government. They are the successive E's. That's clear. But what are the R's?"

"Well, let's see. By the time you began school, had you learned at home what you as a six-year-old might and might not do?"

"Yes, I was pretty well adjusted, though I would sometimes break over."

"Had you learned all this at once, as the result of just one experience?"

"No, it took a great many experiences to teach me. I remember that for quite a while I kept running away, till finally I learned that I had to have permission before I went out of the front gate."

"Did, then, your first experience of running away teach you nothing about government?"

"Oh, yes. I learned that I couldn't run away without being called to account. Eventually I learned to ask permission."

"And after that another round of experiences, perhaps in connection with your brothers and sisters, taught you something about others' rights and the need to respect them."

"Yes."

"So each experience (E) does leave some deposit of learning (R), and each such R does make you look out differently — in some degree — upon the future?"

"Yes, that's clear. I see that each R not only grows out of a preceding E but also helps us face some succeeding E."

"I should like to ask here about the successive R's. Does R_3 sum up R_1 and R_2, or what is the case?"

"Let's answer that by another illustration. Suppose a child, say three years old, is first introduced to dogs by

Building a concept of dog

playing with a playful little white puppy. As he plays (E), he builds up in himself a notion (R) of what a dog is and what to expect. When his mother says that grandmother has a dog, he expects the same kind of small, white, playful dog. But suppose grandmother's dog turns out to be black, though small and playful. What will he now think when he hears that Uncle John has a dog?"

"He will think that Uncle John's dog is small and playful, but he will be in doubt as to the color."

"Does his notion (R_2) after playing with grandmother's dog reject R_1, his former notion of dog?"

"No. In part R_2 confirms R_1. He thinks even more firmly that a dog is small and playful; but in part it changes R_1. He now thinks a dog may be white or it may be black."

"And will the like process continue when he meets large dogs, yellow dogs, fierce dogs, and so on?"

"Yes, it must so continue. I see now that each succeeding R in some measure utilizes all the preceding, but it may correct their deficiencies."

"Isn't it in these different and contrasting experiences that the child comes to notice the different things about a dog?"

"Yes. Suppose Fido hurts his foot and goes limping about? What effect has this on the boy?" *Differentiation of parts*

"He will become more conscious of Fido's feet than before and he will also see how all four feet must work together if Fido is to run well."

"Let me say it a little more explicitly. As the child has from time to time need to think, now of foot, now of tail, now of forelegs, now of eyes, he comes to separate these out of the total notion of dog *Integration of parts* and for the purposes of thought gives them, as it were, a kind of separate existence. This we may call differentiation of parts. Moreover, while the child is differentiating out any one part, as the foot because of the lameness, he is at the same time seeing how this part is connected with the rest: 'Fido needs all four *Differentiation and integration go together* feet to run well.' This we may call 'integration' or 'coördination.' Now I assert that differentiation and integration go hand in hand."

"Yes, that's clear. Now does not this have some effect on the successive R's?"

"To be sure. They become thus ever more complex. They have more and more recognizable parts and the parts are seen to be joined together in ever new ways."

"From what you are saying, the separate parts seem to become known after the child has a notion of a dog and not before?"

"Yes."

"But is not this contrary to what we have been taught about going from the simple to the complex?"

The simple and the complex "Do you mean that a child should build his idea of a dog as he builds a block house, one block or one element at a time?"

"Well, why not?"

"Let's try it and see how it would work. Shall we begin with the feet to build our idea of a dog. Does the child first learn the feet of the dog, and then the legs, joining the latter to the former on top? And does he then learn the body, and join this to the already waiting legs and feet? And does he next add the ideas of tail and head? Does he take each such successive step with no notion of the whole dog till he has thus built it up?"

"That's absurd! You are making fun of me."

"Not of you, but of that way of building up an idea. It *is* absurd, isn't it?"

"It certainly is; but now I am lost, I fear, entirely. How does the child build an idea?"

"Go back to the differentiation we discussed. The child saw the lame foot and so saw foot and feet more clearly than ever before. This differentiation was bringing into clearer relief what was less clearly present before."

"Yes, I see that much."

"But the notion of the dog was all the while a notion of a whole dog even from the first."

"Certainly."

"But it was not so with building the house. The first block didn't make a whole house or anything like it."

"I think I see now. The boy's first experience was of a whole dog and he got a notion of a whole dog. This notion was at first simple enough — and inadequate — but it became more and more complex and more and more adequate as more and more parts or characteristics were differentiated and integrated. However, the notion under consideration was all the time and at each time that of a whole dog."

"Exactly so."

"Well, what has all this to do with 'psychological and logical'? Have you forgotten that? What is the good of all this anyhow? What is going to come from it?"

"We do seem to have gone pretty far afield. Suppose we try to collect it all together. Imagine as regards government a very long series of experience and learning-result closely worked out, stretching from earliest babyhood up to the knowledge of the most learned scholar in the realms of thought. We may picture it in this fashion:

$$E_1 R_1 E_2 R_2 E_3 R_3 \ldots E_{10} R_{10} E_{11} R_{11} \ldots E_{50} R_{50} E_{51} R_{51} \ldots E_n R_n$$

In this the E's mean successive experiences of government, and each succeeding R is the learning result that followed that experience. In every case R grows out of a preceding E and prepares, in some measure, for a succeeding E. Let's look at this series and ask some questions about it. We'll suppose we have before us the growth of the conception of government in a well taught person who comes at length to be a great authority in the subject. I ask first: Is each R made from its preceding E by conscious intent or not?"

"I should say not with conscious intent. Surely as a child he didn't intend to learn. He didn't think about that. He learned, to be sure, but he didn't consciously mean to learn."

"Probably as a child he did not consciously

Place of consciousness intend his learning — though often his parents meant he should learn — but how about his later years?"

"If he is to become a conscious student of the subject, there certainly will come a time when he intentionally studies his experiences in order to draw from them their lessons. Even if he were not to be a scholar, he might still as a man of affairs take conscious note of what was going on so as to profit by it. So the later R's are made with more or less conscious intent."

"Can his parents or a teacher help this process?"

"Certainly. They can help the boy draw proper con-

Can others help? clusions. I suppose in line with our previous discussions they will wish him to be purposeful in his experiences in order that he may better learn. They will also in all probability 'set the stage' or 'load the dice' or otherwise contrive that he have fruitful experiences."

"What do you mean by fruitful experiences? Are some more fruitful than others?"

"Certainly. In fact if parent or teacher or somebody didn't help the child, he would never catch up with what the race during untold centuries has been learning. This means, of course, wise oversight of the boy's experiences."

"Suppose the E's are the right kind, that is, purposeful on the boy's part and fruitful of result, what about the successive R's? How will they differ from each other?"

"As we have already seen, each R in turn is itself more or less of a whole, summing and supplementing and correcting the preceding. They grow continually more and more differentiated within and at the same time more and more fully coördinated. They are also, I suppose, more consciously organized — we might say more and more logical. Not only will each be more carefully drawn as a conclusion from the preceding experiences, but I think each formation of the conception will be more and more consciously made, organized on more and more rational grounds. This is what I mean by saying it would grow more and more logical."

How the successive "results" differ

"Let's go back a minute. How different is any E from its R?"

"If I understand you, they are different kinds of things. Any E is a bit of life itself, actual experiencing, while the R is a result in the mind, an ordering and arranging of what is learned from the experiencing. E is life, R is what is learned from life so arranged as to control better the next experience (a new E) along this line."

"Even a child profits from his experiences, then?"

"Certainly. You might say, if you wish, that each time of life has its own learning, its own arrangement of learned results, its own logic. These successive R's differ as regards organization in degree, but little if any in kind or function."

Logicals

"You apply the term logical to each learning result. Do you do this deliberately?"

"Yes, I think the essence of logical arrangement is effectual organization of experience. I find this in substance — perhaps I had better say 'in germ' — in the learning of even the youngest child. The very essence of learning is for control of subsequent experience. So I am willing to say that each R from the first is, for its stage, logical."

"Am I to infer that by analogy you apply the term 'psychological' similarly to each experience?"

Psychologicals

"Yes, just as the result (R) is organized logically, so is the learning experience by its very nature arranged psychologically, that is, for learning. Perhaps the definition here lies as much in the contrast as in the terms themselves."

"I am not quite clear as to your use of the word logical. Do I correctly understand you that when the words logic and logical are used in their ordinary sense, they refer to the higher reaches of systematic organization, the kind we expect of well-disciplined minds? But when logical is used in contrasted connection with psychological, both terms vary with the development of the person: to each psychological age and experience its own logical arrangement?"

"Yes, that's the way I understand it."

"Won't you state, then, succinctly the difference between the psychological and logical order? I think I know, but I am not sure."

"The psychological order is the order of experience, of discovery, and consequently of learning. The logical order **Psychological** is the order of arranging for subsequent use **order defined** what has already been learned."

"I have heard people discuss whether we should arrange a course in science, say, psychologically or logically. I think I see dimly what they mean, but I should like to see it more clearly. Can you help me?"

"I think so. Go back to our long series written down above, stretching from $E_1 R_1$ up to $E_n R_n$. Let's ask first, what is the difference between a scientist and a **The task of** teacher of science — between what a scientist **the scientist** and what a teacher of science should try to do? Where on this scale would the scientist, as such, live?"

"I suppose toward the end."

"Suppose we say he now has reached R_n and no one has gone further. Then he will try to push ahead and learn still more. He will use his R_n as a basis from which to project an experiment or a series of observations (E_{n+1}). From this new psychological (E_{n+1}) by careful reasoning he will hope to draw some new conclusions. If successful, he will arrange his results in a form to stand criticism and present them as R_{n+1} to the world. This is what the scientist, as such, would do."

"Yes, I see that."

"Now. by contrast, imagine a teacher of science who has gone through the whole series up to and in- The task of cluding R_n; how will he try to bring his son, the teacher say, up to R_n?" of science

"How old is the son and how much does he already know?"

"Why ask these questions?"

"Because the teacher must begin where the child is."

"Do you mean that each learner is at a certain stage on this series and must begin there if he is to advance?"

"Yes, surely. How else could it be done?"

"I agree with you, but is it always so done? What about our textbooks — in physics, for example?"

"What do you mean?"

"Is it not true that most of the older textbooks at any rate took the latest results of science (R_n) and tried to state them simply, then divided this material into thirty chapters and assigned these in turn as lessons?"

"I hadn't thought of it that way, but I believe you are right."

"Why do you say 'older'? I think modern textbooks do the same."

"Possibly so; but already, especially in general science, we see a change coming."

"Well, why shouldn't they make textbooks in the way you describe?"

"Let us see. Suppose the child had reached a development indicated by R_{10}. Is Chapter I (the first thirtieth of

R_n) the same as R_{11}, and Chapter II the same as R_{12}, and so on?"

"Why, no; that would be like building that block house, wouldn't it, a block at a time, and like getting the notion of the dog by beginning with the feet and then adding the legs?"

"I think it would be much like it. And what notion would the child have of physics after a few lessons like this? Do you from this see the difference between the logical and psychological order?"

"I begin now to see. The logical order is taking a mental organization fit for grown-ups, chopping it into pieces, and The logical   giving it a piece at a time to the child to learn. order of   I suppose the idea is that when he gets all the teaching   separate pieces he will then have a whole. But isn't it absurd? It is in fact like building up the notion of the dog by getting first the separate notions of feet, legs, body, tail, and head, and then putting these together. I am glad you gave me that illustration."

"Isn't geometry frequently so taught?"

"Yes, always so, unless there is special preparation for the ordinary geometry textbook. And that's one reason why it often proves so difficult. Of course Euclid's book was for much more advanced students."

"Isn't it true that when R_n is thus cut up into pieces and assigned as so many lessons, memorizing the formulation is about all the child can do?"

"This is often so. The child's E's, then, are not real experiences, only efforts to memorize statements of the results of somebody else's experience. Under such conditions, thinking, real thinking, the thinking of discovery and exploration, is pretty well prevented."

"And if the child doesn't experience, if he has no true E's, he will have no true R's, no really self-organized learning results. Am I right?"

"I think so. I see no escape from that conclusion."

"But are you not going too fast? Do you mean that the child must himself rediscover all that the race has found out? That's impossible!"

"I don't mean to leave the child without help. His process will be immensely shortened by having as a guide some one who knows the field. He is thus saved the costly blind-alley wanderings. But he must ^{The place of} himself face the essential problems if he is to the teacher organize in himself the solutions. On no other basis can he come to have an effectual grasp of the solutions as instruments of further thinking along this line. We can give him, as information, the fact that bichloride of mercury is a poison. He can use this information and save himself from being poisoned; but neither chemistry nor medicine can be taught merely by giving such information. Where knowledge and wisdom and power are sought, there must be much actual facing of difficulties. Experience in a field is necessary for anything like mastery of the field."

"I am not clear on one point. A while back we spoke of the child's having from the first a notion of a whole dog. That seemed clear then. But I fail to see the similarity between that and his work with the science. Do you mean to assert that he has from the first a notion of the whole science and that this undergoes differentiation and integration as we saw in the case of the dog?"

"Yes and no. We do not say that the notion of physics as a science was born the day the child first realized that a stone unsupported will fall, any more than we think the notion of biology was similarly born ^{Experience} the first day he saw the dog. But any vital and is of wholes natural experience has a unity that makes it a whole, whether it be of a falling stone or of a lever or of a syphon. And the child forms a notion of the experience which for him at the time is a whole, however much his more sophisticated elders may feel it as of necessity only a part of a larger whole. Later, if the child is fortunate he will have further fruitful experiences in this realm. Each such will be a whole, but oftentimes will join itself with previous experiences; and the new notion will supplement and correct the old ones. Differentiation and integration will in this manner arise, and at length what you and I call the science of physics will be born. If the boy be so inclined and is still fortunate, this likewise will undergo differentiation and integration and logical articulation with successive experiences until, mayhap, the existing limits of the science are reached. Throughout, if the process be normal, each experience (E) is a whole and each successive R is for our pupil, student, and scholar at that stage likewise a whole, however partial and lopsided that particular R may later appear to him to be."

"But the thirtieth part of R_n isn't felt as a whole, is it?"

"No. It is true that the learned man will give a kind of unity to each logical section of R_n, but even he mainly sees this section as part of the larger whole R_n."

"But it is the boy, the learner, that I am asking about."

"No, indeed; to the beginner the thirtieth part of R_n is neither a whole nor a part."

"I see that it is not a whole, but why not a part?"

"We only see a thing as a part when we see how it fits into the whole. To the novice a part all by itself is merely an ill-conceived whole. He doesn't know what to make of it."

When parts can be seen as such

"What does it mean to learn such things as the thirtieth parts of R_n?"

"For the man who already knows R_n or the most of it, such learning would be a new relating, a seeing of new material in relation to the whole. To him this might well be true learning."

"But I meant to ask about the novice, the beginner. How can he learn these thirtieth parts of R_n?"

"The word learn seems too strong and fine a word to give what he does with such. He cannot see it as a whole for it isn't a whole. Nor can he relate Some it to the whole since he lacks the whole with descriptive which to relate it. Too frequently his so-called learning learning is mostly a memorizing of the words of the book."

"Can't he memorize the ideas?"

"That's hard to say. Strictly speaking no. He cannot get the idea except by some such process as that here described. I mean $E_1 R_1 E_2 R_2 \ldots E_{50} R_{50} \ldots$ He may from related past experiences get glimmering ideas, but closely scanned these are likely to turn out to be words."

"They may fool him, may they not, into thinking he knows something?"

"Yes, and they may fool his elders who ought to know better."

"Do you mean that this is absolutely wasted? That he then learns nothing? If you hold this, how do you explain the fact that most scholars — learned men, I mean — have been brought up on this régime?"

"There are several things to be said. One is that these scholars are the picked intellects that managed to survive. When you ask about them you are ignoring all the casualties left along the line of march. An- How people other thing is that they, being capable, had the have learned power of making a little first-hand experience go a long way. Still a third factor in the explanation, chiefly useful in connection with the second, is that they were good memorizers. Their previous experiences gave them some insight into some parts, as all were successively memorized (verbally). The successive parts were thus in mind until all had been included. Then followed a thinking back and forth, with actual experiences scattered along. In this way they managed in the end, being capable, to build apparently in the wrong order the R_n that they were mistakenly thought to have learned as one whole."

"Do you think this is the way that most people have learned all the various 'logically'organized treatises and the like?"

"Exactly so, so far as these have been learned. But I think most who studied them never in fact learned."

"You seem to imply a peculiar definition to your verb to learn."

"Exactly the definition we have been using all the time. Nothing is for practical purposes learned till it has been made over into one's actual ways-of-behaving. **What it means to learn** Our boys must behave after the manner of physics in order to be able to say that they have learned physics."

"That's a high ideal. If it were enforced, what would become of physics as a subject?"

"It's a high ideal, but it is the only truthful criterion. Any other pretended learning is a fraud and a sham."

"But what would become of physics?"

"Some would learn it much sooner and better than now. Others giving up the sham of pretended learning would accept a humbler and much more useful **The content of physics** learning."

"And what, for instance, might that be?"

"I am not prepared to say, but something like a knowledge of what part science has played in civilization, a greater faith in science as a method and result, so as actually to give up superstitions."

"Do you mean that people really believe superstitions?"

"I do indeed. How many people wince at thirteen at the

table or shun room 13 or avoid Friday for the beginning of a trip or 'knock on wood'?"

"A good many, I suppose, all told."

"Yes, and how many take patent medicines and follow medical quacks?"

"The number is certainly disgracefully large."

"Are the learnings you have named all that you would expect from science in the high school?"

"No, I should wish some knowledge of scientific method, especially of a controlled experiment, and perhaps even more some disposition to experiment in affairs that concern them."

"Is that all?"

"No. I especially disclaimed knowing just what should be expected. But I will say this: if they could get what I have laid out, it would for many, if not for most, be an improvement over what now obtains."

"You are pretty hard on the logical order when used for learning. I judge you don't approve of grammar as most of us learned it."

"I certainly do not. It exactly illustrates what I mean to condemn." The logical order to be distrusted

"Wouldn't you on the whole mistrust definitions?"

"Yes. If I hear that a teacher requires his pupils to memorize many definitions, I have my doubts at once as to that teacher's insight."

"One further question. What does 'psychologizing subject-matter' mean?"

"It refers to the work of the teacher in preparing for the learning of his pupils. In terms of our discussion it means to take a science as Psychologizing subject-matter the scientist knows it (as R_n) and 'unscramble' it into such a series of $E_1 R_1 E_2 R_2 E_3 R_3$ . . . as will lead the learner from where he now is through successive experiences (E) and learnings (R) until he comes to a firm grasp of the science itself. It means to make a path of psychological order from the learner's present state up to a state where he has much experience well organized."

"One last question. You have spoken as if this applies only to science. Does it apply also to our ordinary school subjects?"

Conclusion   "Indeed, it does. I may, by elaboration, say that high school science should certainly begin as general science and be preceded by many experiences preparatory to it — not 'deferred values,' mind you, but experiences in which children live here and now. Geography should be so taught. In our best schools English grammar has already been so made over that little of the nth degree logical is now left. The older grammars were atrocious examples of teaching by the strict logical order. Civics is now being remade thus into citizenship. History teaching is probably scheduled for a similar transformation. Many causes are at work to make over the school subjects more and more into the psychological order. Indeed the best way in which I can now conceive the curriculum itself is as a series of experiences in which by guided induction the child makes his own formulations. Then they are his to use."

"We have much to think over, but I believe it is worth it."

REFERENCES FOR FURTHER READING

DEWEY — *The Child and the Curriculum*, p. 25ff.

DEWEY — *How We Think*, Ch. 5.

DEWEY — *Democracy and Education*, pp. 256–266, 269f.

KILPATRICK — *Source Book in the Philosophy of Education*, No. 481, 482, 483. (These three duplicate in part the three preceding references.)

CHAPTER XIX

MORAL EDUCATION

"I wish we might discuss moral education. I feel the need of clearer ideas on the subject if my teaching practice is to be what I wish it."

"Indeed, I have been much surprised that no mention at all has been made so far of this most important part of all education. I have been watching to see how long we should go before some one would think of it."

"How can you say we have ignored it? I think there has hardly been a discussion that did not consider it."

"I don't know what you mean. When have we discussed it?"

Moral education has pervaded all previous discussions

"From the very first. I could hardly enumerate all the times. The first discussion on the meaning of method turned largely on taking care of the character effect of the attendant learnings. You recall all that was said of concomitant learning. It was pointed out that through these character was largely built."

"So with the discussion on coercion and the building of interests. I remember definitely that we spoke of education in morals being largely a matter of building the right interests."

"Yes, and I recall that in the discussion on the divided self it was specially pointed out that what makes for division of self makes for weakness of character, for inefficiency of moral outlook and response; similarly with the distinction between intrinsic and extrinsic incentives and their character effects."

"And you recall what was said on punishment. I think it is quite right to say that the moral character aspect has been well nigh if not quite the foremost in mind throughout all our discussions. It has certainly permeated everything."

"Now that you mention it I do recall these things, but I wish to have the very terms used, and no dodging. I think too that we use a different psychology when we come to character building."

"I am afraid you will have to go elsewhere if you demand to find a different and peculiar psychology for use in discussing moral education. Character building proceeds along the same lines and uses the same laws of learning whatever aspect you have in mind."

"I have been troubled as to what constitutes the aim in moral education. I have thought all the while it was
The aim in moral education
character, but recently I heard some one say it was conduct. When I think about it I get confused. At which should we aim?"

"If I have to say either, I should say both."

"That's paradoxical enough. What do you mean?"

"Ask yourself which comes first, which is cause and which is effect."

"Why, character grows out of conduct. How else does one become what he is?"

"I say just the opposite, that conduct flows from character. On what other basis could you expect from any one his 'characteristic conduct' as we say?"

"And again I say both, for both are right."

"It's too complicated for me. How can each grow out of the other?"

"Easy enough. Does the hen come from an egg or the egg from a hen? Both. But with a hen and an egg actually before me I do not say that for these two each came from the other. I might say it like this: From a hen (h) comes an egg (e); from this egg (e) another hen (h'); from h' another egg (e'); from (e') another hen (h''), etc. Thus

$$\ldots \text{h e h}' \text{e}' \text{h}'' \text{e}'' \ldots$$

We bring with us into the world the beginnings of a character (C). As soon as this character (or nature) interacts with the outside world conduct (c) ensues. But this conduct (c) changes somewhat the original character (C) and so gives us a somewhat different character (C'). When this character (C') interacts with the outside world conduct ensues. But because the character (C') was different this new conduct (c') is somewhat different. We get then a series like the preceding,

The character conduct series

$$\text{C c} \quad \text{C}' \text{c}' \quad \text{C}'' \text{c}'' \ldots$$

in which each instance of conduct flows from a preceding character and leads to a somewhat new character. Similarly each stage of character came (in part) from preceding conduct and gives rise to a somewhat different conduct."

"How long will this continue?"

"Throughout life."

"At which then should we aim?"

"Again I say at both, but, as between the two, more immediately at conduct. Conduct is character interacting with situation or environment. Character is beyond our immediate influence, but by changing the situation we may influence conduct and thus indirectly influence character and through it subsequent conduct. We shall seek then such conduct as will build the kind of character we approve, hoping from the new character to get the more certainly the kind of conduct that we approve."

Conduct the immediate aim

"Do I understand you to mean that our influence on both conduct and character is indirect, that our direct influence is limited to the situation or environment?"

"Yes, precisely that."

"And that means that, no matter how ethical or spiritual our aims may be, you and I must always begin and direct our influences over others by using physical things, that is by moving them, of course."

Things only can we directly control

"That is true. Talking, for instance, is moving the air in certain ways. Writing is putting ink to paper. A smile is a facial movement."

"I don't just like this idea. It doesn't sound moral. In fact it sounds almost anti-moral."

"If it stayed in the physical movement stage it would not be moral. Fortunately it may get beyond that."

"I don't understand."

"I mean that this gets into character. It is with character that we are concerned. Morals is exactly the tendency of character to respond properly to a given situation."

"Then we aim at character?"

"Yes, but not immediately. Our immediate aim is conduct, conduct of a kind that will build the desired character."

"We seem then to have three aims: immediate conduct, resulting character, and resulting remoter conduct?"

Three aims in moral education

"That's true. We may, if we wish, say that the first two are educational aims and the third is a life aim."

"But we face this resulting remoter life conduct. We shall then aim at it as an educational aim?"

"Quite true; and from that point of view it is perhaps wiser not to distinguish educational aims from life aims."

"I thought we had already agreed that 'education is life.'"

"So we did, and what we have just said is but a new instance of that fact."

"You said that our immediate aim should be conduct of a kind that will build the desired character. Do you believe

people think much about that? It seems to me that mostly
people tell children to keep quiet, for instance, not so much
to change character as to get rid of the noise."

"When parents and elders do so act, are they concerned
then about the children and their future wel- The comfort
fare or about themselves and their own present of parents
peace and happiness?" and elders

"Their own present peace and happiness, I suppose."

"But would you allow children to make life unbearable
for others about them? I wouldn't. I have always suspected
that your whole reforming crowd thought that the whole
world should be turned over to children to do as they pleased
with. Now you have practically admitted it. If I had to
choose between the two I'd say 'Children should be seen and
not heard.' I am tee-totally opposed to your whole wishy-
washy program."

"Yes, we know pretty well where you stand on these
matters; but in this instance at least you conclude too
hastily regarding what some others think. A question of
fact was asked as to what parents and teachers do have in
mind when they restrain children in a certain fashion. The
question of humoring and spoiling children, which is essentially what you raise, we have several times discussed, and
we shall return to it in a moment."

"But I should like to press the question as to whether most
parents and teachers do put their own present peace and
happiness above the character needs of their children. I
don't believe it."

"Any mathematical determination of the instances is
impossible, I suppose, and certainly unnecessary for our
purposes. Would you agree that many parents and teachers
do at times do this?"

"Yes."

"And too often so act?"

"Yes."

"Then we have a real problem to discuss."

"I should like to make a distinction here that seems to me important. As I see it, there are two ways of getting children to keep quiet, or perhaps better, two ways of getting people to respect the rights and feelings of others. One way is to use threats or bribes; the other way is so to change their characters that they of themselves will wish to respect all proper rights and feelings of others."

Two kinds of control over conduct

"A very important distinction, and a capital one just at this point. Which of the two would you say uses the steps of moral education?"

"Why clearly the second, the method of changing the character and disposition."

"The other sounds anti-moral, as was said a little while ago."

Moral education seeks control by character

"Isn't the distinction here much the same as the distinction there? The method of threats and bribes is one that relies merely upon the use of the physical environment; while the other is concerned with the innermost character?"

"Perhaps so, but I was thinking of the distinction between extrinsic and intrinsic incentives."

"Yes, and the distinction between 'external' and 'internal' choices. With bribes and threats the approved conduct is admittedly external and is expected to stay so. The aim of the other is to make the socially approved conduct to be also the internally desired conduct."

"Isn't this the promising path toward the reconciliation of the demands of the individual with the demands of society?"

"Yes; some call this the process of socializing the individual, getting him to the place where he, as an individual,

wishes for himself the things that are at the same time good
for all concerned."

"It might require the revision of some of our institutions,
might it not?"

"Yes, civilization must expect always to be concerned with
these twin problems: on the one hand, building and keeping
its institutions such that they would, if accepted,
make for the good and happiness of all together; Individual
and society
and on the other hand, building in its succes-
sive generations the personal acceptance of such institutions.
These are permanent tasks for mankind."

"I should like to go back to the parents who make
children keep quiet. I don't quite get the different positions or attitudes you think they might take toward their
children."

"It seems to me that there are at least two contrasted
positions: first, that of those who would stop the noise
and are indifferent to the character effect of Two ways of
how they do it; and second, that of those who controlling
seek primarily the character effect and are rela- children
tively indifferent as to whether noise continues or is stopped.
Between these two are many intermediate positions."

"Which would you take?"

"To me it is a question of comparative values and their
combination into the best possible result. We certainly
wish our children not to interfere with the proper rights and
feelings of others. We certainly wish our children to build
the right kind of characters."

"I don't see the contradiction. Why not let the children
practice the consideration of the rights and feelings of others?
This will get both the quiet and the moral growth. Why
not?"

"That's what I say. Make them respect the rights of
others. If they are unwilling, make them. If they still

won't, punish them into it. There's nothing like firmness. I am glad to see you coming round to my position."

"Before you answer that, I'd like to put a case before the group for consideration: A tired father is trying to read in **"Keep quiet** the evening. The children become noisy. The **or go to** mother tells them that father is tired and sug- **bed"** gests that 'we all try to keep quiet so that he may rest and enjoy home.' The children are quiet for a while. Then the noise again. Mother speaks the second time. A third time, father speaks in peremptory fashion: 'Your mother has spoken twice and you don't mind her. I shall not speak again; if I hear any more noise you will go to bed at once. Do you understand?' They do understand and they keep quiet. Now what I wish to know is, first, was this father concerned with character building or with his own peace and comfort?"

"I can tell you. He cared only for his own peace and comfort."

"It would seem so; I don't believe, however, we can tell unless we know more of what he thought. But I think we **What these** can ask a more important question. What were **children** the children practicing?" **practiced** "What do you mean? They practiced keeping quiet and they were learning to keep quiet. He did just right."

"They certainly kept quiet. But I don't think that tells us just what we wish to know. We are thinking of moral character development. What traits, what personal traits, were they practicing? Were they practicing consideration or were they practicing prudence? Consideration for a tired father or prudence in the face of an angry father?"

"Yes, that puts it well."

"It was prudence. You may be sure of that."

"Again I think we can't say, unless we could look within; but this much is certainly clear. They might keep quiet and practice either prudence or consideration. The fact that they keep quiet doesn't tell us what character trait they are practicing."

"You are certainly right about that, and I should like to ask about our homes and schools generally. Do they manage it so that children practice inwardly as well as outwardly the things they should practice? We make children keep quiet and we make them obey promptly, but what are the children really practicing, what are they thinking when they keep quiet and when they obey? These I say are matters too often overlooked, but they are, I think, really the most important things."

"I wish we might go more fully into this matter of how character is built. There are various things I don't quite understand."

"The first thing I should like to ask is the relation of habit to character. Some people seem to take the two as the same, but I thought habit was something rather mechanical, confined to bodily movements."

Relation of habit to character

"Strictly speaking, habit includes all the ways of behaving that we acquire, whether ways of thinking, of feeling, or of bodily movement. So character is simply the aggregate of our habits. I prefer to say the organized aggregate of working habits."

"But the organization itself is simply habit over again, isn't it?"

"So it is, but I wish to call attention to the fact of organization. Character must consider how the aggregate works as an aggregate."

"Why say working habits? Why not just habits?"

"Strictly speaking it would suffice, but I wish to call attention to the fact that character especially contemplates actual working behavior — the habits that really constitute conduct. I say 'working' merely for emphasis."

"Why do you translate character into habit? Do we not know as much about the one as the other?"

"The reason is that the word habit joins us up at once with our whole discussion on learning and how learning takes place. Habit is essentially an S → R bond affair. We thus should get light on how to build habits and so on how to build character."

The laws of learning

"There was so much said on learning that I hardly know what to pick out. What would you say is especially applicable here?"

"I should wish to name three things, the law of exercise, the law of effect, and the law of associative shift."

"You do not omit set and readiness, your old stand-bys?"

"Indeed no. They underlie and condition all discussions where learning is involved."

"What about the law of exercise?"

"I was thinking particularly of a kind of negative way of stating it: We shall not make a habit of any trait unless we practice that trait."

Precise practice

"That sounds too obvious to give much help."

"Obvious sounding or no, it is daily disregarded. I might say it again in two words: *precise practice.*"

"I still don't see."

"Go back to the irritated father. What should a father wish his children to practice in such a case? Consideration or prudence? What did they practice?"

"Clearly he should wish consideration."

"I don't see why you harp so much on consideration or on what the children think. The thing the father wanted was quiet. I say the children practiced keeping quiet. That is precise enough too. What more do you want?"

"Now you bring out into the open the very essence of moral conduct. There are two parts to any moral act and both should agree: first, the outward effect of **The essence** the outward act — quiet in this case and what **of moral** it means to all concerned; second, the thinking **conduct** and attitude — motive and intention some prefer to call it — that go along with the outward act and join it up with character as a whole."

"Might we not say that this thinking and attitude are exactly what give *character* to the act?"

"You are right, and this helps us to see what morality is. We might say it in slightly different words as a unified self *vs.* a divided or badly organized self. Our aim **The inte-** is such an integration and organization of all **gration of** the habits in character that the full character **character** shines out in each act, speaks through each act."

"Is that why you are so concerned here with the thinking and attitude involved?"

"That's part of it, but there's more yet. The fact that they keep quiet doesn't tell whether the children are practicing love or hatred, affection or fear, consideration or mere prudence. We wish quiet for the father, but we certainly are also concerned that the children build love and affection and consideration and especially an acting in connection with these and in obedience to these."

"This, then, is what you mean when you say 'precise practice'?"

"I mean that if a trait is to be built, as affection, we must practice *precisely* that thing, affection."

"You mean too that if the child practices hatred or fear he is not building love or affection?"

"Exactly so. 'Whatsoever a man soweth that shall he also reap.' There is no truer saying."

"Then what do you say of most school discipline?"

"At best most of it fails to have children practice desirable traits. Much of practice builds positively bad traits."

"Do you call prudence a bad trait?"

"Prudence in affairs is a very important trait, slow in the building, too; but when we use 'prudence' as in our discussion here we mean that the children may be doing an outwardly good act, but are inwardly thinking of themselves, of saving themselves from threatened punishment, and of course are thinking but little, if any, of their father and his feelings."

"Then the badness of this kind of prudence is its selfishness?"

"Yes."

"And the father might, it is likely, have been forcing upon his children the practice of selfishness?"

"Yes, that's what I mean."

"And do you think the results bear out your contention?"

"Life is very complicated and ascribing this or that bad trait to this or that procedure is at best an uncertain affair."

"But if you had to say?"

"If I had to say, I should say this: that there is in our American political and social life a very great deal of selfishness, of prudence in this bad sense. Many men
will do anything they can 'get away with.' If we had wished to build this trait in our citizens we could hardly have chosen a school and family discipline better suited to do it than that too frequently found."

"Do you mean the kind used by this father?"

"Yes, I think many children have seldom practiced at home or in school any conduct except on the shut-up-or-go-to-bed basis."

"But isn't it hard to get children to be quiet on any other basis?"

"It may well be, but I insist that you cannot reap what you have not sowed. It is practice, precise practice, that builds. Nothing less will suffice."

"Then moral education must very largely concern itself with securing the right inner attitudes."

"Yes, that is a prime objective."

"And mere outer behavior will not suffice?"

"It certainly will not."

Moral education much concerned with attitudes

"Then you would not try to get pin-drop order and quiet?"

"I abominate it."

"Do you really dislike quiet?"

Pin-drop order

"In itself, no; when it is got at the expense of moral character, yes."

"Does this maxim of 'precise practice' partly explain why you wish children to practice responsibility?"

"Yes. I wish them to build that very desirable and complex thing called responsibility. Then I must wish them to practice responsibility of many different kinds and conditions."

Practicing responsibility

"One thing troubles me. You use a good many general terms like 'selfishness,' 'consideration,' and 'responsibility,' but my study of psychology has taught me to be careful of such."

"And you are right to be troubled. I often fear that I shall be misunderstood. Such general terms are shorthand terms covering a great many particulars. I am quite justified in wishing unselfishness say as a characteristic; but I am wholly unjustified in letting you think that practicing unselfishness in one thing means unselfishness everywhere else."

Dangerous use of the general

"The general law of transfer of training holds here, does it not?"

"Yes, unselfishness built up in one situation will carry over into another related line only in the degree that there are common elements."

Transfer of
training
involved

"But you still wish your child to practice a proper unselfishness in each thing that he does?"

"Yes, indeed."

"If a good many particular cases of unselfishness are built up, may not the child generalize from these and so help in building up a more generalized trait?"

"Authorities differ somewhat. I should say yes, provided the child is old enough to generalize and does generalize, and provided then there be practice in obeying the generalization."

General-
ization

"Will a name help?"

"Yes, indeed. The terms 'fair,' 'no fair,' 'fair play,' and the like help boys greatly to generalize the notion."

"And the more consciously the notion is held the better promise of transfer to a new case?"

"Yes."

"Does this mean that moral education differs according to the age of the child?"

"Practically, yes, very greatly."

"We distinguished earlier the outer act from the inner attitude that accompanies. While the child is very young, what he is to be taught to do or not to do, has to be very simple and very definite. 'Father's book — don't touch it.' 'Ink — don't touch it.' As he grows older, reasons can be named in connection."

Moral edu-
cation differs
with the age
of the child

"But you would, all the while, wish the child to practice from higher rather than lower motives, wouldn't you?"

"A good general rule is to use the highest that will work."

"You mean that you would go down the line till you got one that would work?"

"Your question is too difficult for a single answer. In general, avoid severe measures. Many slight pains if invariable will teach generally better than one big one."

"You mean better, all things considered?"

"Yes, especially considering the attendant responses. I am very anxious that my child love me and that he build up a very firm belief in my fairness and in my sympathy. These things have to be considered."

"And you would pay more and more attention to the child's thought and attitude response as he grew older?"

"Yes, that's it."

"I thought we were going to discuss the Law of Effect."

"So we are, but I fear our time is up. We can take that next time."

"How shall we sum up what we have gone over this afternoon?"

"We first saw that moral education is not a separate kind of education but essentially a part or rather an aspect of all education. We have constantly had this moral aspect in mind in our previous discussions. Summary Conduct and character changes follow each other in endless turn throughout life. Each act of conduct was conditioned by the existing character and helped to build a new character. Since human control is direct only of physical things our immediate aim has to be present conduct, that it be such as to build good character. It is, however, probably right to say that in moral education our prime aim is character building, for character is our safest hope for future conduct. We saw that, sad to say, many parents and teachers are so much concerned with the immediate outward effects of their children's conduct that they jeopardize and even damage their children's character development in order to secure their own peace and comfort.

"Habit is the unit element of character. To build character then is to build the right habits of thinking and feeling as well as of outward behaving. To this end exercise is a prime consideration. Precise practice of any trait is necessary if that trait is to be built into habit and character. It is then not sufficient that children practice merely outwardly good behavior. The inner attitude is an essential part. This is a factor often overlooked, and as a child grows older should loom larger."

"Did you say we should next time discuss the Law of Effect?"

"Yes, and associative shift."

"It seems to me that this matter of moral education is very complicated."

"So it is, and the end is not yet in sight."

REFERENCES FOR FURTHER READING

KILPATRICK — "Disciplining Children," *Journal of Educational Method*, 1: 415–421 (June, 1922).

DEWEY — *Moral Principles in Education.*

KILPATRICK — *Source Book in the Philosophy of Education*, No. 537, 538, 541, 542, 544, 552, 557.

JAMES — *Talks to Teachers*, Ch. 8, 15.

DEWEY — *Democracy and Education*, Ch. 26.

THORNDIKE — *Principles of Teaching*, Ch. 11.

CHAPTER XX

MORAL EDUCATION — *Concluded*

"I believe we agreed to discuss to-day the action of the Law of Effect in moral education."

"Before we begin I have a question. After our talk, I went away feeling that in this matter of moral education parents and teachers have less actual control over their children than most of them think. Am I right?"

Law of Effect in moral education

"I don't quite get your meaning."

"I mean that many in charge of children set their teeth and say that these children *shall* learn to do thus and so, in effect *shall* build this or that into their characters. Now from our discussions I get the idea that the parent's part is only indirect.

Control by parents indirect only

The thing that counts most, at least with those above early childhood, is what the children themselves feel and think when they are acting."

"Exactly so. What the children think and feel as they act is probably the largest factor in determining what traits shall go into their characters."

"And this accompanying inner attitude, I understand you to mean, is largely beyond the control of parents and teachers."

"Yes, that is what I meant."

"You mean that we cannot of our will *make* children practice this or that feeling?"

"Yes. Often and often does a parent stand helpless as the child seems bent on wishing wrong things."

"Part of this helplessness of parents and teachers we saw when we were discussing 'precise practice.' We cannot make children practice what we will."

"Yes, is there something else?"

"That's what I was thinking. The Law of Effect still further lessens the power of parents and teacher."

"How so?"

"In this way: the Law of Effect says that whether any act shall grow into a habit and so become part of character or grow into aversion depends on the actor, the child."

"You mean on whether it gives him satisfaction or annoyance?"

"Yes, and this is most certainly beyond the mere say-so of parents."

"We may by our bribes or threats make children act outwardly in a certain way, but we do not in this fashion make the act satisfactory to him. That's for the child to say. Something in him decides."

"And not only may he feel aversion, but our efforts at force may even increase this aversion?"

"Yes."

"Then I don't see what we can do. If we cannot make children behave, what is left?"

"Your question is clear cut and brings the issue out into the open: If we cannot *make* children behave, what is left?"

"Ought we not to remember, in connection, the two contrasted kinds of conduct?"

"Which two?"

"The conduct that comes only from threats or bribes, and the conduct that comes because the individual chooses **Two ways** that kind of conduct, being himself that kind **of securing** of person." **conduct**

"And which does moral education seek?"

"Clearly, the second. That man only is to be counted

honest who of himself chooses the path of honesty, being himself that kind of person."

"And to build this kind of honesty one must practice it?"

"Yes, and not only that, but must practice it with satisfaction."

"You believe in that maxim I see, 'Practice with satisfaction.' "

"Indeed I do."

"Doesn't it combine the laws of Exercise and Effect?"

Practice with satisfaction

"Yes, though of course it gives only the positive side of effect. We must not forget the negative side: 'Practice with annoyance builds an aversion.' "

"Doesn't this 'Practice with satisfaction' still further limit the power of parent and child?"

"Yes, it is the child's satisfaction or annoyance that counts, and we cannot control that."

"I thought you were going to tell us poor parents and teachers what to do; instead of that you still further lessen our power."

"That's true. If 'Practice with satisfaction' is the governing rule, and if parents cannot make their children *practice* and cannot make *satisfaction attend,* then they do seem helpless. They are ruled out on both counts."

What parents and teachers can do

"What can they do?"

"They can work within limits along both lines. They can help bring the practice and they can help bring the appropriate satisfaction or annoyance."

"How can they help?"

"They help the practice mainly by giving children opportunities."

"And the satisfaction?"

"This mainly comes from the same opportunities."

"It all sounds rather weak to me, but I should like to hear more about it."

"I mean that morals is a matter of living with people, living with other people in such way as to bring the greatest happiness to all."

Meaning of morals   "And the way to build morals is to practice living?"

"That's exactly what I mean. To build morals, children should have the opportunity to practice a rich and varied social life."

"But shouldn't there be some way to tell the wrong from the right?"

"Most emphatically, yes. They must practice, and must know when they go right and when they go wrong, and **Discriminative practice necessary** they must be glad when they go right and sorry when they go wrong."

"There's your 'practice with satisfaction,' I see."

"Yes, 'Practice the right with satisfaction' and 'Practice the wrong with annoyance.' "

"And something must tell them the right from the wrong?"

"Yes, but the more nearly they see it for themselves the better."

"You mean that, living together, it is easy for them to see that some things are right because they work well and others are wrong because they work ill?"

"Yes, on the whole they can see what they ought to learn; but of course we have to help."

"I see now what you mean. We help them to practice by helping to provide opportunities for them to live."

"Yes, and we help them to feel glad or sorry at the right thing by helping them to see how things work."

"Do you mean then that what you call living must be the main reliance of moral education?"

"Yes."

"And you mean to say that moral instruction and punishments are not the main reliance?"

"I do certainly mean that. I do not exclude either moral instruction or punishments; but these, I say, cannot form a steady diet for moral growth. They are more like tonics and medicines; rather to be used on the physician's prescription when things have unfortunately got into a bad way." *Punishment like medicine for emergencies*

"I thought we were going to discuss the Law of Effect."

"We have been discussing it. It's contained in the proper working of social living."

"I don't see it."

"Suppose some children are building a house and one boy lays down his hammer for a moment and another boy wrongly takes it off. It is likely enough that the first boy will resent this. A situation of social stress arises. The wise teacher will now interfere as little as possible, but yet enough to see that the group as a whole makes the right *Group enterprises include inherent moral education* distinction and decides rightly as to what should be done. If Boy Number 2, as will often happen, remains for a while blinded by his own step, the other boys who do see clearly will (or may be led to) insist that he accept the group judgment. His wrong has brought annoyance."

"But it was the judgment of the other boys and not his own opinion that controlled him. This seems a clear case of coercion. Why shouldn't the teacher decide at once? He can very likely make the distinctions plainer than the boys can. I don't see the need of group living, as you call it."

"In the first place, the group enterprise gave the opportunity for the hammer to be taken. Many and varied group enterprises will mean many and varied chances to practice group morals. The hammer episode was but one false step to many right steps of coöperation and the like. All the others were instances of 'practice with satisfaction' and accordingly of strengthening and building social habits."

How the group helps

"But the hammer episode is still an example of coercion, isn't it?"

"We have, I think, discussed this once before. The boy who took the hammer doubtless did have at the outset a mind-set that upheld his conduct. If the teacher — and not the other boys — had decided against him, his mind-set might easily have continued. It certainly would have continued if the other boys had sided with him against the teacher. But as the group decided against the boy, his opposing mind-set was weakened. You know it is hard for us to hold out against our own crowd. By the next day the opposition and any trace of resentment has probably gone down before the united opinion of the group."

"It is very interesting to me to think that all the nine hundred and ninety-nine social relationships that involve no appreciable social strain are still educative for morals. I hadn't thought of that before. I had fixed my attention on the single thousandth instance."

Wealth of moral education in group activities

"It is interesting, but we have to distinguish. Some of those nine hundred and ninety-nine have already been so well learned that there is little more to learn about them. But out of varied group enterprises there must of necessity arise novel situations and novel aspects of old situations and novel connections of old materials. Most of these will probably be met in the right fashion. If so, each one represents positive moral growth."

"But is it not true that the more attention we give to the situation, the better the learning?"

"Yes, on the whole that is true; but conscious attention can result in a right decision as truly as in a wrong decision. As the conscious right decisions are likely to be more numerous than the conscious wrong decisions, what was said of the positive learning still holds."

"And when the wrong decision comes before the group, if the teacher is wise and tactful, most of the group will decide rightly and this under very conscious attention. So even of the individual wrong act, the class as a whole will get positive moral growth."

"Your mathematical discussion of the proportion of positive moral learning is very interesting. I had not thought of it that way."

"But all this positive moral learning depended, did it not, on the opportunities the children had for actual social living?"

"Yes, mainly on the existence of group enterprises."

"And the hammer episode tells what you mean by providing opportunities and helping to guide the process of moral choices?"

"Yes."

"And 'precise practice,' 'Practice the right with satisfaction,' and 'Practice the wrong with annoyance' are all involved."

"Exactly so."

"I am troubled about a further thing."

"What is that?"

"Those children who wouldn't keep quiet when the father was tired. Isn't it true that they ought to be made to practice keeping quiet, even if only for prudence' sake, rather than be allowed to practice a dis- How coercion regard of their father's rights and feelings? If may do good they practice disregard and 'get away with it,' is not that a case of 'practicing the wrong with satisfaction'?"

"It may sometimes be so, and we certainly should not allow children to practice the wrong with satisfaction."

"Doesn't this complicate the question of moral education?"

"Yes, it does. But we have said all the time that the parent must if possible bring it about that the child practice the right with satisfaction, and that if he should practice the wrong, annoyance should attend. Your question shows the complications that may arise, but introduces no new principle."

"Will not a child who learns to keep quiet for prudence' sake learn more readily to keep quiet for consideration's sake than will one who learned selfishly to disregard the feelings of his father?"

"I think you are right. At any rate it may so happen."

"It is thus a case of associative shift?"

"It may be."

"Do you mean by associative shift that one first learns to do a thing for one motive and later shifts to doing it from another motive?"

Associative shift in moral education

"This does take place in associative shift, but the positive factor of association is necessary else associative shift will not take place."

"I don't get your meaning."

"You recall Pawlow's dog. His mouth watered because the tempting morsel was placed on his tongue. At the same time a bell was rung sharply. The two happened thus in association many times until at length the bell alone sufficed to make the dog's mouth water. The shift was made, but association was an important element."

"You think then that the children might begin by keeping quiet through fear of punishment, but later come to keep quiet from consideration only?"

"Yes, if the children are young enough and the thought of consideration be constantly associated."

"Why young?"

"Older children can make better distinctions. They may see so clearly why they act in the first case that no shift will take place."

"Then the shift is not certain to take place?"

"Indeed it is not certain."

The shift not certain to take place

"What about prizes and rewards in this connection?"

"I think they belong just here if anywhere."

"You are opposed to them?"

"On the whole, yes."

"But you think they may at times serve on the principle of associative shift?"

"They may."

"Would this hold of the badge and distinctions of the Boy Scouts and other various organizations that use such?"

"So far as I can see, yes. The badge or distinction may induce a child initially to do a certain desirable thing. After the child begins doing it, the activity may come to be directly interesting. If so a shift has taken place."

Prizes and rewards and associative shift

"And you would approve this?"

"Approve is a strong word. If these things take place in this fashion and if there seems no other better way in which to build the interest, then I should approve."

"You call it all building interests?"

"It is, I think, essentially that — so building a trait into one's character that thereafter one wishes to do the thing in and of itself."

Moral education largely building interests

"You think then of buttons, badges, honors, distinctions and the like as scaffolding?"

"Exactly so. We may put up a scaffold if that is the only

way or the best way to build the house, but it is the house
we expect to live in and we mean to tear the scaffolding

Rewards and
honors as
scaffolding down."

"If taking down the scaffolding causes the
house to fall, we have failed?"

"Exactly so; that's a good test."

"I wish we might go a little more thoroughly into the
question of morality. I don't know how much is habit and
how much is thought and I don't know which comes first,
habit or thought."

"Which comes first depends partly on the age of the
learner. With a very young child an almost bare habit is

Habit and
thought in
moral edu-
cation possibly the most we can get. As the child
grows older more thought is possible. After
a while true moral deliberation is possible."

"You put thought after habit then?"

"In this matter of growing up, yes. But there is more
to be said."

"You mean that the older person meeting a like situation
the second or third time shouldn't have to deliberate?"

"Yes. Suppose I, a grown man, pass a fruitstand and
have to deliberate whether or not I shall slip off an apple
while the vendor's attention is distracted. Suppose further
that I do decide not to take an apple. What do you think
of my honesty?"

"I should hesitate to trust such a person. At his
time of life he should have settled this question long
before."

"You mean that this moral deliberation, if it had ever
been necessary should long ago have gone over into fixed
habit with uncertainty gone?"

"Yes, and in this sense thought precedes habit."

"I believe I see now the different time relations between
habit and thought in morals."

"You speak of moral deliberation, would you mind saying a further word about it?"

"I am glad to do so. The process is much the same as that of the complete act of thought previously discussed, but there are certain novel points we may well dwell upon. **Moral deliberation**

"Moral deliberation occurs when we find ourselves pulled in contradictory directions. We must act, but we do not have available an appropriate moral behavior pattern — we do not see a course which promises to conserve all the values at stake. In such case we take up the opposed lines of action, asking of each: If I do this, what will happen? When we have thus, in imagination, followed out each course as far as we can, we then compare the two opposed lines of foreseen consequences and choose the one that seems best to us."

"How does one decide as between the two contrasted lines of expected consequences? How do we tell which is better?"

"It would take us afield into ethics to answer this question. I will only say that each one decides as to good and bad out of his philosophy, that is, according to what manner of man he himself is."

"And after one has chosen, what then?"

"If the moral character has been well built, the appropriate response then takes place. One acts according to his decision."

"I seem to see three things in the working of a good moral character: first, a sensitivity as to what may be involved in a situation; second, a moral deliberation to decide what should be done; and third, the doing or effecting of the decision so made." **Elements in the good moral character**

"The first and third make me think of $S \rightarrow R$."

"How so?"

"One becomes the more sensitive to the stimulus of any S → R response, the more often, the more promptly, and the more satisfactorily he acts upon it. Obey a stimulus and we become the more sensitive to it. Disregard it and we become callous to it."

"That's good. Now how about the third?"

"The third emphasizes the other aspect of the S → R response. We will respond (R) to any situation (S) in the degree that the connection between the two has been well built."

"From this it would seem that we should form a great many S → R responses covering as well as may be the moral field. If these are well formed we shall then be morally sensitive to their demands as seen in any situation. If there is no contradiction in the resulting demands we shall then act in response to the stimuli felt to be present."

"You mean we shall act in response to a stimulus if the appropriate response bond connection has been built?"

"Yes, that's right."

"And we deliberate if we find ourselves pulled into contradictory responses by the S → R bonds called into action?"

"Yes, deliberation is to find if possible which response will best meet the demands felt in the situation."

"It seems to me that, fastening attention on the S → R conception, we may restate the foregoing in a way to give us helpful suggestions for moral education?"

"How would you restate it?"

Three constituents of the good moral character

"As I see it, we should seek to build three things:

"1. A stock of ideas to describe and identify the moral situations likely to arise.

"2. Skill in judging such matters so as, if need arise, to decide efficiently which idea best fits a given situation, and if the case be novel what response is appropriate.

"3. A stock of responses joined appropriately with the ideas above described so that when a particular idea has been selected its appropriate response will follow."

"I understand you mean this as a program of moral education?"

"Yes."

"Would some of the ideas have more idea content than others?"

"Indeed, yes. Go back to the symbol $S \rightarrow R$. So far as I can see, any idea under (1) above may serve as an S, and these would vary from the barest sign up to the completest system of philosophy."

"And similarly with the R's?"

"Again, yes. They would vary from the slightest look of recognition up to the most elaborate and inclusive scheme ever worked out for bettering civilization."

"You called this a program for moral education, how would you go about it? What would you do?"

"I should expect to build, as occasion offered, the ideas with their appropriate responses, and to develop, as fully as was feasible, the widely varied skills in judging of such matters."

"Will the ideas help in judging?"

"Yes, they form the basis upon which judgment must work, but actual skill must be developed."

"How do you build ideas in this field?"

"Just as anywhere else. First of all, the child will get at least a crude idea from hearing about a thing or hearing a term used. With this crude idea as a nucleus, he should have opportunity to try it out under such varied conditions as (a) will show where it is strong and where weak, where adequate and where inadequate; and (b) will fix the strong and adequate points and piece out the weak and inadequate points."

How ideas are built in the moral realm

"I was thinking that our discussion of psychological and logical is pertinent here."

"It is pertinent. The alternating series of psychological and logical is exactly the process of building more and more adequate ideas."

"These two ways of building ideas are the same way, are they not?"

"Substantially so. Each succeeding logical is an idea, and each next psychological more or less tests that idea."

"All this means actual experience, doesn't it?"

"Yes, much and varied actual experiencing."

"Do you mean we cannot use other people's experiences in building ideas?"

"No, this repeats a discussion we had once before. We can use a certain proportion of vicarious experiences, but there must be a large substratum of first-hand experiences to begin with, and as often as feasible we should test our resulting ideas on the hard facts of first-hand experience."

"How about books or stories or pictures?"

"So far as concerns the building of ideas about morality The use of and the practicing of judgment on such ideas, books, stories, books and the like may be of great assistance. and pictures Literature and history and biography all furnish rich material for this purpose."

"You seem to have limitations in mind."

"I was thinking of the need for first-hand experience in order to build item 3 of the program, the stock of responses. How moral We cannot build a response without responding, responses so we are severely limited here. Situations are built reported in books and elsewhere afford but a colorless and unreal responding. A little is possible. A child may say, 'If I ever get a chance I'll do thus and so.' This has some effect, but such effects are slight in comparison with actual responding to actual situations."

"Your conclusion then for moral education is that we need much actual practice in life situations?"

"Yes, many varied social life experiences calling forth abundant life reactions from the participants."

"Does this mean a change in our ordinary schoolrooms?"

"Indeed it does. The ordinary school with fixed desks, with lessons mostly memorized from books, with the teachers settling practically every question — such a school situation furnishes so little opportunity at real living as practically to starve the children morally." *The ordinary schoolroom not adapted to moral education*

"Does this account for the wide demand for moral instruction and for lessons in citizenship and the like?"

"It certainly has much to do with it. If we had set out to devise a system that would prevent moral development we could hardly have surpassed our hitherto prevalent practice in this respect."

"You think then the public school cannot build morals?"

"Indeed, I do not. I think it has abundant possibilities."

"You mean it has possibilities but has not tried to realize them?" *The public school and moral education*

"Exactly."

"What should it do?"

"Get a change of heart in superintendent, supervisor, and teacher as to what is of most worth. Stop stressing skills and facts to the hurt of everything else. Make our schools into social institutions. Encourage coöperative enterprises. Change the curriculum from extrinsic to intrinsic subject-matter. Seek *Changes needed to get moral education* activities that challenge the deepest interest and the highest powers of the children. In it all and through it all seek to make our children increasingly sensitive to the moral aspects of life. Seize every opportunity to build in them a sense of responsibility for group values."

"I accept practically all you say, but I am troubled to hear no discussion of duty. Do you not believe in building

Place of duty in moral education

a sense of duty in children?"

"A sense of duty well built is a great moral asset, and I should try to build it."

"You seem lukewarm. I think duty the greatest thing in morals if not the sum of it."

"Duty may in a certain logical sense be the sum of morals, but it does not follow that we should make moral education depend on building one all inclusive notion of duty."

"You would disapprove such an effort?"

"I certainly would. I consider duty in this all-inclusive sense to be correspondingly lacking in specific content. It

Duty, honor, etc. as reinforcements

is probably best conceived as a general notion which along with such similar conceptions as honor, plighted word, 'what will people think,' can be built up to the place where they have distinct value for reinforcement purposes. Frequently one's moral strength is just balanced. To feel that the matter at hand is a duty, to be able to say 'My honor demands it,' to think 'I have given my word' — any one of these may save the day *provided* we have previously built a strong response to duty or honor or plighted word as the case may be."

"Then we must be careful to build such a reliable response to duty for example?"

Sense of duty must be built

"Yes, and it is not easy. Many a parent has for a long time hurt any use of the term duty by making it hateful to the child. It is here as elsewhere, 'practice with satisfaction.' "

"Do you not believe in direct moral instruction then?"

Direct moral instruction

"If you mean by direct moral instruction using some textbook with set lessons, no."

"But what about a set time when moral matters are so discussed as to clarify concepts in the field?"

"Opinions differ. My own opinion is that this may be
done with older children if you have a very good teacher to
take charge of it; but great care must be taken that it not
be expected to take the place of intelligent oversight of
actual moral living."

"You think that the main reliance must be zestful social
living properly directed?"

"Exactly so."

"And that means a change of heart, as you
said, among school people?"

The main
reliance in
moral edu-
cation

"Yes. We must put first things first."

"You mean value habits and attitudes above skills and
facts?"

"Yes."

"But you would not disregard facts and skills?"

"No, but I would give them their due subordination in a
scheme of fruitful living."

"And is your last word for moral education zestful social
living properly directed?"

"Yes, zestful social living under the guidance of those who,
on the one hand, appreciate social moral values and, on the
other, love children and know how to lead them."

"Zestful social living under wise guidance. This must be
our main reliance."

REFERENCES FOR FURTHER READING

See references at the end of Chapter XIX (page 326).

CHAPTER XXI

Some Concluding Questions

"Could we not to advantage sum up what we have been talking over this year?"

"Or better still, why not consider certain points that will round out our ideas as to what to do about it all?"

"What point had you in mind? Possibly we can do both."

"One thing I should like to ask about, and that is the word 'project.' I have heard a great deal about the 'project method.' If I understand it, that's what we have been talking about a good deal of the time, but I don't believe any one has used the word even once."

The term "project"

"Do you know why?"

"No, why?"

"I can't answer for any one else, but I have been following the practice I observed at the university where I studied under a man who has done a good deal to spread the idea. I remember, too, his advice."

"And what was that?"

"He said the merits of purposeful activity depend on how well it will work if given a fair chance and not at all on the name assigned to it and still less on who first used the name. He refused to get stirred up by disputes, and he would not use the term 'project' at all till the doctrines had all been discussed, so insistent was he that we not mistake the name for the thing signified."

"Don't you think, however, a name has a good deal to do with the spread of an idea?"

344

"It may very well so act. A pat name attracts attention. People ask then what it means."

"Yes, and many natural born faddists take it up at once in order to be 'up with the times,' just as young people wish to wear 'the latest thing.' "

"Can a good thing be a fad? I thought a fad **Fads** was just an empty show."

"Certainly, a good thing may be a fad. If those who practice a thing don't know or care why they use it but simply do it to 'get on the band wagon,' as the politicians say, or to draw attention to themselves, then that thing is to them a fad."

"I heard a great scholar in literature say that we nowadays make a fad and fetish of spelling. He said uniform spelling was not necessary, that Shakespeare didn't know how to spell even his own name or, perhaps better, he spelled it almost any way that the fancy of the moment struck him."

"Well, can't we get on with the project? Do you mean that when we were discussing purposeful activity and simultaneous learnings we were discussing the project method?" **The project method**

"Exactly so."

"I thought a method was a device. I should hardly call purposeful activity a device."

"Method is differently conceived by different people. There are some, as we saw, who believe in education as mere preparation for future living and therefore are **Method not** concerned as to how best to get their daily or **necessarily** weekly quotas of extrinsic subject-matter **a device** learned. These people are almost sure to think of method as a matter of device. But there is a much broader notion possible. You recall our discussion of the 'Wider Problem of Method' [Chapters I and IX]. It was there brought out that *how* we influence the child, the way we speak to him, the kind of house we provide, all his surroundings, in general all the ways in which we treat him — all these things have great effect on the many simultaneous responses he makes, inwardly and outwardly. And from these many responses comes his character."

"If I understand you, all that we do to the child or let happen to him that stimulates him in any way is to be thought of as having *method effect?*"

"Exactly so. And it is in this broad sense that our wish to use child purposes is a matter of method. We believe that this way of treating children stimulates them helpfully in very many ways."

"You defend then the term 'project method'?"

"If it is to be thought of as a device for the 'painless putting across' of prior chosen subject-matter, no, I abominate it. I saw recently a book telling how to use the project method in religious education that illustrates this wrong use. But if it be thought of as the purposeful way of treating children in order to stir the best in them and then to trust them to themselves as much as possible, yes, I approve it. But the term 'project' must not be allowed to distract attention from the reality back of it. It is the reality and not the name that concerns us."

"Did this book of which you speak use 'purposeful activity' as its definition of the project?"

"No, I thought it found another definition better suited to its device idea."

"How many different types of projects are there?"

"For myself I recognize four types useful to distinguish."

"You don't deny there are other schemes of classification?"

Types of projects "No, indeed. There are many other useful classifications. These four are chosen to show that the different typical procedures are provided for."

"Let us keep in mind that a project is an instance of purposeful activity — it is the pursuit of a purpose. Then first of all contrast producers with consumers. The Producer's Type I is the Producer's Project, in which the Project purpose is to produce something. This varies through the widest conceivable range in importance, from the smallest child's most temporary sand house to the making of a nation or a world association of nations — in material that may be used, from the stone in the walk under our feet to the spiritual yearning of a prayer. Wherever there is activity dominated by the purpose to produce, there we have a project of Type I."

"You don't limit projects then to things made with hands?"

"I most assuredly do not. Life is not so limited. Our educational outlook must be as broad as the whole of life. Wherever purpose can go there we find projects. The next is Type II, the Consumer's Project. Consumer's In this the purpose is to consume, to use in some Project way, to use and enjoy. A small boy has the opportunity to see fireworks. His purpose makes his eyes follow the rockets high into the air, as he looks eagerly to see the bomb burst. The boy is, as regards production, merely passive; but he is very active in consuming, taking in, enjoying what some one else has produced. An artist paints a picture, a producer's project. I and others come to see and enjoy, a consumer's project."

"Do not some object to calling this a project?"

"Yes, they are basing their definition on something other than purpose. The question with me is simple: Is there a purpose dominating this boy as he faces the fireworks? And the answer clearly is 'Yes.' That there are educational implications is clear as soon as we turn to literature or the appreciation of music or other works of art. If the learner has no purpose to take in and enjoy, there will be little learning, little if any growth in taste."

"Did not some get the idea at the first that this second type was limited to what we ordinarily think of as esthetic appreciation? I notice you give enjoying fireworks as your example. This is hardly an esthetic pleasure."

"I am not sure that the enjoyment of fireworks is not esthetic; but I do think the wording in an early account of this topic was probably misleading on this point."

"You said there are four types."

"Yes, shall we go on? Type III is the Problem Project, where the purpose is to solve a problem, to clear up some **Purposeful** intellectual difficulty. Historically and indi- **problem** vidually this is probably to be thought of as **work** an outgrowth of Type I. Almost any purpose to produce, especially if it be educative, will involve some difficulty which in turn will call for thinking. The difference then between Type III and Type I is that Type III consists wholly of the problem, while Type I typically involves fashioning, with the problematic thinking only incidental."

"Is every problem then a project?"

"No, I may recognize a problem without purposing to solve it. If so, that problem is no project for me. It becomes a project to me only as I purpose to solve it and do pursue the purpose."

"Might some activity begin as a project, but the purpose die away and the activity so end as a mere task?"

"Yes, if the purpose dies and the teacher still requires the completion of what was begun, then it becomes a task."

"This means that we cannot objectively apply the term 'project' as a label—'Once a project always a project'?"

"Yes."

"Isn't this a drawback? Doesn't it vitiate your definition?"

"No, it does not vitiate the definition. Nor do I think it a serious drawback. If I were more concerned with objective labeling than anything else, I might Learner's be troubled. But it so happens that I am attitude an more concerned with the learning of my pupils essential than I am with what you call objective label- factor ing. I wish then a term that points to what I conceive to be the essence of the learning process, the learning's attitude. When the purpose has gone, the learning process has much deteriorated. The excellence of the purpose definition is that it calls attention to this essential attitude on the part of the learner."

"Do not some overlook this in assigning problems?"

"Indeed, yes. With young people it is only in slight degree that problems can be assigned. Assigned problems as a rule remain teacher's problems; they do not thereby become pupil's problems. Purpose cannot be assigned."

"Then any one who advocates extrinsic subject-matter is likely to leave purpose out of his project definition?"

"Yes, I think so."

"Isn't this just the difficulty with your project method, that it limits assignment?"

"Yes, both its difficulty and its excellency. Its excellency is that it looks facts in the face without The factor blinking. It tells you that in following the of purpose assignment plan, you lose the advantage of the limits pupil's favorable attitude. It merely discloses assignment difficulties that were there all the time. It doesn't make the difficulties; it discloses them."

"It seems to me that you are 'side-stepping' now. I see what you mean. Purposeful activity is undoubtedly the best way to learn if only you have or can get a strong enough purpose in the child. But we cannot always get this, and when you tell us — as your project method does — to use only child purposes, then we do strike difficulties, because you are refusing to allow us to use other ways of dealing with children."

"Did I ever tell you to use nothing but child purposes? Did I ever say you must not use other ways of dealing with children?"

"That's what I have understood. You have advocated purposeful activity and you have decried coercion and punishment. What else am I to understand?"

"I am very glad you have brought this out, because I do not wish to be misunderstood and apparently I have been. What I have said I still say. Purposeful activity furnishes better learning conditions than coercion — better for the primary learnings, better for associate and concomitant learnings. But I have never said you can get purposeful activity just by wishing it or by decreeing it. If you have the purpose working with you or if you can get it, then you will get better learning. If not, then you must do the best you can, taking everything into account."

"Then you are just holding up an ideal. You don't expect us to attain it? You are dealing with pious wishes?"

"No, that's not what I mean."

How pursue ideals

"But you admit that it is an ideal and cannot always be obtained?"

"Yes, but let us look more closely before we speak of pious wishes. Consider health. It too is an ideal."

"Yes."

"And you don't expect all people always to attain it?"

"No, there are difficulties that hinder. People are either ignorant or wilful or unfortunate. No one has perfect health all the time. Still less can all the people have it."

"Do the difficulties mean that our advocacy of health is a mere pious wish, that we must not seek health? Suppose I am at the head of the city board of health, what shall

I do about the ideal of health and these difficulties you name? Suppose an actual epidemic is on. Many of the citizens are ignorant and prejudiced. My help- **Ideals and** ers are too few. Some of them are ill-prepared **difficulties** for the work at hand. What shall I do?"

"You must do the best you can with the conditions as they are."

"I must seek my ideal even though I cannot attain it perfectly?"

"Yes, by seeking you'll get more than if you don't seek."

"And the difficulties and hindrances, must I yield to them or shall I seek to lessen their power and influence?"

"Clearly the latter, but you must not disregard them."

"Then if I understand you, whenever I face an actual situation I must take as my beginning the facts as they are. In this sense ideals and hindrances all go in together to determine what I must do. I must no more overlook a difficulty than I overlook my ideal (my aim, my end)."

"Yes, I begin to see what you mean. Go on."

"But as I look to the future, ideal and difficulties must be treated differently. My ideal — my end and aim — I must, if it is feasible, preserve and hold entire. The difficulties I must seek to reduce and as far as possible get rid of altogether."

"Yes. That is the way of meeting any actual situation."

"So now with purposeful activity. It is my ideal for my pupils. I shall make it my end and aim. But my very devotion to my ideal must make me pay all **Certain diffi-** necessary attention to the difficulties that stand **culties to be** between me and my ideal. I must know that **faced** pupils, as they now are (and in some measure as they always will be), will at times purpose hurtful and not helpful things. Textbooks oftentimes are not made for people with purposes but for the other kind. I must know that much if not most of the machinery of school promotions and the like are based on finishing set tasks. I must know that this machinery has been of slow growth, that superintendents, supervisors, teachers, pupils, boards of education, and parents are all accustomed to it and — to speak plainly — prejudiced largely in favor of maintaining it without much change."

"You make out a long list of difficulties. I wonder you are not discouraged before you begin."

"The real list is much longer, yet I am not discouraged. My ideal is, I believe, founded on essential human nature. If so, then so long as it is disregarded there will be dissatisfaction and unhappiness; wherever it is used properly, satisfaction and happiness."

"But you have not told us what to do."

"The answer is simple, though the road be hard and long. We must work *toward* the ideal whenever and wherever we can."

"You admit then that we must often compromise?"

"Indeed, yes. It is the only way to be true to the ideal."

Pursuing ideals through compromise

"But can't you make it plainer what to do. I still don't understand."

"I'll try. Imagine a scale. I think we used it once before. It is arranged like this: At one end (I) is the complete basis of intrinsic subject-matter and purposeful activity; at the other (E) is the com-

E _____ I

pletest kind of extrinsic subject-matter with assigned tasks and coercion, looking only to a distant future. We are to try, each in the place where he works, to live as high up towards I as our skill and the situation allow, and also try to carry the whole educational scheme in which we work further up toward I. But we are going meanwhile to 'carry on,' we are going to keep things going. This means that we shall, partly for lack of insight and skill on our part, partly by reason of outside conditions, have to live and act at times further down toward E than we like."

"Does this mean that if I have to teach a certain thing this term and it does not come purposefully — up toward I — then I am to move on down toward E and if need be assign it as a task?"

"Yes, if it must be taught this term and there seems no other and better way of doing it."

"Then you lay all your ideals on the altar of expediency?"

"That's a rather unkind and I think misleading way of putting it. I recognize facts because I must, and I then use them in such way as to further my ideal. Sup- **Facing facts** pose I wish to be on the other side of a brick wall, I don't ignore the wall or pretend that it is not there and walk ahead as if it were not there. If I did so act, I should never get on the other side. The wall won't be treated that way. No, I recognize the facts, I look for a door or a scaling ladder. Recognizing what I can move and what I cannot, I adapt myself to the situation and so in some measure control it. But all the while I hold to the aim of getting on the other side of the wall."

"Won't you illustrate with school matters?"

"Willingly. Suppose I have to give my pupils weekly grade marks. The regulations require it. Then I'll try to manage these marks so that they will do as little harm as possible. Instead of calling attention to them as if they were the be-all and end-all of school work, I'll try to distract attention from such extraneous incentives and fasten it on the inherent interests of the work itself."

"Suppose the course of study fixes just what you have to teach and leaves you little or no time for anything else. What would you do?"

"That I admit is about as hard a situation as I could have to face. I did face it once for a year, and like young

How deal with a fixed course of study

Hannibal of old I then 'swore eternal enmity' to such a scheme — a vow, I may add, that I have kept. Usually I should advise one to leave such a system if possible. If, however, you cannot, then stay and accept facts as they are, but use all your power to change affairs. And work along a variety of lines. First, use all the leeway the situation allows you in dealing with your own class, and that's more than you might at first think. Second, get as many people as you can in the system to study and learn about better things. Third, agitate — properly — for better regulations. If you are tactful and persistent, you may accomplish much."

"I don't see what leeway you could find to use under such conditions."

"Oh yes, there is much that could be done. Encourage thinking in your pupils. There is always some chance to think. Be on the lookout for problems lying within the course of study. Use such for all they are worth. Encourage some out-of-school projects. In matters of discipline utilize the pupils' assistance as much as you possibly can. The case of pupils' marching discussed some time ago [page 54ff.] actually took place during that bad year. In certain more mechanical matters, the work might be arranged on an individualized basis."

"By the individualized basis you refer to such work as we find in the Dalton and Winnetka plans. You approve them then?"

Individual- "Not on the whole or as inclusive schemes,
ized work but where we must regularly deliver fixed quotas of subject-matter we may well use certain of their devices to advantage. I did it twenty years ago. Under

such circumstances there is, I think, much about them to commend."

"But you object to all fixed quota schemes, if I understand you?"

"On the whole, yes; and my objection is deeply rooted."

"Is such individualized work given no place in your ideal scheme? I should think there would at times be distinct need for drill."

"I agree heartily that there is definite need for drill, and Type IV which we have not discussed contemplates it. This is sometimes called the Drill Project, though I prefer to call it the Specific Learning Project. Type IV In it the purpose is to acquire some item or degree of skill or knowledge."

"You mean, for example, to attain a certain speed and accuracy in column addition?"

"Yes, that would illustrate it."

"Then I don't see why you object to the Winnetka plan. That is exactly what I understand they do under this plan."

"What I object to is having such drill in advance of the need for it and apart from a situation where it is felt to be needed, or at any rate apart from a recognition of the need. After pupils meet a situation calling for column addition and come to realize their need for drill in order to attain a desired standard of speed and accuracy, then I should say use it."

"And would you object to calling their attention to the standard norms in addition work say?"

"By no means, provided I was satisfied the so-called standards represented proper work for my pupils at that time. You recognize that most "Standard" norms so-called norms merely represent existing practice; that is, what can be got under present curricular and teaching conditions. Whether they should be accepted as standards is quite another matter."

"I don't understand you. Do you mean to say that a norm worked out statistically from say 100,000 school children is not a standard? I am surprised. I thought that such statistics proved it to be a standard and that it had to be accepted."

"You understand me correctly. I do not without special consideration accept such norms as standards. Don't you see that your 100,000 children merely represent the results of present efforts at classroom teaching. But present efforts may be wrong. Possibly we should not put column addition where it now is taught. Counting thousands or even millions of children doesn't tell us whether it belongs where we have put it. It only tells us what we get when we do put it there. I do not say that all 'norms' are so got, but for any one to claim that the norms so got are binding standards would be ludicrous if it were not tragic."

"You spoke as if Winnetka had only individualized study. Don't they also have group work there?"

"Yes, they do and, as far as I can learn, this group work is carried on excellently, with much of the spirit that we have here been advocating. I wish they could see their way clear to emphasizing more strongly the group-work side of learning and reducing the other to distinct subordination to it."

"You think that some of their self-teaching and self-testing devices may be a permanent addition to educational practice?"

"Yes; the idea may be, at any rate. But I should wish all such used, as was said above, only after the need had been felt. I fear, too, they try to reduce more subject-matter to this basis than is wise."

"That brings up the idea of the separate school subjects.

Shall we not have to give them up if the ideas of purposeful activity and intrinsic subject-matter be adopted?"

"As hitherto conceived and taught, yes; sep- Separate
arate subjects for children would have to go:" school

"I don't see why. We shall forever need subjects
arithmetic, for example. Why not teach it openly and
avowedly? Why slip about and pretend?"

"You don't understand me, I think. Arithmetic we shall
always need and shall always teach and we shall teach it
openly. The point is this. We learn better — certainly
as a rule — when we face a situation calling for the use of
the thing to be learned. Other things being equal then, we
shall try to teach our arithmetic as it is needed; that is, in
connection with situations of actual need. The effect of this
will be to find arithmetic in many little pieces scattered along
the path of life. These we shall teach as we meet them. As
we accumulate in this way a store of arithmetic some of the
pupils, particularly the more mathematically inclined, will
from time to time put the pieces together and form wholes
more or less complete. Later some will specialize in the
subject."

"Is this our discussion of psychological and logical over
again?"

"Yes."

"Do you think arithmetic learned in this haphazard way
will be held in mind for use as well as if it were learned more
systematically?"

"Yes, I think so, though I don't much like your term
'haphazard.' I think that what is learned in a life situation
has cues and feelers joined to it that promise best for its
future use. I think that what is learned from a systematic
course in a book is in danger of lacking these life connections
and so it is in danger of lying idle in the mind when the
occasion arises to use it."

"I have heard some say that the organization of experience into subjects is an artificial affair and that in ignoring subject division lines we are just back to life experience. What do you think?"

"I think it is true. No person ever finds arithmetic or geography or history by itself in life. It always comes embedded in a situation involving much more. It seems to me wiser to learn it as we find it thus embedded, for then we shall the better recognize it the next time we meet it in life. That's what I meant by the 'cues and feelers' above."

"But how are you going to get drill and system on any such basis?"

Drill   "I thought we had answered that before. We get the needed drill on any operation after we have met it and have seen the need for it. Our drill then can respect the 'cues and feelers' and so preserve its 'natural setting' connections. The child's attitude toward it is almost surely better."

"But what about the systematic organization of subject-matter?"

"That too, we have answered. System should come after the separate parts have been met in their life connections.

Systematic organization of subject-matter   You will have to go back to some things that were said [page 297] on differentiation and integration of parts. Each person must make his own system if it is to be of service to him."

"It is in just such things as this that you and all who believe as you do seem to me to go wrong. You persist in thinking that the individual can ignore the race experience. You know very well he can't, but you go on acting as if he could."

"No, we don't propose to ignore the race experience. On the contrary, I think the race has worked out better systems than any one of us is likely to make. And the race experience envelops us all the while. Whoever talks, uses the race experience, or whoever uses a tool. Whoever uses such words as 'whole number,' 'fraction,' 'decimal,' is using the race-experience system. We cannot live in this world without learning and using what the race has worked out. But to take such things as they come, naturally, discuss them, see what they mean, use them, and so gradually build up each one himself for himself the system into which they fit —this is to give one a control over his thought system that no amount of memorizing other people's formulations can give."

"I still don't quite see. Take geography. The scientific textbook writer can surely surpass your pupils in making a scientific system of geography. Why not use his system? Why throw it away?"

"How do you mean to use his system?"

"Learn his book just as it is written."

"That is what I hoped you would say. Don't you know that most of that beautiful system fails to strike the pupil at all? The system that he brings from the textbook is still the one that he makes as he feels the need himself of systematizing."

"Wouldn't you encourage the pupils to make actual systems?"

"Indeed I should, and I should wish them to get suggestions from well made books, from any source in fact that would help."

"Wouldn't they merely borrow?"

"If their effort at system making was merely formal, yes, they would. That's what they now do, and I should then be just where the ordinary teacher is. But I should try to have them make a system only after the felt need for system had arisen. Then, if they borrowed, I'd hope they would not merely borrow but would borrow helpfully."

"Then you would wish your pupils in the end to organize their geography into a unifying system?"

"So far as such a system is helpful, yes. For mere formal examination purposes, no. I think as pupils get mentally older they will wish to bring together what they know in ordered form. I should naturally expect this tendency and encourage it."

"Would you use any textbooks in your school?"

"Again a difficult question. Many textbooks of the present day aim only at presenting children with **Textbooks** pre-digested thinking. Such I should not use, or at any rate I should not use them as was intended by their authors."

"But what kind would you use?"

"Only time and fuller experimentation can tell. At present I can only prophesy, and you know what a bad business that is. I can see several different kinds possible. One kind would be simply a reading book, one that would tell in a fascinating way the story of history or geography or travel or adventure, or of insect life — all the other wonderful things that have come down to us. Another would be a compendium of ready reference or possibly a systematic treatise to be consulted as need might arise. Still another would be a book that raised questions, stimulated inquiries and activities. And still another one would contain self-directing and self-testing drill material."

"Where can we get such books?"

"Most remain to be written perhaps, but a goodly beginning has been made if we know where to look."

"Don't you think that the classes in your school would have to be so small that the cost would be prohibitive?"

"No, I don't see it that way. Of course we don't now spend a due proportion on our schools. People give lip service to education, but as a whole the country spends

more on its motor cars than on the education of its children. However, I see no good reason for supposing that very small classes are necessary or even desirable. I think after we have sufficient experi- *Size of classes*
ence at it, this method, considering the service
rendered, will take care of numbers quite comparably with other methods. Probably most city elementary classes are now too large. All such would have to be cut down."

"How about a course of study? It couldn't be printed and given out in advance, could it?"

"Not as hitherto understood."   *The course of study*

"What kind could we have?"

"This is another one of our very difficult questions. I can only suggest a tentative program, a kind of compromise measure, if you wish. It might be something like this:

"1. A clear account of the theory, with emphasis on the new kind of aims.

"2. A few specimen projects of various sorts worked out in detail to show the kind of thing to be expected and why, with a study of the correlative outcomes.

"3. A list of suggestive projects much larger than could possibly be used, with appropriate reference materials and suggestions for equipment.

"4. Some account of outcomes reasonably to be expected, with emphasis on habits, attitudes, and appreciations, since these have too generally been overlooked — such outcomes not to be held up as immediate objectives but to help the teachers and pupils estimate their own progress.

"5. Some self-teaching and self-testing drill material with statement of correlative desirable standards."

"You call this a compromise?"

"Yes, I should fear lest the formulated outcomes and drill procedures be wrongly used; but probably, at the first, public opinion would demand them. Then I should expect further experience to tell us better how to make out the course of study. I distrust my ability to prophesy."

"Wouldn't there be great trouble in adjusting pupils who go from one school to another?"

Adjustment
when pupils
change
schools "No, interestingly enough, our scheme would have less trouble at this point than the usual plan. You see it is the precise specification of subject-matter quotas that give the trouble now. As soon as this lock-step is broken, adjustment is much easier. 'Social age' seems as good a single factor as any, possibly making special provision for the two extremes."

"You said earlier something about the new aims. I wish we might discuss the matter of objectives. It isn't Objectives at all clear to me. You believe in knowledge and skills, you say, but you would add also habits, attitudes, ideals, and appreciations. These, then, would constitute your list of objectives as I understand it. Am I right?"

"Yes and no. I am afraid of your way of stating it. For the purpose at hand I reckon three kinds of objectives: more immediate, more remote, and intermediate. Habits, skills, attitudes, knowledge, and other personal traits I am calling the intermediate objectives. If matters go well, they are not to be sought immediately. The immediate objective is to secure a good instance of present child life, gripping and sufficiently difficult to 'lead on.' The more remote is life too, succeeding life raised to a higher level because of the traits learned in the immediate experience."

"I am lost entirely. How can you call an instance of present child life an objective? I thought an objective had to be something to be learned. Am I all wrong?"

"So far from being all wrong, you have most of the practice on your side, but I still hold to my statement, so I must

defend myself. What is an objective? In military terms
it is typically a minor aim, a specific position the taking of
which forms a part necessary to the attainment of a larger
whole. So here, my first (immediate) objective is a gripping
experience that promises to 'lead on.' I must get this in
order to attain my further aims. Suppose I attain this
objective, then my second (intermediate) objective is the
acquisition through this experience of certain desirable
traits, as knowledge, skill, habit, or attitude. These I must
get in order to attain my still further aims (more remote
objective) of a higher level of living. The intermediate
traits have been satisfactorily got only as they eventuate in
this higher living."

"This seems to fit with the discussion of the 'continuous
remaking of life.' "

"Yes, it is meant to fit exactly there."

"But I don't yet quite understand. Do you first set up
certain traits as items of knowledge or certain habits or
skills that you wish and then hunt about for some experience
that will teach them?"

"No, that is exactly what I don't do. That would give
traits an immediacy of aim which I wish to deny. It's life
I wish to put first. So I seek first some fruitful **Experiences**
experience. Having got that going, I seek to **the immedi-**
direct it, if need be, so that the pupils will **ate objective**
grow from it and through it — so grow that they will
henceforth live a richer life and have more control over
the process."

"How do you decide which experience is to come
next?"

"On my theory we cannot decide in advance of the occasion for action — not helpfully as a rule."

"On what bases do you decide when the time does come
to act?"

"I value experiences according as they are (*a*) gripping; (*b*) sufficiently novel to involve before finished an extension

How to
appraise
experiences of present outlook and abilities, remaining, however, within the range of success; (*c*) in relation to preceding experiences, so varied as to keep life from being too one-sided. The experience that promises most under these heads I prefer."

"And you expect to get desired traits from such experiences?"

"Yes, when one lives zestfully and successfully through a novel experience he will learn along many lines. These learnings when sorted out and properly labelled become what we are calling traits."

"But what I don't see is how you pick your experience to get desired traits; you seem to say that you seek the experience first and then take whatever traits follow, but surely you don't mean that."

"That is exactly what I do mean. I do ask that the successive experiences be varied enough to take care of the different sides or aspects of life; but as a rule I consider traits only when the experience is under way and I am wishing the child to get the most possible from the experience. Even then the trait may very well be rather my adult sophisticated way of looking at the matter. I may not mention any trait, as such, to the child. He is supposed to be concerned primarily with making a good job at the present affair and only secondarily concerned with learning."

"Your word 'trait' bothers me. What do you mean by it?"

"I mean by 'trait' any one learning outcome worth naming, such as skill, habit, fact, knowledge, ideal, attitude, or appreciation. The word 'trait' is merely a general term to represent any one such learning outcome."

"Do you have then no place for minimum essentials? I thought everybody had come to admit that there were certain traits, I suppose you would call them, that are essential to good living in society and that these must be got. But you seem to deny it." *Minimum essentials as now conceived*

"Let me first ask you a question. Did you ever see included in any actual list of minimum essentials such things as truthfulness and honesty or only certain abilities as reading, writing, spelling, and certain facts in history and geography?"

"I had never thought about it before, but I believe only the latter. In fact, as I come to think about it, minimum essentials are practically those things that a child must learn if he is to be promoted. I am sure I never saw truthfulness included, or honesty."

"Why not?"

"I am not sure. I don't know whether it is because we cannot compel a child to learn truthfulness. I mean we cannot assign it as we can spelling and make him practice it before us — drill him on it — till he gets it. Or whether it is because we think untruthfulness doesn't prevent him from doing next year's work."

"You think, then, minimum essentials refer perhaps to the things essential to our school machinery and its smooth running rather than to things essential to life?"

"I don't know. It looks that way."

"Do you think truthtelling less essential to life than certain words in the spelling list or certain common facts in history or geography?"

"No, I certainly don't."

"Now I'll answer your question about my attitude toward minimum essentials. I think there are certain things so useful for future progress in school and life, both immediate and more remote, that we should use compulsion if need be to get them, so important that if they are not got otherwise there would eventually come a time when we should, if need be, drop practically everything else and compel the learning of them. If you wish to say these are minimum essentials I have no objection, provided I be allowed to have my own definition in mind when I use or accept the term."

Another notion of minimum essentials

"Would you mind telling us some things you would include in this?"

"By no means. Only I cannot give you a complete list. I think, in fact, it would differ with each child and the conditions surrounding him. My general list for all would certainly be very much smaller than you are accustomed to think. Reading would be the main such essential, the ability to manage ordinary reading matter. Counting, making change, column addition should be included. These are not all, but the list would be short."

"What would you do about honesty and truthtelling?"

"There would be a long list of things which I should seek insistently as opportunity presented, but I would not include them in the same list with these assignable things."

Other desirable traits

"You don't mean to stop your other list with those few things?"

"No, but I wouldn't include all the arithmetic or the 'facts' that you are accustomed to see on such lists. This list I should keep short, so short in fact that only rarely would the teacher need to consult it."

"Are you not departing from your conception of the continuous remaking of life when you admit even this short list of 'minimum essentials'?"

"No, because I wish them as means to growth here and now, or as means to the present remaking of life. Without them and their unique contribution the reconstruction of experience is sadly hampered. I must have them in order to attain my aim."

"Then why not start out at once and get them? 'Eventually, why not now?'"

"If they can come intrinsically, all is better. If they cannot be so got, then I suffer a loss, but I can save something else by compelling these. All the while I am pursuing my aim."

"Would you mind telling your general aim of education?"

"I am glad to do so. My aim as I work with children is to have them live more richly and successfully right now in the belief that this will mean most to them and to others both now and hereafter." The aim in education

"Your word 'successfully' is an unusual one in this connection. What is successful living in the case of a child? It is a word I am more used to seeing applied to grown-ups."

"I dare say you are right. But the question is a good one: What is successful living in the case of a child? What do you say? Is the present included or only the future?"

"Both, I suppose. I should say that a child lives successfully when he lives happily and makes others happy about him. That takes care of the present. As for the future I should say that what he does now must be the kind that prepares also for the future."

"That sounds good. Do you notice that you have said in general terms what I said earlier about how to choose among activities? If an activity is gripping and is carried out successfully the present will, as a rule, be happy. If it requires more than present outlook and achieved abilities and in comparison with preceding activities is sufficiently varied, it will prepare for the future."

"You wish then to get both present and future together in one statement?"

"Yes."

"But do you mean that a child should never look ahead. How about planning for a fishing trip? Or an older boy's trying to choose his life work?"

The child's look ahead "I wish especially to encourage planning ahead. In fact every plan to make or do anything is a look ahead. The more mature the child, the further ahead he can and will look. As the boy gets up toward manhood the choice of a profession may be a most gripping project."

"Didn't we discuss this under the head of the growing interest span?"

"Yes [pages 183 ff.], it is exactly the same."

"In trying to get present life and future into one statement are you trying to care for what we called 'the continuous remaking of life'?"

"Exactly so."

"If you were going to introduce these ideas into a school system where they had not been tried, what would you do?"

How introduce the idea "First of all, I don't believe in forcing them in. That isn't the kindly way to do anything, and it seldom succeeds. If I were a superintendent or supervisor, I should take note of the teachers already working most nearly along these lines and encourage them **Encourage those already at work** to do even more. Then I should get other teachers somewhat interested to visit these and try some of the things they saw. I should encourage all to study the theory underlying, with the hope of building a general interest in it."

"Do you think you would get far if you had hard and fast subject-matter requirements?"

Relax subject-matter requirements "No, these would have to be relaxed. To some quite capable teachers I should give a very free rein and study the results. In meetings with the teachers I should stress the finer and subtler outcomes and try to remove some of the felt strain to get the more mechanical and accordingly the measurable outcomes."

"Are there no specific things a teacher might do?"

"Yes, there are three specific lines to follow. One is to make over gradually the ordinary class work — we discussed this once before — looking out for every chance to base the work on problems."

"You say 'gradually.' Are you afraid you might go too fast."

"Yes, and properly so. This idea has its technique and it is different from the old way. No teacher can shift suddenly. Besides a failure that results from going too fast does more harm than any other kind."

"What else? You said there were three **No sudden** lines of advance?" **shift**

"Another is to get permission to set aside a half hour or an hour as a 'free-work' period. Tell the pupils they may take the time for any worthwhile activity, but each must first get your permission for his **A free-work period** project. At first most can't think of anything worthwhile. They are not used to thinking constructively, you see. So you must say: 'If you can't think of anything, I can'; and then you must have ready some good suggestions."

"What's the special advantage of this period?"

"It serves several purposes. It gives the teacher a chance to try out the plan on a small scale. Teacher and pupils both will have to learn. Again it will serve as a seed bed for suggestions to be used in other school periods. If the teacher is successful, projects soon will be undertaken which require more time. They can then run over to English or history or science according to where they most belong. Finally after a short period succeeds it can be extended gradually to cover as much of the week as it seems wise to run on this plan."

"You again speak cautiously."

"Yes, we live in the world with a great many other people, most of whom are thoroughly committed to the old way. This must go slowly. Besides there must be much experimenting before we know how to care for everything on the new basis."

"You said there were three lines of advance. We've had two."

"Yes, the third is extra-curricular activity. We can use this to distinct advantage. Perhaps eventually the line
Extra-curricular activities between curriculum and extra-curricular activity will shift. Surely it must become less definite than now."

"Do you honestly, deep down in your heart, expect this new idea to supplant the old? Do you think it can really be made to work?"

"Indeed, I do. It is coming. There's hardly a school in this country that is not moving in this direction. The distance moved in a generation is great; and the better the school and the more in touch with modern thought, the greater on the whole has the movement been."

"What are you most afraid of?"

"That we shall move too fast."

What to fear   "Fear you'll move too fast! I don't understand."

"I fear the *why* of it all will not be sufficiently understood or the *how* of it sufficiently worked out before people are boasting that they have it. In other words I fear it will be made a fad."

"The faddists will be among the professed friends of the movement. What can the avowed foes do that will most retard it?"

"Hold to the old-fashioned fixed quotas of subject-matter. Continue to measure success in terms of it. Insist on holding to this while they pretend to allow freedom to experiment."

"You think that extrinsic subject-matter is the crux on which the new and old positions turn?"

"Yes. Intrinsic subject-matter and purposeful activity with education as the continuous remaking of life to ever higher levels — these three pretty well constitute the new position." *The crux of the matter*

"Are you not sorry that we've reached the end?"

"Reached the end? We haven't reached the end. There's plenty more. We have merely stopped. It is the term that has ended."

REFERENCES FOR FURTHER READING

"Dangers and Difficulties of the Project Method: A Symposium," *Teachers College Record*, 22 : 283–321 (September, 1921).

LIST OF REFERENCES

BOOKS

ALEXANDER, THOMAS. *Prussian Elementary Schools.* Macmillan. New York, 1918.

BONSER, F. G. *The Elementary School Curriculum.* Macmillan. New York, 1920.

CHARTERS, W. W. *Curriculum Construction.* Macmillan. New York, 1923.

COLLINGS, ELLSWORTH. *An Experiment with a Project Curriculum.* Macmillan. New York, 1923.

CUBBERLEY, E. P. *Changing Conceptions of Education.* Houghton Mifflin. Boston, 1909.

DEWEY, JOHN. *The Child and the Curriculum.* University of Chicago Press. Chicago, 1902.

DEWEY, JOHN. *Democracy and Education.* Macmillan. New York, 1916.

DEWEY, JOHN. *The Educational Situation.* University of Chicago Press. Chicago, 1906.

DEWEY, JOHN. *How We Think.* Heath. New York, 1910.

DEWEY, JOHN. *Interest and Effort in Education.* Houghton Mifflin. Boston, 1913.

DEWEY, JOHN. *Moral Principles in Education.* Houghton Mifflin. Boston, 1909.

DEWEY, JOHN. *School and Society.* University of Chicago Press. Chicago, 1915.

GATES, ARTHUR I. *Psychology for Students of Education.* Macmillan. New York, 1923.

JAMES, WILLIAM. *Principles of Psychology.* Holt. New York, 1890.

JAMES, WILLIAM. *Talks to Teachers.* Holt. New York, 1899.

KANDEL, I. L., (editor). *Twenty-Five Years of American Education.* Macmillan. New York, 1924.

KILPATRICK, W. H.   *The Project Method* (pamphlet).   Teachers College, New York, 1918.

KILPATRICK, W. H.   *Source Book in the Philosophy of Education.*   Macmillan.   New York, 1923.

MERIAM, J. L.   *Child Life and the Curriculum.*   World Book Company.   Yonkers-on-Hudson, 1920.

STEVENSON, J. A.   *The Project Method of Teaching.*   Macmillan. New York, 1921.

THORNDIKE, E. L.   *Education.*   Macmillan.   New York, 1912.

THORNDIKE, E. L.   *Educational Psychology.*   Teachers College. New York, 1913–14.

THORNDIKE, E. L.   *Educational Psychology, Briefer Course.* Teachers College.   New York, 1914.

THORNDIKE, E. L.   *Principles of Teaching.*   Seiler.   New York, 1911.

WOODWORTH, R. S.   *Dynamic Psychology.*   Columbia University Press.   New York, 1918.

WOODWORTH, R. S.   *Psychology.*   Holt.   New York, 1921.

PERIODICALS

Journal of Educational Method.   World Book Company.   Yonkers-on-Hudson.

Journal of Philosophy.   Journal of Philosophy.   New York.

Teachers College Record.   Teachers College, New York.

INDEX

Absent-mindedness, 113.

Aims, in education, 187, 191–92, 257, 362–67; in moral education, 312–13, 314–15, 325; immediate objectives, 362–64; intermediate objectives, 362, 364; remoter objectives, 362; minimum essentials, 365; child's look ahead, 368.

Alexander, Thomas, quoted, 125–26.

Annoyance, not same as pain, 32. *See also* Effect, Law of; Regret.

Appreciation, significance of, 135, 197; how built, 129; cannot be assigned, 101, 119, 129, 288; cannot be compelled, 194. *See also* Attendant learnings; Attitudes; Concomitants.

Arithmetic, teaching of, referred to, 356–58.

Architecture, influence of, 122–23.

Assignability, 101–2, 129, 287–88.

Associate suggestions, defined, 102; value of, 104; how got, 129; how treated, 104–5, 106; follow readiness, 133; marginal responses, 113. *See also* Attendant learnings.

Association. *See* Associative Shift.

Associative Shift, discussed, 38–41, 179–80; varies with age, 335; in moral education, 334–36; prizes and rewards, 336–37.

Athenian method, 109.

Attendant learnings, discriminated and defined, 102–3; influenced by readiness, 132; place of, on coercion-interest scale, 167–68; influence of, on character, 311. *See also* Associate suggestions; Concomitants; Primary learning.

Attitudes, how built, 63, 71, 105–6, 119, 120–35; importance of,

99–100, 101, 123, 135, 197, 343; non-assignable, 101; effect of coercion, 89–91; not yet measured, 107; give character to an act, 321, 327. *See also* Attendant learnings; Aversion; Concomitants.

Aversion, 85, 87, 89–90, 97–98, 118, 328.

Behavior, defined, 277; outer, not sufficient, 323. *See also* Ways-of-behaving; Conduct.

Behavior-pattern, 280. *See also* Ways-of-behaving.

Bonds. *See* Connection.

Broad problem of method. *See* Wider problem of method.

CAN, 190, 197–99, 268.

Character, analysis of, 337–39; how built, 318–25; always being built, 108; strength of, 153–54; character-conduct series, 313, 325; habit and character, 319, 325; habit *vs.* thought, 336–37; integration of, 321; in relation to attitudes, 100, 311, 321, 327; influence of ritual on, etc., 124. *See also* Moral education; Selfishness.

Charters, W. W., referred to, 203.

Child, essentially active, 150–51; child *vs.* teacher activity, 206–12, 212–14, 247; child *vs.* subject-matter, 273; controlling children, 317–19; frontier *vs.* modern, 254–62; childhood a waste period, 283.

Choosing, how valuable, 152–54, 208, 210–11; internal *vs.* external choices, 161–64, 316; continuity in, 165; accepting a situation, 165–66; varies with age, 183–84, 185, 201. *See also* Purpose.

Citizenship, characteristics demanded, 126–27, 129; teaching

AMERICAN EDUCATION:
ITS MEN, IDEAS, AND INSTITUTIONS
An Arno Press/New York Times Collection

Series I

Adams, Francis. **The Free School System of the United States.** 1875.

Alcott, William A. **Confessions of a School Master.** 1839.

American Unitarian Association. **From Servitude to Service.** 1905.

Bagley, William C. **Determinism in Education.** 1925.

Barnard, Henry, editor. **Memoirs of Teachers, Educators, and Promoters and Benefactors of Education, Literature, and Science.** 1861.

Bell, Sadie. **The Church, the State, and Education in Virginia.** 1930.

Belting, Paul Everett. **The Development of the Free Public High School in Illinois to 1860.** 1919.

Berkson, Isaac B. **Theories of Americanization: A Critical Study.** 1920.

Blauch, Lloyd E. **Federal Cooperation in Agricultural Extension Work, Vocational Education, and Vocational Rehabilitation.** 1935.

Bloomfield, Meyer. **Vocational Guidance of Youth.** 1911.

Brewer, Clifton Hartwell. **A History of Religious Education in the Episcopal Church to 1835.** 1924.

Brown, Elmer Ellsworth. **The Making of Our Middle Schools.** 1902.

Brumbaugh, M. G. **Life and Works of Christopher Dock.** 1908.

Burns, Reverend J. A. **The Catholic School System in the United States.** 1908.

Burns, Reverend J. A. **The Growth and Development of the Catholic School System in the United States.** 1912.

Burton, Warren. **The District School as It Was.** 1850.

Butler, Nicholas Murray, editor. **Education in the United States.** 1900.

Butler, Vera M. **Education as Revealed By New England Newspapers prior to 1850.** 1935.

Campbell, Thomas Monroe. **The Movable School Goes to the Negro Farmer.** 1936.

Carter, James G. **Essays upon Popular Education.** 1826.

Carter, James G. **Letters to the Hon. William Prescott, LL.D., on the Free Schools of New England.** 1824.

Channing, William Ellery. **Self-Culture.** 1842.

Coe, George A. **A Social Theory of Religious Education.** 1917.

Committee on Secondary School Studies. **Report of the Committee on Secondary School Studies, Appointed at the Meeting of the National Education Association.** 1893.

Counts, George S. **Dare the School Build a New Social Order?** 1932.

Counts, George S. **The Selective Character of American Secondary Education.** 1922.

Counts, George S. **The Social Composition of Boards of Education.** 1927.

Culver, Raymond B. **Horace Mann and Religion in the Massachusetts Public Schools.** 1929.

Curoe, Philip R. V. **Educational Attitudes and Policies of Organized Labor in the United States.** 1926.

Dabney, Charles William. **Universal Education in the South.** 1936.

Dearborn, Ned Harland. **The Oswego Movement in American Education.** 1925.

De Lima, Agnes. **Our Enemy the Child.** 1926.

Dewey, John. **The Educational Situation.** 1902.

Dexter, Franklin B., editor. **Documentary History of Yale University.** 1916.

Eliot, Charles William. **Educational Reform: Essays and Addresses.** 1898.

Ensign, Forest Chester. **Compulsory School Attendance and Child Labor.** 1921.

Fitzpatrick, Edward Augustus. **The Educational Views and Influence of De Witt Clinton.** 1911.

Fleming, Sanford. **Children & Puritanism.** 1933.

Flexner, Abraham. **The American College: A Criticism.** 1908.

Foerster, Norman. **The Future of the Liberal College.** 1938.

Gilman, Daniel Coit. **University Problems in the United States.** 1898.

Hall, Samuel R. **Lectures on School-Keeping.** 1829.

Hall, Stanley G. **Adolescence: Its Psychology and Its Relations to Physiology, Anthropology, Sociology, Sex, Crime, Religion, and Education.** 1905. 2 vols.

Hansen, Allen Oscar. **Early Educational Leadership in the Ohio Valley.** 1923.

Harris, William T. **Psychologic Foundations of Education.** 1899.

Harris, William T. **Report of the Committee of Fifteen on the Elementary School.** 1895.

Harveson, Mae Elizabeth. **Catharine Esther Beecher: Pioneer Educator.** 1932.

Jackson, George Leroy. **The Development of School Support in Colonial Massachusetts.** 1909.

Kandel, I. L., editor. **Twenty-five Years of American Education.** 1924.

Kemp, William Webb. **The Support of Schools in Colonial New York by the Society for the Propagation of the Gospel in Foreign Parts.** 1913.

Kilpatrick, William Heard. **The Dutch Schools of New Netherland and Colonial New York.** 1912.

Kilpatrick, William Heard. **The Educational Frontier.** 1933.

Knight, Edgar Wallace. **The Influence of Reconstruction on Education in the South.** 1913.

Le Duc, Thomas. **Piety and Intellect at Amherst College, 1865-1912.** 1946.

Maclean, John. **History of the College of New Jersey from Its Origin in 1746 to the Commencement of 1854.** 1877.

Maddox, William Arthur. **The Free School Idea in Virginia before the Civil War.** 1918.

Mann, Horace. **Lectures on Education.** 1855.

McCadden, Joseph J. **Education in Pennsylvania, 1801-1835, and Its Debt to Roberts Vaux.** 1855.

McCallum, James Dow. **Eleazar Wheelock.** 1939.

McCuskey, Dorothy. **Bronson Alcott, Teacher.** 1940.

Meiklejohn, Alexander. **The Liberal College.** 1920.

Miller, Edward Alanson. **The History of Educational Legislation in Ohio from 1803 to 1850.** 1918.

Miller, George Frederick. **The Academy System of the State of New York.** 1922.

Monroe, Will S. **History of the Pestalozzian Movement in the United States.** 1907.

Mosely Education Commission. **Reports of the Mosely Education Commission to the United States of America October-December, 1903.** 1904.

Mowry, William A. **Recollections of a New England Educator.** 1908.

Mulhern, James. **A History of Secondary Education in Pennsylvania.** 1933.

National Herbart Society. **National Herbart Society Yearbooks 1-5, 1895-1899.** 1895-1899.

Nearing, Scott. **The New Education: A Review of Progressive Educational Movements of the Day.** 1915.

Neef, Joseph. **Sketches of a Plan and Method of Education.** 1808.

Nock, Albert Jay. **The Theory of Education in the United States.** 1932.

Norton, A. O., editor. **The First State Normal School in America: The Journals of Cyrus Pierce and Mary Swift.** 1926.

Oviatt, Edwin. **The Beginnings of Yale, 1701-1726.** 1916.

Packard, Frederic Adolphus. **The Daily Public School in the United States.** 1866.

Page, David P. **Theory and Practice of Teaching.** 1848.

Parker, Francis W. **Talks on Pedagogics: An Outline of the Theory of Concentration.** 1894.

Peabody, Elizabeth Palmer. **Record of a School.** 1835.

Porter, Noah. **The American Colleges and the American Public.** 1870.

Reigart, John Franklin. **The Lancasterian System of Instruction in the Schools of New York City.** 1916.

Reilly, Daniel F. **The School Controversy (1891-1893).** 1943.

Rice, Dr. J. M. **The Public-School System of the United States.** 1893.

Rice, Dr. J. M. **Scientific Management in Education.** 1912.

Ross, Early D. **Democracy's College: The Land-Grant Movement in the Formative Stage.** 1942.

Rugg, Harold, et al. **Curriculum-Making: Past and Present.** 1926.

Rugg, Harold, et al. **The Foundations of Curriculum-Making.** 1926.

Rugg, Harold and Shumaker, Ann. **The Child-Centered School.** 1928.

Seybolt, Robert Francis. **Apprenticeship and Apprenticeship Education in Colonial New England and New York.** 1917.

Seybolt, Robert Francis. **The Private Schools of Colonial Boston.** 1935.

Seybolt, Robert Francis. **The Public Schools of Colonial Boston.** 1935.

Sheldon, Henry D. **Student Life and Customs.** 1901.

Sherrill, Lewis Joseph. **Presbyterian Parochial Schools, 1846-1870.** 1932 .

Siljestrom, P. A. **Educational Institutions of the United States.** 1853.

Small, Walter Herbert. **Early New England Schools.** 1914.

Soltes, Mordecai. **The Yiddish Press: An Americanizing Agency.** 1925.

Stewart, George, Jr. **A History of Religious Education in Connecticut to the Middle of the Nineteenth Century.** 1924.

Storr, Richard J. **The Beginnings of Graduate Education in America.** 1953.

Stout, John Elbert. **The Development of High-School Curricula in the North Central States from 1860 to 1918.** 1921.

Suzzallo, Henry. **The Rise of Local School Supervision in Massachusetts.** 1906.

Swett, John. **Public Education in California.** 1911.

Tappan, Henry P. **University Education.** 1851.

Taylor, Howard Cromwell. **The Educational Significance of the Early Federal Land Ordinances.** 1921.

Taylor, J. Orville. **The District School.** 1834.

Tewksbury, Donald G. **The Founding of American Colleges and Universities before the Civil War.** 1932.

Thorndike, Edward L. **Educational Psychology.** 1913-1914.

True, Alfred Charles. **A History of Agricultural Education in the United States, 1785-1925.** 1929.

True, Alfred Charles. **A History of Agricultural Extension Work in the United States, 1785-1923.** 1928.

Updegraff, Harlan. **The Origin of the Moving School in Massachusetts.** 1908.

Wayland, Francis. **Thoughts on the Present Collegiate System in the United States.** 1842.

Weber, Samuel Edwin. **The Charity School Movement in Colonial Pennsylvania.** 1905.

Wells, Guy Fred. **Parish Education in Colonial Virginia.** 1923.

Wickersham, J. P. **The History of Education in Pennsylvania.** 1885.

Woodward, Calvin M. **The Manual Training School.** 1887.

Woody, Thomas. **Early Quaker Education in Pennsylvania.** 1920.

Woody, Thomas. **Quaker Education in the Colony and State of New Jersey.** 1923.

Wroth, Lawrence C. **An American Bookshelf, 1755.** 1934.

Series II

Adams, Evelyn C. **American Indian Education.** 1946.

Bailey, Joseph Cannon. **Seaman A. Knapp: Schoolmaster of American Agriculture.** 1945.

Beecher, Catharine and Harriet Beecher Stowe. **The American Woman's Home.** 1869.

Benezet, Louis T. **General Education in the Progressive College.** 1943.

Boas, Louise Schutz. **Woman's Education Begins.** 1935.

Bobbitt, Franklin. **The Curriculum.** 1918.

Bode, Boyd H. **Progressive Education at the Crossroads.** 1938.

Bourne, William Oland. **History of the Public School Society of the City of New York.** 1870.

Bronson, Walter C. **The History of Brown University, 1764-1914.** 1914.

Burstall, Sara A. **The Education of Girls in the United States.** 1894.

Butts, R. Freeman. **The College Charts Its Course.** 1939.

Caldwell, Otis W. and Stuart A. Courtis. **Then & Now in Education, 1845-1923.** 1923.

Calverton, V. F. & Samuel D. Schmalhausen, editors. **The New Generation: The Intimate Problems of Modern Parents and Children.** 1930.

Charters, W. W. **Curriculum Construction.** 1923.

Childs, John L. **Education and Morals.** 1950.

Childs, John L. **Education and the Philosophy of Experimentalism.** 1931.

Clapp, Elsie Ripley. **Community Schools in Action.** 1939.

Counts, George S. **The American Road to Culture: A Social Interpretation of Education in the United States.** 1930.

Counts, George S. **School and Society in Chicago.** 1928.

Finegan, Thomas E. **Free Schools.** 1921.

Fletcher, Robert Samuel. **A History of Oberlin College.** 1943.

Grattan, C. Hartley. **In Quest of Knowledge: A Historical Perspective on Adult Education.** 1955.

Hartman, Gertrude & Ann Shumaker, editors. **Creative Expression.** 1932.

Kandel, I. L. **The Cult of Uncertainty.** 1943.

Kandel, I. L. **Examinations and Their Substitutes in the United States.** 1936.

Kilpatrick, William Heard. **Education for a Changing Civilization.** 1926.

Kilpatrick, William Heard. **Foundations of Method.** 1925.

Kilpatrick, William Heard. **The Montessori System Examined.** 1914.

Lang, Ossian H., editor. **Educational Creeds of the Nineteenth Century.** 1898.

Learned, William S. **The Quality of the Educational Process in the United States and in Europe.** 1927.

Meiklejohn, Alexander. **The Experimental College.** 1932.

Middlekauff, Robert. **Ancients and Axioms: Secondary Education in Eighteenth-Century New England.** 1963.

Norwood, William Frederick. **Medical Education in the United States Before the Civil War.** 1944.

Parsons, Elsie W. Clews. **Educational Legislation and Administration of the Colonial Governments.** 1899.

Perry, Charles M. **Henry Philip Tappan: Philosopher and University President.** 1933.

Pierce, Bessie Louise. **Civic Attitudes in American School Textbooks.** 1930.

Rice, Edwin Wilbur. **The Sunday-School Movement (1780-1917) and the American Sunday-School Union (1817-1917).** 1917.

Robinson, James Harvey. **The Humanizing of Knowledge.** 1924.

Ryan, W. Carson. **Studies in Early Graduate Education.** 1939.

Seybolt, Robert Francis. **The Evening School in Colonial America.** 1925.

Seybolt, Robert Francis. **Source Studies in American Colonial Education.** 1925.

Todd, Lewis Paul. **Wartime Relations of the Federal Government and the Public Schools, 1917-1918.** 1945.

Vandewalker, Nina C. **The Kindergarten in American Education.** 1908.

Ward, Florence Elizabeth. **The Montessori Method and the American School.** 1913.

West, Andrew Fleming. **Short Papers on American Liberal Education.** 1907.

Wright, Marion M. Thompson. **The Education of Negroes in New Jersey.** 1941.

Supplement

The Social Frontier (Frontiers of Democracy). Vols. 1-10, 1934-1943.

Date D·